Light Invisible

Light Invisible

Satisfying the Thirst for Happiness

M. V. Lodyzhenskii

Translated by Mother Magdalena
of Novo Divievo Monastery
Spring Valley, New York

Holy Trinity Publications
The Printshop of St Job of Pochaev
Holy Trinity Monastery
Jordanville, New York
2011

Printed with the blessing of His Eminence,
Metropolitan Hilarion First Hierarch
of the Russian Orthodox Church Outside of Russia

HOLY TRINITY PUBLICATIONS
The Printshop of St Job of Pochaev
Holy Trinity Monastery
Jordanville, New York 13361-0036
www.holytrinitypublications.com

ISBN: 978-0-88465-187-1 (paper)
ISBN: 978-0-88465-199-4 (ePub)

Library of Congress Control Number 2011921025

This book is dedicated to Olga Alexandrovna Lodyzhenskaia

CONTENTS

PREFACE TO THE ENGLISH LANGUAGE EDITION

Many parallels can be seen to exist between the cultural and intellectual life of the Russian Empire at the dawn of the twentieth century and of modern Western societies in the first decade of the twenty-first century. The Russian Empire was beginning to feel the impact of the industrial revolution and the increasing material wealth it was providing for parts of society. Intellectuals and others claimed that there was a spiritual vacuum and reacted against the Orthodox Church, which for them was moribund and did not offer a solution to their deepest spiritual needs. A similar crisis can be seen in the contemporary West, where our material needs are satisfied to a greater extent than ever in human history, but a fundamental spiritual vacuum exists to which the "established churches" of Christendom are not seen as providing any real solutions.

In the Russian Empire in the late nineteenth century, many were dabbling with Eastern religions, Theosophy, and the occult in a way that bears comparison to the ongoing interest in vampires, angels, and demons in our own society. Against this backdrop, Mitrofan Lodyzhenskii (1852–1917) emerged with a trilogy of books that sought to penetrate to the heart of the human condition. He demonstrates that through the incarnation of the God-Man Jesus Christ, a "Light Invisible" has broken into the world. This Light has been appropriated by the saints in the Church, engendering a radical transformation in human understanding and orientation. We, too, can change our present way of thinking and acting so as to embrace this Light.

Lodyzhenskii was once a follower of Theosophy and dabbled in Eastern religions. This book is a witness to his return to Orthodox faith and life. *Light Invisible*, which first appeared in Russian in 1912, is the second book of a trilogy entitled The Mystical Trilogy, the first volume of which is *Super-Consciousness and Paths to Its Acquisition* (1906) and the third is *The Dark*

Force (1914). In his preface to the second edition of *Light Invisible* (Petrograd, 1915), Lodyzhenskii wrote,

> Our book *Super-Consciousness*, explaining mysticism in general and its main subdivisions, enters into this work as its first volume. The third volume of the trilogy, *The Dark Force*, printed in 1914, concerns investigations of super-consciousness developed in conjunction with evil human passions and investigations of demonic mysticism. Although all of these books are interconnected, each one represents a separate treatise with which the reader may become acquainted independent of the other parts.

The reader should be aware that the translator and editors did not have access to the same editions of the Russian language books used by the author when he wrote this book. Furthermore, not all of these works exist in English translation, and where they do it is not always possible to cite a corresponding reference. For example, the texts published in Russian as the *Philokalia* are not identical to the collection published in English.

Additionally, the author followed a Russian cultural and intellectual practice in which it is not considered essential to give all details of the source material but simply an indication of its origins. Therefore the bibliography and endnotes at the end of this English edition are listed to facilitate the reader's understanding or indicate as closely as possible a source for further reading and study.

INTRODUCTION

Let him become a fool, that he may become wise.

For the wisdom of this world is foolishness with God. —1 Cor 3:18–19

Who of us has not read the revelations of the Gospel about the Logos? Who does not remember the words inscribed there? "In the beginning was the Word (Logos), and the Word was with God.... All things were made through Him, and without Him nothing was made that was made. In Him was life, and the life was the light of men."[1] And who of us has not tried to comprehend the profound meaning of these utterances?

First of all, what involuntarily impresses itself on our thoughts after reading these sayings is what is understood here by the Logos as power—power creating the universe, and along with it, power creating "light" in man. What kind of "light"? Of course, the light of reason, the light of true knowledge, the light illumining the soul of man.

After this, another question arises that is not easily resolved: the question of what constitutes this knowledge of truth, where it is, and how it is apprehended. In other words, what knowledge contains the light of men, brought by the Logos, that light which, according to the words of the Gospel, shineth in darkness; and the darkness comprehended it not?

And so we will have to resolve the question of what comprises this knowledge of truth. But here man's skeptical mind suggests to the seeker of this truth that the knowledge of truth in general is relative, that because all philosophical systems have as their main goal to know the truth, that this merely leads to the conclusion that every person has his own truth. "What is truth?" said Pilate long ago.

First of all, what we can answer to these doubts is this—that John the Divine, in beginning his message, speaks not of truths constructed by man under the conditions of his earthly reason, but rather speaks of the Gospel truth, coming to man from without—by way of a special perception, namely: Here it speaks of "the light of man," brought by the Logos, and not of the light of relative truths, constructed on those data that give man's intellect its imperfect and, in the majority of people, its limited consciousness. And, of course, we would say further that "the light of man" brought by the Logos is not that light of understanding that is given to us, for example, by materialistic philosophy that maintains that in the world exists only physical matter and that indisputable truth consists in the existence of this matter alone.

Nor in the same way is this that light of truth preached by other philosophical systems, acknowledging truth only in the sensations of our five senses, acknowledging truth only in our cerebral thinking and consciousness. Of course, the Gospel does not speak of such truths, and we, beginning with its fundamental principle about the Logos, will not direct our thoughts to searching for truths in these systems. After all that we set forth in our book *Higher Consciousness,*[2] these and similar interpretations of truth cannot satisfy us. If we were convinced that besides our ordinary consciousness there is higher consciousness, then the above-cited interpretations, proceeding from the sphere of limited human consciousness, seem to us to be one-sided, not encompassing all the endlessly rich manifestations of earthly life and of the soul of man, manifestations not only in consciousness but also in higher consciousness. These interpretations are, in fact, interpretations of limited horizons; these ideas are examples of the constructions of philosophers, overlooking, as is characteristic of their limited view, a great many things in the world, although imagining in their conceit that their understanding comprehends the whole fullness of knowledge.

Not so is the Gospel truth, contained in the above-cited sayings about the Word. The Gospel truth is much broader than these relative truths; it encompasses the higher spiritual world and the whole existence of the universe. Not so is the truth of the Logos, creating "the light of man"—the light which is not extinguished by the darkness of human errors and contradictions. To know this truth, we would say that a completely different way of comprehending is needed, a way of renouncing man's small horizons is needed, a way of spiritual aspiration into "another world," a way of aspiring according to those landmarks posted by the great aviators of the spirit—the Christian ascetics.

And the truth of the Gospel will be understandable to us when for its solution we turn to their works, to these sources born not of our limited consciousness, but of a broadened consciousness, when we turn to the instructions of these people, going the dynamic way of their whole life toward the Christian Logos. These people have broadened their consciousness to what for us with our ordinary consciousness are extraordinary limits; they have attained great power in understanding and explaining the truth of the Gospel. "The soul sees God's truth according to the strength of its life," says St Isaac of Syria[3] or, translating this saying into our language, in order to know divine truth, according to St Isaac of Syria, the activity of a holy life is needed, the power of penetration unweakened by sin, the power perceiving truth through brilliant intuition.

And indeed, upon acquainting ourselves with the words of Christian ascetics (compiled in the *Philokalia*), we found therein these brilliantly expressed explanations of questions concerning the Gospel truth.

In the forefront, we must place the philosophical sayings of the sixth-century ascetic Abba Dorotheus, expressed in his particular scheme. Although we have already set forth these sayings in our book *Higher Consciousness,* nevertheless, we consider it necessary to cite them now, because in them we see the wonderfully profound realization of the attempt to clothe in philosophical form that which was given by Gospel revelation. Said Abba Dorotheus,

Imagine a circle, the middle of which is the center and coming out from the center radii, rays. The farther these radii go from the center the more they separate and move away from one another; and on the contrary, the closer they move to the center, the closer they come to each other. Suppose now that this circle is the world, the very center of the circle is God, and the straight lines (radii), leading from the center to the circumference or from the circumference to the center of the circle are the paths of people's lives. And here also, the saints enter into the circle toward its center, wishing to come closer to God; the more they enter in, the closer they come to God and to one another.... The same goes for moving away from the center. When people move away from God, to the same extent they move away from each other and the more they move away from one another, the more they move away from God. And such is the quality of love: the more we remain outside and do not love God, the more each person is removed from his neighbor. But if we love God, then the closer we come to God with love toward Him, the more we unite with love to our fellow men; and the closer we unite with our fellow men, the closer we unite with God.[4]

Pondering the profound meaning of this saying, it would be impossible not to recognize that the Gospel revelation about the light of the Logos, about the "light of men," is expressed here in all its fullness. According to Abba Dorotheus's scheme, a man imbued with spiritual love, uniting men in God,[5] lives in the sphere of the Logos, that is, in the sphere of that power which, according to the Gospel, creates the "light of men." This mystical circle of Abba Dorotheus is the symbol of this higher sphere. A man, comprehending this sphere with his whole being, in this way already begins to extricate himself from that circle of ideas in which he thrived before. He already begins to live outside that circle, the center of which he imagined himself to be, contraposing the whole world to his own consciousness.

This consciousness, which had seemed to him to be the fullness of everything, he now recognizes to have been fostered under the conditions of an incomplete point of view. He sees that his reason, which had seemed to him to be so powerful, has been trained in a limited sphere and is abnormally developed. Such a person now turns his whole psyche into the consciousness of another reason—*higher reason,* illuminated by the Logos. And this reason, conceived in the rays of divine grace, radiating out from the center of world life—this reason, developing within a person, itself becomes like its own source—the Logos. And so the reader now sees that thanks to the brilliant scheme of Abba Dorotheus, we are able to some extent to understand the previously cited words of the Holy Gospel—"in Him (the Logos) was life; and the life was the light of men."

The aforesaid scheme of Abba Dorotheus at the same time represents a striking example of how human thought, illumined by the light of higher reason (the Logos), finds a way even in a graphic representation to explain the relationship between the Godhead and men, and in this way helps people to feel that, besides the sphere of the egotistical intellect (the mental world), in whose power live the overwhelming majority of people, there is yet another sphere—the sphere of the Logos, an ego-aspiring sphere (the spiritual world), into which a human being can penetrate only by developing within himself higher reason, akin to the Logos, reason fed by divine love.

In the thirteenth chapter of our book *Higher Consciousness,*[6] we cited the writings of the Russian philosopher Nicholas Berdyaev, defining the relationship between the higher reason (the Logos) and the lower reason (ratio). May we remind the reader of the main principle expressed by Berdyaev. He says, "Apostle Paul gives eternal kinds of reason—'let him become a fool, that he may be wise,'—and again: 'the wisdom of this world is foolishness with God.'"

Berdyaev says further, "There is limited reason, common sense, reason of the rationalists; and there is divine reason, the reason of the mystics and saints." The greatest Christian and pagan philosophers, for whom philosophy was holy, recognized the existence of a higher, divine reason, the Logos, in which the subject and object are identical and revealed the action of the Logos in man.

In many parts of this present work, we will be using the terms *higher reason* and *lower reason* (Logos and ratio); therefore, we recognize the need to speak of these concepts in more detail, to determine the characteristics of these reasons and their mutual correlation.

We will begin with the lower reason (ratio). Already in the fifth century, the Christian ascetic St John Chrysostom, in one of his homilies about purity of faith, also said that "the nature of rational reasonings is similar to a labyrinth—nowhere does it have an end and it does not allow thoughts to be firmly established on any kind of foundation."[7]

These words are remarkable. Contrasting "the nature of rational reasonings" with the strength of purity of faith and with the strength of spiritual intuition, Chrysostom expressed with these words his judgment of the insignificance of the small reason (ratio) in the business of comprehending spiritual truths, truths lying at the base of existence. According to the meaning contained in St John Chrysostom's statement, if man's reason does not have living roots in religious feeling, then it is condemned to fruitless wandering in a labyrinth.

Here it is interesting to note that for this argument we find support in what is now recognized by many as philosophy, laid down already by Descartes, which contraposes one's rationalistic thinking to existence, and imagines finding the fullness of all knowledge in one's thinking alone. To philosophers of this doctrine, human thought represented a self-contained, firm basis, as if absolute, capable by its pure logic of comprehending truth. Meanwhile, human thought by its very nature is of the same essences as that reality which it is studying, and this thought cannot be a self-contained force, but is rather a derivative force, dependent upon many forces, and mainly upon moral and other impulses governing the thought of man. And if this thought were torn away from its living roots, nourishing it in man, then all that would be left would be merely rational arguments, "the nature of which," as Chrysostom says, "is similar to a labyrinth and does not allow thoughts to be firmly established on any kind of foundation."[8] Besides this, thought that is separated from existence can even go so far as to negate the very existence that it is studying, leading away from the understanding about the world to an understanding of ideas about the supposed world, to an understanding of ideas perpetrated in the mind of man. Several rationalists have even reached the possibility of such a negation.[9]

But such a philosophy, of course, could not and cannot be sound. Its very instability is observable now in that crisis of philosophical thought in the West, which is now being experienced by this new philosophy after Kant's philosophical ideas were exhausted in the teaching of his epigones.[10] A picture of this crisis is very cleverly reproduced by one of the Russian philosophers, Vladimir Ern, in his work *Struggle for the Logos*. Incidentally, in the aforesaid work we read the following characteristic excerpt, summing up in condensed form the main conclusions pertaining to this question:

> A tree in order to live must have both roots going into the earth and foliage and flowers which bathe in the azure heavens; and it perishes if its trunk is separated from the roots and branches. The new philosophy of the West, determined from the very beginning by the principle of its own philosophizing of the ratio, in the name of this principle, began already with Descartes and Bacon to hack away at the roots and branches of the living tree of human philosophy. This dual process of tearing away (from the earth and from the sky), predetermined by the very concept of the ratio, passes historically through stages of increasingly greater development and reaches its height in the monumental philosophy of German idealism. Hegel once and for all fells the tree; the flow of creative life forces is stanched, and the proud edifice of European philosophy collapses with catastrophic force. The whole of subsequent European philosophy is an attempt to *give life* to the dead: to sprout new shoots on a trunk which is already dead. From this comes the unparalleled fall of philosophy after Hegel, the development of scholasticism and epigonism.[11]

The exceedingly interesting characteristics of this very same crisis are noted by another Russian philosopher, Vyacheslav Ivanov. "As the result of neo-Kantian research," says this philosopher, "the subject of cognition, which the person has turned into, sees himself locked in an indissoluble circle. Everything within the circle is relative: everything outside the circle is indeterminate data," and this position leads to the negative conclusion, necessitating concurrence with the positions of the Hellenic sophist Gorgias: "There is no existence: even if there were, everything would be unknowable; even if it were knowable, it would be inexpressible and incommunicable." Vyacheslav Ivanov concludes that to live as such gnosiology teaches is impossible.[12]

Externally, the crisis of this new philosophy is manifested in the fact that the movements of philosophical thought have splintered at the present time into many disputing schools, unable even to agree upon exact terminology that would make it possible for them to understand one another.

And this whole tower of Babel has come about because people are cruelly mistaken when they try to find the origin of all truth in the formalistic logic of our lower reason, as if it were always and everywhere capable of being the undeceived instrument of human thought, capable also of being an impartial judge in all matters.

Even if this reason has been able to catch exact laws in indifferent mathematics and in its kindred astronomy, if it has gropingly reached an approximate, from the point of view of form, knowledge of physical laws,[13] if it has perfected technology and begun to rule nature, yet it is still a long way between this and its ruling the truth in the matters of existence, in the matters of a human soul, which in many ways will always be for him an insoluble mystery. Our intellect proves powerless also in solving questions closely connected with man's soul, moral questions. In our book *Super-Consciousness,* we listed graphic examples of the wanderings of human thought, stricken with the disease of atheism, which is highly characteristic of the lower reason. We presented cases of the sort of labyrinth of human logic that human thought, when torn away from religious roots, can reach when resolving moral questions.[14] We will not list new examples at this time.

That which we presented before is sufficiently convincing. One should note that all these examples of abnormal manifestations of human thought do not represent peculiar exceptions, because the lower reason, *by virtue of its very essence*, by its very nature, cannot by its own forces alone gain an understanding in such matters. These qualities characterizing the nature of the lower reason can be studied by analyzing the very essence of the reason.

―――――

We will attempt to do this analysis. Let us examine the characteristics inherent in the lower reason.

Let us begin with a most interesting definition by A. Besant, relative to this subject. She says that the human intellect, clearly distinguishing "I" from "not I," comprehends in full measure only itself, and all else "it conceives as outside and foreign to itself."[15] Testing this definition on oneself, each of us must agree with the truth of this definition. And if this is so, then it would undoubtedly follow that essentially the intellect's *first and fundamental characteristic is to shut itself off from the outside world, to shut off subject from object.*

From this fundamental characteristic of our reasoning (intellect)—to comprehend subject and object as separate—are born other characteristic features: its egocentricity and its egoism. Let us explain this at greater length. Proceeding from its small "I," the intellect of each person is first of all inclined in its "I" to maintain its own point of view, is inclined to think of itself as the center for which exist all its surroundings in the world. Shut off from all that constitutes the "not I," the human intellect is inclined to look upon its own abilities and strengths primarily from only a one-sided point of view, namely, from the point of exercising its own right to influence the world outside itself. The less this right is bound by the hindering conditions of the outside world, the more freely this right is exercised.

Thereupon, man who has developed within himself such a consciousness, if with his egocentric views and strivings collides with someone similar to himself, blocking his way, then it is perfectly natural that with his whole being he would be inclined to say to the latter, "I exist, don't bother me. You with your existence interfere with my life; go away or disappear."

Furthermore, in connection with these natural qualities of the lower reason—to be egocentric and egotistical—within it is developed the quality to think of itself not dispassionately, but rather with a certain pleasure in itself brought about by attained results obtained through struggle, in the consciousness of its *own* strength, of its *own* power and superiority. The spirit of self-asserting pride is indeed a natural attribute of lower human reason. All its thinking is usually accomplished in the consciousness of its *own* significance in the work of comprehending truth and in deluding itself with this, its own significance. But just as soon as the lower reason begins to delight in the thought of this significance, it becomes inclined to value the truth not as such, but rather as its *own creation,* and that is why in the overwhelming majority of cases it loses the true criterion between truth and delusion.

This tendency of human of human reason (the lower reason) to be proud was most definitely expressed by Christian ascetics; they condemned this reason that exaggerated its own significance. We cite the following example from the *Philokalia* collection. The seventh-century ascetic St Maximus the Confessor calls the kind of *thinking* that is imbued with feelings of its own significance *proud philosophizing.* And contrasting this philosophizing with divine knowledge (which according to our terminology is given by the higher reason), he says that this proud philosophizing is made up of two forms of ignorance or lack of knowledge—ignorance of God's help and ignorance of its own infirmity. This results in man's being deprived of "Divine and human knowledge."[16] Similarly interesting in regard to this subject is a saying of the Apostle Paul. The Apostle Paul says, "Love edifies," but "knowledge puffs up" (is proud).[17]

Besides the aforesaid qualities of the lower reason (egocentricity, inclination to egotism and pride), it is also necessary to point out that because of all the conditions of our life, the human intellect, as we already explained in our book *Super-Consciousness,* is nurtured in an atmosphere far from conducive to the development in man of impartial, undarkened speculation. This atmosphere in which people live, including philosophers, is an atmosphere of vanity, and we all know how difficult and sometimes even impossible it is for a person to separate himself from vain associations inherent in his ratio. If during the time of the first Christians the ascetics said that it is difficult to avoid vain thinking, for whatever one does to drive it out becomes a new source of its movement,[18] so now when no one fights against vain thoughts, but on the contrary, everyone develops them within themselves, these thoughts are indeed that atmosphere in which human thinking moves in the overwhelming majority of cases, striving in this fog of vanity and the illusory notion of its own importance to realize the impossible—to see clearly and orient itself unerringly in matters of truth.

We repeat: people are cruelly mistaken when they suppose that human intellect has the quality of always being objective, that it can easily free itself from such associations as mentioned above. No matter how vigilant or steadfast a person may be, these associations in the majority of cases nevertheless penetrate his field of consciousness. Even outstanding human minds are not spared from error when they take as a free decision of their own consciousness such conclusions that have as their root the thirst of the intellect to glorify itself and ascribe exaggerated importance to its powers. The doctor of philosophy Carl du Prel says that the vast majority of people do not have objective thoughts, but only thoughts begotten of their egotistical will, interest, and need, so that a large portion of scientific books even now merit the censure expressed by Baron Verulam in the words "One cannot call the human mind pure light because it experiences within itself the effect of the will and the senses."[19] Into this sphere of the will and senses enter mental passions, the power of which we discussed in detail in *Super-Consciousness,* and "these temptations will not cease for as long as the world stands," says the Christian ascetic St Isaac of Syria.[20]

Here it would be appropriate to mention the characteristic opinion of the lower reason expressed by this ascetic. According to St Isaac's terminology, he calls the lower reason "the first degree of knowledge." He says that "in this knowledge is planted the tree of knowledge of good and evil, eradicating love. Its qualities are arrogance and pride. It is conceited, but meanwhile it walks in darkness—and values its own importance in comparison with what else is on earth and is unaware that there is anything better than itself."[21]

That the lower reason (ratio) is often not impartial in matters of philosophical investigation is demonstrated to us by the whole direction of positivist philosophy that so fascinated people during the last century, regarding which our great writer L. M. Tolstoy ventured to say that the positivist philosophy of Kant was enthusiastically received by people mainly because *it strove to justify the evil existing in human society.*[22]

Finally, if we acknowledge that the intellect of only a few exceptional people is capable of being impartial and pure in its judgments concerning questions of existence, questions relating to the human soul, then this reason, by virtue of its powers, cannot be considered an instrument capable of resolving such questions, because man's very intellectual resources are greatly limited in this regard. This truth is being acknowledged by the philosophical schools having considerable success of late in the West. Thus, a representative of one of these schools, Henri Bergson, in his philosophical investigations seriously questions the significance of the intellect in understanding matters of the life of man's soul and proposes another instrument for this cognition, an instrument that by its very nature is the complete opposite of the intellect, namely, intuition. In the future development of this instrument, he sees the key to the aforesaid understanding. In his work *Creative Evolution* (*L'evolution créatrice*), Bergson maintains that intuition goes in the direction of life itself, yet intellect goes directly opposite, that in humanity, of which we are part, intuition has been almost completely subjugated to the use of the intellect, that if this intuition has been retained, then only vaguely and sporadically, that it resembles a nearly burned-out lamp which blazes up from time to time for just a few moments. "True, this light is faltering and weak," says Bergson, "but all the same it brightens *that darkness of night where we are left by the intellect.*"[23]

It is impossible not to agree with Bergson's opinion, for in fact how can, for example, the intellect comprehend manifestations of the soul such as creative inspiration; how can all such things be understood by human reasoning, which by its very nature is bound to investigation in a static state, to investigation in a schematic form, bound to its own formalistic logic?

———

Let us now go on to the higher reason. As we proceed to elucidate this understanding and the inherent qualities of the higher reason, we should begin with the following proposition.

Primary truth, determining the meaning of life, illuminating man's consciousness with its light, proceeds not from rational thinking, but rather from man's heart (from his emotional sphere). The heart apprehends truth in its own special way, through its own special process of penetration, its own special intuition that for our brain is elusive and incomprehensible. In this process of intuitive penetration—a process whose root (nourishment) lies in the sphere of emotions (the higher emotions), a process conceived in the heart, unpolluted by evil passions, but rather warring with them—consists the work of the higher reason, the germ of which lives in the heart of every man. The germ of this higher reason living within the heart can be developed by man to a point of consciousness, that is, to a special and completely independent-from-the-brain sensation of a man's higher "I" in the sphere of his heart. Each of us could realize this truth by means of experimental self-observation, if we were to undertake the enormous task of cleansing ourselves from evil human passions. But at the present time we can barely find within our intelligentsia people capable of such experiments. For proof of this proposition, it is necessary to turn to other data.

Let us recall Tolstoy. Let us recall that part of Tolstoy's confession where he says that his attraction to God (his search for God) had its source not in reasoning, but in the heart.[24] This attraction was not a rationalistic striving; on the contrary, it was completely unconscious for his intellect. The germ of this attraction was hidden in Tolstoy's higher reason. In spite of the rational life to which Tolstoy had then given himself, and which he admitted in his confession had nearly driven him to suicide—by virtue of his special qualities as a writer of genius, his higher reason could not be stilled in him completely. Nevertheless he lived and worked, this higher reason dwelling in his heart and by irrational means (not by way of the brain, but from the heart) making its demands to know truth in God.

To corroborate this thesis of the higher reason, we will recount the following experiences taken from the lives of ascetics, going the way of a righteous life, cleansing their heart.

In our book *Super-Consciousness,* in the section on mental prayer,[25] while discussing the conditions for attaining it we cited instructions, worked out by the practice of asceticism, that during prayer the person praying should extinguish the consciousness of his lower reason (cerebral consciousness) and kindle another consciousness—consciousness of the life of the heart. As the readers recall, Gregory Palamas and others express this instruction in the form of this requirement: "Force your mind from the head down into the heart and keep it there." In answer to the question "What does it mean to kindle consciousness in the life of the heart?" we answered, that in order to understand this, one must remember that the heart of the ascetic who has entered upon the path of mental prayer is in no way that heart possessed by people of this world, barely living the life of the heart. We then said that he who lives the life of the heart feels, for example, the words of St John Chrysostom, "May the heart swallow the Lord and the Lord the heart, and these two will be one." Such a one understands the life of the heart, understands the meaning of the expression "the heart is kindled" or "consciousness was kindled in the life of the heart."

Now these instructions on the state of a person at prayer, under which condition is kindled the consciousness of the life of the heart, also explain the matter of the higher reason that we are discussing. Consciousness in the life of the heart that burns so strongly during the high moments of mental prayer and of which the ascetics tell is indeed, by its very essence, consciousness of that higher reason about which we are now talking. But only during prayer, thanks to the influence on man of divine grace, does the life of this higher reason manifest itself in any exceptional degree of fullness and strength. The perception of this life under these conditions is so intense in itself that man is not aware of the other, cerebral consciousness (ratio). Expressing it another way, spiritual super-consciousness, of which we spoke in our book *Super-Consciousness,* is indeed by its very essence consciousness of the higher reason—but consciousness carried to its very highest point, to the manifestations of man's highest faculties (spiritual vision).

In each of us glimmers the germ of this higher reason—reason that can develop in the exalted feelings of the heart—feelings of love and unity. But consciousness of this is not given to all, for our life passes entirely in the rational sphere (in the mental sphere), profoundly poisoned by the egoism of each and every one of us. And the overwhelming majority of people live half-anesthetized to their higher "I," half-anesthetized to their higher reason. But if under any circumstances in a man's life, his higher reason were to leave this lethargic condition (as with Tolstoy who felt in his heart a striving toward the Divinity), and if this reason begins to grow in a man, then his whole being, all his views on the world and his surroundings, all his wisdom are transformed. Then a man is as if reborn.[26] Aspiring in his heart toward the Logos, he begins to give himself up to a great purpose, a great service—to be, according to his strength, a bearer of His life, poured out in the world. Such a man perceives the world as the sum total of powers originating from the one divine center, perceives the occurrences of human life as transitional stages to the revealing of a higher life in people, the revealing in them of that universal (church) consciousness that Abba Dorotheus expressed so brilliantly in his scheme. One should note that the aforesaid development of the higher reason is accomplished independently of the level of a man's intellectual development. The Christian ascetic St Macarius the Great mentions in his works such cases when an ignorant person (i.e., a man who is uneducated, with an undeveloped lower reason) is reborn spiritually, is transformed into a wise man and hidden mysteries are made known to him, but essentially he is ignorant. And this wisdom, maintains St Macarius, surpasses by its loftiness natural knowledge that is acquired by the efforts of philosophical thought.[27]

Having elucidated how one must understand the term *higher reason* (Logos) as opposed to the lower reason (ratio) or, as the Apostle Paul says, "the wisdom of this world," we will now talk about the most characteristic qualities of higher reason.

On the basis of experiences from the lives of Christian ascetics, one should first of all say that to the higher reason belongs this characteristic quality: the ability to sense and to know God. The sixth-century ascetic St Isaac of Syria says that "man partakes of the experience of God through the experience of the feelings of the spiritual mind."[28]

Of this ability of the higher reason to sense God, Anthony the Great speaks in the following characteristic saying, "As the body having no eyes is blind, does not see the sun illuminating the whole earth and sea, cannot enjoy its light, so the soul not having a good mind [the higher reason] or a good life [nourishing this mind] is blind: does not know God . . . and cannot enter into His delight through incorruption and eternal blessings."[29]

One should note that in the great majority of cases, the process of this realization of God by man is accomplished not at once, but through consistent and gradual development. For a person awakening to the spiritual life, beginning to live by means of the higher reason (or rather its germ)—the first sensations leading to a knowledge of God are usually expressed vaguely and weakly, like the far-off dawn of the approaching light. But with the clearing of vision and striving toward the sun (applying to this, of course, man's own efforts), this perception is developed. The germ of the higher reason begins to grow, warmed by the rays of the super-universal power called by Christian theologians *divine grace*. And so develops the ability of this reason to sense the Godhead. Man's first vague sensation of Divinity is transformed into a powerful emotion toward God. Then, as expressed in the words of

St Anthony the Great, man already "knows God and enters into His delight through eternal blessings."

––––––––––

In connection with this quality of the higher reason—to sense and to comprehend God—there are some richly gifted people progressing toward perfection by way of lofty endeavors (spiritual struggle) within whom may develop a special faculty of this higher reason—the faculty of "spiritual vision" to penetrate into the higher spiritual world, the faculty which we called in our book *Super-Consciousness, spiritual super-consciousness,* of which we spoke there in detail.[30]

Concerning this super-consciousness, we ascertained that it develops in a man's heart through the action of divine grace, and namely in this means of its development consists the difference between the aforesaid super-consciousness and mental (natural) super-consciousness, the organ of which—the intellect or lower reason—dwells in the brain. (With this latter super-consciousness, a yogi strives to master astral and mental powers through his own personal influence and through impulses coming from himself, the yogi, and not owing to the power of divine grace overshadowing a Christian ascetic.)

As we also made clear in our first book, spiritual super-consciousness developed in man's higher reason is an emotional–mystical condition, extremely difficult to communicate to our ordinary consciousness; and the only way to represent these sensations is by means of analogies that give a remote idea of these sensations.[31] The aforesaid faculty of the higher reason for spiritual super-consciousness can engender still other mystical faculties—the faculty for clairvoyance, for prophecies, for spiritual visions, for so-called miracles, and for higher spiritual ecstasies—about which we also spoke in *Super-Consciousness*[32] and about which we will also speak in Chapter 7 of this book. Regarding these faculties, we already ascertained in *Super-Consciousness* that they differ from analogous faculties of yogis (e.g., clairvoyance) in that they appear in Christian ascetics by way of the heart, as gifts of divine grace, as the result of the ascetics' prayers, and as the consequence of their naturally vitalized religious intuition. They are in many cases involuntary and unexpected for the ascetic. Whereas with yogis (and with occultists) they are attained, as affirmed by the Hindu ascetic Vivekananda, through exercises of the brain—are attained through special gymnastics of the psychic powers, having as its goal to bring a person to a certain predetermined ultraphysical perception and influence, and besides—which are attained through these gymnastics, totally independent of whether the yogi believes in the Divinity or even rejects God.

_____

One of the very highest qualities belonging to the higher reason, which in our age is beginning to be the most stifled within man, is the presence in him of *inner conscience*. This inner conscience is a special feeling of man's fear of inner reproach, reproach of the heart living by the higher reason, unable by its nature to reconcile itself to evil. The ascetics attach great significance to this conscience.

Abba Dorotheus says, "Having created man, God instilled in him something Divine—something similar to a spark, a thought having within itself light and warmth—a thought enlightening the mind and showing him what is good and what is evil. This is called conscience and it is a natural law."[33]

In our times this conscience, this lofty inner feeling of the heart, is substituted in the great majority of cases by another conscience, another sensation, characteristic of the lower reason, fear not of inner reproach, but of outside reproach, that is, of judgment of an evil deed that could be expressed by surrounding people. Fear of such a reproach has a close analogy with fear in general of any repression for an evil deed. A man fears losing his importance among people in the same way he fears civil or criminal answerability. Only here punishment does not play a role but rather fear of feeling the damage to his self-love, his vanity. And guarding one's self-love is the main stimulus of the outer conscience. The ascetic Bishop Theophan the Recluse says the following concerning this outer conscience, which he calls the *worldly conscience*: "There a man has in mind only himself and his temporary relationships, but here (with the inner conscience), on the contrary, he completely forgets himself and everything temporary and sees only the insulted God.... There he grieves that he was shamed before people, but here that he has shamed himself before God."[34]

Here we see the results of the influences of the inner and outer conscience. If it comes from the inner conscience, then this conscience (an attribute of the higher reason) is for people a stimulus to inner truth as well—not for show, but in reality. All sincerely religious people are indeed bearers of this inner truth. Now, the outer conscience (an attribute of the lower reason), built on the fear of punishment or the fear to his vanity or self-love, cultivates in people the mere semblance of truth that sickens a man's pure moral feeling.

This semblance of truth we see in just about everything that surrounds us, but it is manifested in especially characteristic form, for example, in our judicial institutions. As K. P. Pobedonostsev wittily observes,

> In the aforesaid institutions we see the machine for the artificial manufacture of truth, *but truth itself is not visible in the triumphant bustle of machine production,* is not audible in the noise of the wheels of the enormous mechanism.... Judges meet in session in majestic awareness of their priestly worthiness, and, like soothsayers of old, listen for as long as the attention lasts; the lawyers orate, leading magnificent words and high-flown phrases along the narrow corridors and pipelines of artfully designed thinking, in advance weighing in hard cash each one of their long-winded sessions; long, tedious hours of wordy torture drag on, but meanwhile the main victim of this torture, *ill-fated truth,* must cross over into the promised land by the thin hair of Mohammet's bridge: woe to him who in this crossing relies on his own powers. Only he is right who, having first mastered to perfection the artistry of an acrobat, manages not to stumble and fall on the way."[35]

———

A most characteristic quality of the higher reason, distinguishing it from the lower reason, is its unusual simplicity and striving toward sacrifice.

We all know from experience how complex is man's cerebral thinking; we know how convoluted is man's reasoning and how it is burdened by a multiplicity of associations from intruding ideas. In direct contrast to this complexity, the higher reason possesses the quality of simplicity. Speaking of the books of the Gospel, St John Chrysostom says, "For whom is it not clear all that is contained in them: who upon hearing, blessed are the meek, blessed are the merciful, blessed are the pure in heart and so forth, will need a teacher in order to understand any of what was said."[36]

To explain what Chrysostom says here, we cite the following words of Theophan the Recluse. He wrote, "Truth is akin to the spirit. Simply and sincerely expressed, she will find it; but furnished with images, configurated and embellished, she will remain in the fantasy—entangled in ponderings and proofs, will be detained in the reason, not reaching the spirit and leaving it idle."[37]

This quality of simplicity in the higher reason is especially manifest in spiritual super-consciousness. St Isaac of Syria in his description of the divine mystical state says that in such a state of super-consciousness, the soul may be transported into a bodiless (superphysical) sphere, might touch the depths of the intangible sea, get to know the wonderful wisdom of God's activity, the wisdom of His governing the nature of creatures both mental and physical, *"to comprehend spiritual mysteries with a simple and subtle mind."*[38]

"The Godhead simple, incomplex, indescribable," says another ascetic, St Gregory of Nyssa. "And similar to God human nature (striving toward the Logos) in this case is made simple, indescribable and in the true sense of the word single, so that within it the visible and the secret are the same, the concealed and visible are one."[39]

It is also interesting to note that characteristically the higher reason in its relationships with all its surroundings reveals a completely original feature, distinctive to itself, namely its striving toward sacrifice, for this reason is nourished by divine love, is nourished by lofty emotions, whose nature consists wholly of forgetting oneself for the benefit of one's neighbor. Meanwhile, the nature of the lower reason is inclined, on the contrary, to reveal itself not in sacrifice, but in grasping, in the struggle for egocentric superiority, in the struggle for power and possession of material goods. Therefore, the pleasure of the higher reason and the pleasure of the lower reason are two very different things and are incommensurable with one another, by virtue of the satisfaction that a person experiences.

The Gospel—a book originating in the Logos, a book of the higher reason—is thoroughly infused with the spirit of sacrifice and love and gave to the world awareness of the higher heavenly joys of the higher reason—joys which up until the Gospel the world did not know, living as it was in the sensations of paganism, in earthly pleasures. "With the appearance of Christ on earth, with the shining forth of the Gospel," says our Russian publicist V. V. Rozanov, "all earthly fruits suddenly became bitter. In Christ the world became bitter, precisely from His sweetness."[40]

It still remains for us to say that the higher reason possesses the quality, together with its growth and development, of modifying the very ratio, converting it to itself, adapting man's lower reason to its own higher purposes.

First, with the development of the higher reason in a person, the lower reason ceases to imagine itself to be a self-sufficient power and thus begins little by little to renounce its egocentric and egotistical qualities.

In place of the striving toward acquisition with which it was chiefly preoccupied, the basis of sacrifice and striving toward it began to take root. Having been made a function derived from the higher reason, it inevitably is raised to religious consciousness.

Furthermore, it begins to assimilate the truth that higher wisdom comes first of all not through theoretical constructions but through the exerting of all human powers in man's struggle with his evil passions. He also begins to realize that when a man's heart becomes purified, then his reasoning, which contains the full strength of logical thinking, is able to acquire the divine qualities of the Logos—the qualities of its penetration and simplicity. "Purification of the mind—this is perfection," says Macarius the Great. "Enter into your mind, the prisoner and slave of sin, and examine what is on its bottom, in the depths of your thoughts—I mean that serpent nestled in the so-called secret places of your soul."[41]

Finally, such human reasoning, illuminated by the light of the higher reason, if it enters into the realm of philosophical thought, becomes the creator of a philosophy completely different from rationalistic; it already becomes the creator of a philosophy, the principles of which proceed from the intuitive penetration of the higher reason. "The real basis of truth," says William James, "is always formed by our impulsive faith, but our verbally expressed philosophies—these are merely a series of formuli in which faith is clothed. Spontaneous, intuitive conviction hides *in the depths of our soul*, but logical arguments are only its surface manifestation. Instinct commands and leads—reason follows submissively."[42] According to the law indicated by James, a Christian philosophy is created. The instinct of the higher reason, hiding in the depths of our soul, shows Christians their origin—the Logos; points to Him as to the Divinity, governing the world; and shows this Divinity as the all-good conscious Person, in His limitless love coming down to the needs and sufferings of people striving toward God and who by His grace are being made His children. And here a philosophy is created subject, as is every other philosophy, to the norms of logical thought, but based on this instinct of the higher reason. A philosophy is created that is in harmony with the higher sphere of the Logos (the scheme of Abba Dorotheus). A philosophy is created that is not an individual or personal matter, as we say in the rationalistic systems. The Christian philosopher already philosophizes in a different way. His reasoning creates thought subject to the highest power—to the power that stands above his personal, egocentric strivings. The thought of such a philosopher is created subject to a higher principle—to the Logos.

We have already cited a striking example of such a philosophy, quoting the sayings of Abba Dorotheus about his marvelously profound mystical scheme. Here, in this scheme, the life of the world consists not of the small "I" of each person, but rather in the great "I" of the universe—in the "I" of the personal and all-good Divinity.

"As the sun serves for the sensual, so God serves for the mental," says another Christian philosopher, Gregory Palamas, "and He is the first supreme Light, illuminating all reasoning nature."[43]

Now rationalistic philosophers, proceeding in their philosophy from the lower, personal "I," in essence repeat the mistake of Ptolemy's system. "Ptolemy's system has long ago gone out of fashion," says K. P. Pobedonostsev, "but ... doesn't the newest philosophy fall into the very same muddle again from the same gross mistake that it takes *man* as the center of the universe and forces all of life to revolve around him, just as during the time of Copernicus science forced the sun to revolve around the earth?"[44] Christian philosophy was conceived by the great words of St John the Divine that we quoted in the first lines of this chapter. This philosophy developed in the teaching of Christian ascetics; they profoundly understood its significance in relation to other philosophical systems. Already in the fourth century Christian philosophers had a fully conscious attitude toward their philosophy. Thus St Gregory the Theologian in his biography of St Basil the Great talks about Christian philosophy in the following expressions: "Our philosophy is serious and profound; it is at odds with the world and strives to be united with God, gathering treasures in heaven and not on earth."[45]

Beginning in the fourth century, this philosophy received its subsequent development in the works of the Christian ascetics. Contained in the extensive Russian collection of their works, called the *Philokalia*, are writings by thirty-eight ascetics, dating from the fourth to the fourteenth centuries, inclusive. In the aforementioned writings one senses the collective mind of the saints of the Eastern Church, their interpretations and sayings imbued with the spirit of unity in the Logos.[46] A systematic summary of the most important of these sayings have been set forth in the thirteenth and fourteenth chapters of our first book, *Super-Consciousness*.

For those of our readers who are not familiar with the aforementioned book, we feel it is necessary to say here a few words about it. The book *Super-Consciousness and Paths to Its Acquisition* was written for the purpose of explaining that (1) besides the perception of normal consciousness, there also exists the perception of a broadened consciousness or super-consciousness; (2) although the ability to perceive the latter is inherent in every person, however, in the majority of people it abides in a latent state; and (3) there exist various kinds of super-consciousness, of which the highest form, giving man feelings of real joy and unutterable happiness, is *spiritual super-consciousness*.

In our above-mentioned work, the starting point leading to these conclusions and to this terminology was the definition of normal consciousness as established by science, of consciousness proceeding from the affirmation of one's "I" and, contraposed to this affirmation, the concept of "not I," that is, the concept of the outside world, surrounding man. In other words, in our work we took as the point of departure man's consciousness, proceeding from his "I," as from the fundamental center, or *egocentric consciousness*. At the same time we expressed then that our book was written not so much for people who acknowledge the necessity of religion, but is for everyone in general, though he be not a believer, yet who is not deprived of a clear sense of his own soul as a special substance. Proceeding from these propositions and on the basis of the data we have worked out, in the second half of our book (chs. 12 and 13) we came to the conviction that the most perfect way of realizing the attainment of higher super-consciousness, spiritual super-consciousness (giving man the highest happiness), *is the way shown by Christian ascetics*. Later, having set forth this path in detail and acknowledged the height and greatness of its basis—the Christian religion—by doing this we then left the stage of indifference toward the Christian religion. We became its adepts, mastering its principles; and then we acknowledged the indisputable superiority of Christian asceticism over what is far more renowned at this time, Hindu asceticism (Raja yoga).

Having mastered all this, we now enter into the realm of Christian philosophy, now as its confirmed supporters. We now enter this realm of philosophy, constructed not on the egocentric "I" but on the great "I" uniting people in God. We enter into the realm of philosophy, deriving its revelations from the sphere of the higher reason, into the realm of philosophy, of which one of its chief principles is acknowledgment of the Logos—Christ, recognition in Him of the spiritual center, which gives men spiritual life.

Therefore, now in our present work, we must change our original point of view. Now we will direct our conversation primarily from the point of view of Christian philosophy. But of course this will not stop us from examining the facts under investigation from different angles for the purpose of their full illumination.

———

Together with changing our basic point of view, we must also broaden our terminology. Above, we just now explained in detail the meaning of our terms the *higher reason* and the *lower reason*. In addition to this, we will talk here also about what for us is an essential concept, contained in the term *mysticism*, a term that will often be encountered in this book.

In the present work, in which we will be discussing the lives of Christian saints, we will use the word *mysticism* from the point of view of Christian philosophy.

The word *mysticism* was used from a Christian point of view even by Vladimir Solovyov, who gave several pointers regarding this subject in his article "Mysticism."[47]

Vladimir Solovyov gives the word *mysticism* two interpretations, dividing the concept into (1) practical or experimental mysticism and (2) mysticism as a special kind of religious–philosophical cognitive activity. Solovyov defines *practical mysticism* as the aggregate of phenomena and actions, which in a special way bind man to the secret essence and powers of the world, independent of the conditions of space, time, and physical causation.

Concerning mysticism *as a special kind of religious–cognitive activity*, Solovyov defines this mysticism as the possibility of direct association between the cognizing subject and the absolute object of cognition—the essence of everything or the Divinity. Furthermore, in giving indications on how one should correctly use the word *mysticism* in Christian philosophy, Solovyov says that from the Christian point of view mysticism is divided according to the worthiness and significance of the object and the environment of the mystical interaction *into divine, natural, or demonic mysticism*.[48] These categories of mysticism, according to Solovyov, coincide with our categories of super-consciousness. Therefore, we accept them in their entirety:

1. By *divine* or *higher mysticism* we understand the mysticism of man's conscious communion with the spiritual sphere (the sphere of the Logos), the mysticism of man's unity with the Godhead (the Logos), mysticism overshadowed by the power of divine grace, that is, namely that which we call *spiritual super-consciousness*.[49]

2. By *natural mysticism* we understand mental mysticism or *mental super-consciousness*,[50] attained through the power of heightened human thought (Raja yoga). Although this sphere of super-consciousness presents a certain refined substance as compared with the physical world, just the same, in its essence it is of the sphere of the material world.[51] This aforesaid mysticism differs from divine mysticism mainly in that this state can be attained by human powers without the help of divine grace.

3. By *demonic mysticism* we understand those states attained by means of astral powers, fed by man's evil passions (astral super-consciousness).

We should explain here that Solovyov's understanding of the word *mysticism* embraces all that we understand by the word *super-consciousness*. Therefore, Solovyov's expression *mysticism* and our *super-consciousness* concur with each other, although we defined the word *super-consciousness* in a completely different way than Solovyov defined the word *mysticism*. Solovyov proceeds from the Greek word[52] (neuter-gender plural from the adjective *mysterious*). But we, in using the word *super-consciousness,* proceeded from what science understands by the word *consciousness*, drawing an analogy between consciousness and super-consciousness.

In concluding this introduction, we will say a few words of how we are arranging the plan of our work.

The purpose of the present book which we have called *Light Invisible* is to represent holy people's lives, which were filled with selfless activity and high spiritual strivings for the good of one's fellow man, filled with manifestations of spiritual super-consciousness.

Here one should note that the number of saints venerated by Christians is extremely large. In the *Menologian* alone there are about 2,000 biographies. The materials for studying the lives of the saints—patrologies, the *Menologion,* lives of the church fathers, and finally the works of the saints themselves—open up such an enormous field for research that it was necessary to settle on a plan for making possible the curtailment of the work in order to fit our research into one book. Therefore, after having familiarized ourselves with the necessary material, we chose the following way in which to fulfill the task.

First of all we talk of what we understand by "Light Invisible," and we also speak about the main types of saints—the contemplative type and the active type (Chapter 1)—explaining the common bases for determining these types.

Then, from all the lives of the saints we chose to give an account of the life of one of the greatest saints to illuminate the world—the great Russian ascetic, Seraphim of Sarov. We are dwelling on this Christian ascetic because Seraphim is a saint close to us in time. Information about him is quite extensive; there is rich material. Besides this, Seraphim is interesting to us as a type of saint living according to the directions of the Christian ascetics in the *Philokalia,* such directions with which we became familiar in detail when writing our book *Super-Consciousness.*

In recounting the life of Seraphim (Chapter 2), we speak in detail of his mysticism, and in order to depict in relief this side of the ascetic, we considered it advisable to draw a comparison between the mysticism of Seraphim, characterizing the asceticism (spiritual striving) of the Eastern

Church and the mysticism of one of the most celebrated saints of the Western Church, Francis of Assisi, characteristic of all Catholicism (Chapters 3 and 4). Besides this, we have devoted one chapter (Chapter 5) to explaining the common difference between the mysticism of the Eastern and Western Churches.

In the following chapters (Chapters 6 and 7) we switch to other saints of the Eastern Church, acquainting the readers with such features of their lives that supplement the type of saint studied by us in Seraphim. In addition, we speak here in detail of the joys of higher mystical life. For this we used the material given to us in the writings of the famous ascetic of the eleventh century, Symeon the New Theologian.

In Chapter 8, we cite characteristic examples of the deaths of ascetics. In this same chapter, we dwell on a theme of profound interest to us, namely, how the saints died as compared with the death of the Russian writer, Tolstoy, also striving toward spiritual attainment at the end of his life.

Finally, in the last chapter we talk of the strugglers for the Logos, that is, those who in spiritual endeavors and by their word devoted themselves to the work of defending Christian beliefs and ideas, thereby helping to strengthen them in the public consciousness.

All the while, along with the sublime scenes from the lives of the Christian ascetics, we have been relentlessly pursued by other thoughts. We have been pursued by images of our own miserable reality. We have been pursued by comparisons of manifestations of "light" described in the present book with the darkness of our real life, and these comparisons involuntarily burst forth in our writings.

And at the end of the last chapter we tell of the kind of struggle for the Logos that is anticipated in our present era and the movements of this era that are the most hostile to Christianity.

Regarding the secular and religious literature that we used for our work, there is a detailed list of writings and books from which our references have been taken at the end of this book in the bibliography.

CHAPTER I

Light in the Darkness

And the light shines in darkness, and the darkness did not comprehend it. (John 1:5)

I f we compare some typical opinions that have come into use in our everyday life with the opinions by which people of Christian spiritual endeavors are guided on their way, then we are faced with really startling contrasts, indicating how sharply our rational life in the ratio differs from life in the Logos, of which speak the Gospel and Christian saints. For this, let us take several examples.

One cannot go a certain way, not having become that way oneself, says human reason in the consciousness of its own might. The more one dares, the more one receives.

Christian saints say, "We must always be firmly convinced that there is no way we can attain perfection through our own works and strivings . . . if God Himself does not help us in this."[1]

Happiness lies in power and possession, says our reason. We place our stakes only on the rich and powerful; the representative of governmental power guides our thoughts.

"The All-good God left the strong, wise, and rich of the world and chose the weak, simple, and poor by His great and unutterable goodness," say the Christian ascetics.[2] "Come to Me, all you who labor and are heavy laden," we read the words of the Holy Gospel.[3]

"I'm not some kind of beggar who has to pray.[4] I'm not a useless pariah who has to waste time on this," says the man of proud riches and acquisitive energy.

"If you deprive yourself of prayer, "says St John Chrysostom, "then it is the same as if you were to take a fish out of water, for as water is in this life, so is prayer to you."[5]

––––––––

There is nothing more unpleasant than the feeling that people call humility, says our reason. Humility is self-abasement. The first quality of a human being consists in his preserving his dignity and not losing self-respect.

"If there is no humility in a man then he will not inherit the kingdom of God," say Christian ascetics.[6]

––––––––

Poverty is loathsome, says our reason. Anyone who does not knock himself out in the pursuit of money we consider a powerless man, devoid of ambition.[7]

"If you have more than is necessary for your daily needs," says the sixth-century ascetic St Isaac of Syria, "give to the poor. Nothing so draws the heart to God as alms, and nothing so produces peace in the soul as voluntary poverty."[8]

––––––––

The growth of interest on capital is an entirely lawful act, says our reason. Interest on capital has been consecrated by the practice of government loans; they have entered into all human economic relations.

"Children! Do not lend money on interest," instruct the Christian saints.[9] "If, having given someone a loan, forgive him, then you will be an imitator of Jesus' nature, but if you ask for it back, then Adam's nature; now if you take interest, this will not even be according to Adam's nature."[10]

Enough of these comparisons. The startling contrasts between our rationalistic life and the spiritual life are strikingly illuminated by the examples presented. Life in the ratio and life the Logos are like two different worlds, having nothing in common with one another.[11]

Although he may strive for perfection, man, when using his own powers structured on rational will, cannot extricate himself from the moral contradictions from which his whole life is woven. Now we all feel and recognize that in man's soul every thread of his higher motives is criss-crossed with threads of egoism; every moral act is poisoned with the venomous admixture of a self-loving motive. Man is unable to renounce all this with his own powers—for this help is indispensable, strengthening him in his spiritual endeavor.

Christian ascetics see this help in the action on man of spiritual world-embracing power that they call *divine grace*. Not only do they believe in this power, but also they know it and feel it through their spiritual super-consciousness.

For our part we cannot but acknowledge that this power is undoubtedly a real force, because we know that it has called forth and does now call forth great and real consequences. Christian ascetics lived their lives, which are examples of the action of extraordinary spiritual energy surpassing human nature, not according to the pattern of our lives. Against the background of our commonplace lives, the lives of the saints, proceeding according to the way indicated by the Savior of the world, deriving strength for their ascetic endeavors from divine grace, appear before us as light piercing through darkness.

This light flared up especially brightly during the first age of Christianity—in the age when it was ignited from its Great Sun, enlivening the spiritual world, when this Sun, the Logos Himself, became incarnate as man.

"That Christ overturned the whole history of the world is a fact which the whole world must acknowledge," says Nicholas Berdyaev,

> and this must be acknowledged not only by the conscious Christian world, but by the world alien to Christ, hostile to Him. Christ captivated the world, mesmerized it; from Him proceeded folly, incomprehensible to the heathen, even to this day. It was as if humanity went out of its mind, out of its heathen natural mind, and was captivated by the mysterious person of Christist.... In the history of the world a cosmic upheaval took place, a truly new epoch began, and this miraculous role of Christ cannot be explained by those who see in Him only a man, though a most unusual one. And the whole baptized Christian world, even having lost the higher religious consciousness of who Christ was, feels mystically that hidden in Him is a great mystery, that bound up with Him is the greatest problem of world history. Let them mentally compare Christ with Buddha, Socrates or Muhammad, but just the same deep down they feel that this is not the same, that with

the coming of Christ the cosmic structure of the world was changed, that a power entered the world which was not of this world.... The most positivistic historians know that after Christ the axis of world history changed its direction; Christ became the theme of world history. The whole fabric of human existence lost its resemblance to the threadbare heathen fabric. After Christ the history of the world went not according to the path of least resistance, as the positivist historians would like to think, *but according to the path of most resistance*, according to the path of resistance to all the sinful order of nature.[12]

But beginning after Christ, the movement of human history according to the path of greatest resistance was not a linear process. The era of maximum tension of the human spirit has given place to the era of its slackening. And if, as we see this now, a period of general moral decline sets in along with its attendant intensification of human suffering, if we now find ourselves at the trough of the wave, then we can expect its upsurge, for consciousness of the life of the spirit, implanted deep in the hearts of men by the Great Sower of good, lives in the masses. And one must say that it lives especially vigorously in the soul of the Russian people, feeling within itself the power of the higher reason, an elemental power, that cannot be opposed. Christ said that the gates of hell shall not prevail against the church which He raised, and the Russian people profoundly believe these words of the Savior. No matter how refined evil may become, no matter what new forms it might take on, the life of the Russian people will continue to follow the path of greatest resistance to this refined evil.

Meanwhile this evil, which in essence is that old heathen evil, would not even think of surrendering to Christianity. It again begins to dominate, only it pursues its goals in different, secret ways. For this it has long ago changed its former tactic of direct violence against Christianity. Alongside the all-visible triumph of Christianity, this evil strove to steal its way into the Christian organization itself and there undermine its basic roots. And it did, in fact, steal its way in and began accomplishing its destructive work. Christianity became tainted with superstitions and produced the Inquisition. It deviated into papism and soulless heathen Caesarism.[13] Besides this, according to the keen observation of the publicist M. O. Menshikov, Christianity has now reached the point of Christ-damning Nietzscheism, to freemasonry that is hostile to Christ, to positivism that denies Christ, to the complete unbelief of agnostics and nihilists, to the total godlessness of anarchists.[14] On the one hand, we see that in place of the heathen power of the sword holding the world in its iron embrace, instead of the power of direct violence, a different power has ascended the throne, the *power of gold*, soulless force, the might of indirect violence, power based on the torment of need. And here we are, masters of this gold (or, rather, subjugated by this evil) again at the trough of the wave.[15] The calm of darkness has enveloped our intelligentsia, the calm of people's isolation, the calm of cold reason, the calm of *stony insensibility*.[16] And if on the backdrop of the heartlessness of the dominant classes life now flares up, then this is chiefly only in the manifestation of vice that is so highly regarded on the exchange of human vanity—subtle vice putting on a mask of goodness. And therefore moral sufferings have not lessened; they are all the same sufferings of the heathen world. As at the end of ancient times, people are tormented by mental anguish and the horror of unbelief. So our intelligentsia, unable to figure out and understand where in all of this lies the root of evil, with irony tosses at believers the reproach, "This is what Christianity has brought the world to!" And they say this without understanding the essence of the matter, completely blinded by their cold autocratic ratio, which the intelligentsia has made its sinless deity.

Given such a general state of affairs, protest against evil, heathen force, against life based only on reasoning, must of course again flare up, and it will flare up. But will this be soon? What kind of envoys of the Higher Power will come to us? Will these be people of meek love and profound religious mysticism, such as, for example, St Seraphim of Sarov was? Or instead will we hear finally the burning, protesting speech of a preacher, kindling the hearts of men, such as was the great Christian homilist St John Chrysostom?

For these fiery preachers to come, maybe we need special exceptional conditions, maybe we need an acute intensification of human torment and oppression of life. Maybe for this we need mighty armed conflicts, brought upon man by his heathen ratio;[17] maybe we need terrible social upheavals of nations, when finally everything will begin to shake, when no one will be sure of the next day. And maybe only then the speeches of fiery preachers, powerful in the higher reason, will be heard and felt.

However, enough of all these oppressive thought about the evils of the world and the calamities to come. Even without this, life is joyless and we cannot escape it; we are called on to endure it with Christian patience. This is a great force, if it is combined with love and prayer to the Logos—a force essential for active struggle, the energy of which should be first of all directed toward self-amendment.[18]

And so, enough of these bitter reflections, depressing the soul. Let us refresh ourselves with bright and joyful occurrences that have illumined and still illumine the world. Let us look at examples of Christian strength, as manifest in the lives of ascetics and saintly people. Let the light of their lives, contrasting with the darkness of our own, uphold our faith and enliven our love. This light, emanating from the great saints, is, as it were, a reflection of another higher and for us invisible sphere, of another *higher and for us Light Invisible*. And it is inextinguishable, this great *invisible-to-physical-eyes light*. Darkness cannot comprehend it.

———————

One of the main divisions that we first of all come into contact with when studying the lives of the saints is how their lives' paths relate to two basic types of ascetic endeavor: the *contemplative* type and the *active* type. These types are determined by the distinct character of the ascetics' spiritual love and the various means by which this love is attained. While investigating the saints' biographies, we see that the path of development of their spiritual lives proceeded either through the cultivating within themselves first of all love for God, or through the developing within their heart, mainly, love for our brethren—our fellow men. To explain what has been said, let us recall the scheme of Abba Dorotheus that we discussed earlier. The summarizing points of this scheme are as follows: (1) "the closer we come to God in love for Him, the more we are united in love with our neighbor" and (2) "the more we are united in love with our neighbor, the more we are united with God." This summarization elucidates the essence of the matter under consideration; it point out the two main paths to perfection: the *active path* passes in works of love for one's neighbor; the *contemplative* or *ascetic* path is accomplished when the spiritual striver goes toward his goal through the direct cultivation within himself of immediate love for God. Such a path leads to mystical revelation, to the mystical contemplation of the Divinity and His powers. But here we must again make one more important digression from our main theme.

We find it necessary as a preliminary to our ensuing discourse to express several ideas regarding the mystical language that we will have to use at times in our present work.

Just now we used the expression, "to the mystical contemplation of the Divinity and His powers." The reader has every right to ask what one must understand by these words. But to acquire an approximate understanding of divine mysticism, it is essential at least to some extent to understand what the process of the aforesaid mystical contemplation is; namely, how do we experience it?

To this we must answer that to understand what mystical contemplations is, and how we experience it, we have only one path—this is the path of analogies, and the most vivid analogies, besides. And only in these analogies can this understanding be expressed.

Christian ascetics also resorted to analogies. But because in the era of their creativity their general knowledge of things of the visible world was primitive and far from rich, the imagery of ascetics could not have much variety. As regards this, we the people of the twentieth century are more fortunate. With the development of aviation and everyone's being aware of what *aviation* represents, applying this word to spiritual contemplation makes it possible through analogy to sense what spiritual aviation is. The concept of the wireless telegraph gives us a certain understanding of clairvoyance, of the possibility of influencing people at a distance by the power of thought or the power of spiritual intuition, and so on. Our knowledge is growing, and along with it our ability to make analogies is broadened.

Thus, we now have more extensive means than the Christian saints had with which to represent the kind of experiences that mystical contemplation gives to man. Although such great saints as, for example, St Isaac of Syria tried as best they could to convey with their concepts the sensations of this contemplation, yet their communications regarding this is for us still unclear; it requires quite an effort to comprehend their deep meaning. The imagery of St Isaac was completely understandable to his contemporary Christians, sensing mystical perceptions experientially, having developed within themselves a mystically musical ear. But for us in our era—an era carried away by the intellect, when mystical language, the language of feelings and higher emotions, is rarely heard, and when in the vast majority of the intelligentsia there is a total lack of mystical understanding—the words of St Isaac of Syria sound obscure; they rarely touch one's soul.

Let us take for example just the following words of his description of the mystical state during contemplation, of which we spoke above (mystical contemplation of the Divinity and its power). St Isaac of Syria represents this mystical state with his own particular analogies in this way: he says that in this state, man's consciousness "can be carried away into the bodiless realms, can touch the depths of the intangible sea."[19]

Upon reading these last words, involuntarily we ask the question "What is this 'depths of the sea' and what is this 'sea' that St Isaac talks about?"

As soon as we begin to sense the meaning of these words and understand St Isaac's thoughts, along with it, we feel the urge to transmit his thought to the reader in the clearest way, to convey it using our own more varied imagery.

We will now make an attempt in this direction. Let us see if it is possible, by using analogies more understandable than those of St Isaac, to influence our incipient mysticism, so that this mysticism, at least to some extent, could sense the meaning of St Isaac's words about "the depths of the intangible sea" and, further, that the words that we used above when speaking of mystical revelation, namely the words *contemplation of the Divinity and His powers,* communicated to our readers the meaning closest to reality, with the greatest possible clarity.

With this purpose in mind we will attempt to do everything within our power, and may the readers not be surprised if we now make an excursion into an unexpectedly different realm—into a realm that has now been quite thoroughly investigated and that has its own contemplations, not so very remote from mystical—contemplations of a vast and sublime world. Stated briefly, we will attempt to make a small excursion into the world of stars as perceived by astronomy.

Here it would be apropos to note that in general it would not do us any harm if at least once in a while we were to think of this world. People who live in cities usually forget about it altogether, absorbed as they are in the impressions of their artificial life—impressions of the street, their dwellings, and palaces, and their entertainments—absorbed in their small human affairs and vain lives.

To begin our excursion we will not dwell on the overall pictures of the starry heavens, ever fascinating in their grandeur, but rather we will look at just a small part of it, if only through binoculars. Let us look at one of the multitude of star clusters in the heavens, namely, on the star cluster that in astronomy is called Pleiades, popularly known as *stozhari.*

And so, diverting ourselves for a while from worldly impressions, we go outdoors one dark, starry night; find in the heavens the bright spot which is called the Pleiades; and direct at it our small viewing instrument. If the reader has never in his life tried this, then I can assure him that he will see something totally unexpected; before him will appear a sight of amazing beauty that will stagger his imagination. He will see in the small field of vision of the binoculars a cluster of flashing diamonds, and each of these flashing diamonds is a whole solar system. There, in just this field of vision of the binoculars, he will see a multitude of them. I speak from experience: Until one becomes accustomed to the impression of such a sight, it is difficult to tear one's eyes away from the amazing Pleiades.

But now let us switch over from contemplating the Pleiades to other impressions of the world of stars—to phenomena that man quite rarely has the opportunity to contemplate. Let us switch over to mysterious phenomena arousing awe-inspiring impressions, let us switch over to the eclipse of heavenly bodies and to the appearance in the sky of what we call *new stars*. We refer to what the astronomer Max Wilhelm Meyer has to say about this in his popular book on astronomy, *The Making of the World*: "People must have experienced horror at the sight of one of our large heavenly bodies suddenly being eclipsed, even though this phenomenon did not last long. Such occurrences deeply shook their conviction of the eternalness and inviolability of the heavenly bodies. Let us add to these transient phenomena the sudden blazing up of a *new star*, which disrupts the primordial tableaux of a constellation."[20] Meyer says further on, "Whatever assumptions we might make for the purpose of explaining the blazing up of a *new star*, one is for certain: that this flaming star represents the funeral torch of some perishing world."[21]

Another popularizer of astronomy, N. P. Azbelev, in his book *Unity in the Structure of the Universe* represents even more picturesquely the moment of the blazing up of a new star. He says,

> One of the countless multitude of worlds in the starry universe: at a distance of hundreds of *light years*[22] from us, during the process of its gradual extinction, emitted a convulsive sigh of unwilling farewell to life, the star began to burn. This sign was instantly passed on into the sensitive ether, which with its high speed waves carried news of it into boundless space to other worlds.... After hundreds, and maybe even thousands of years of tireless travel these waves met the earth (a *tiny particle of matter* in the innumerable mass of suns and other "earths") and transmitting this news to it in passing, sped further and further on."[23]

The brief astronomical depiction gives us an idea of the boundlessness of the universe in which we live and in which from time to time worlds are buried, the news of which burial we receive through the appearance in the sky of a new star, as Meyer expresses it, the "burial torch" of one of the perishing worlds.

We all know that man worked with his lower reason for several thousands of years in order to comprehend all this, and here he finally searched out these facts and has communicated them to us. And now in order to sense approximately the boundlessness of creation, we should take the aforementioned pictures of the world of stars, which transferred our ordinary point of view from our earthly life to the point of view of the boundlessness of the universe. Consequently, we see that our earth, which to us seems so enormous, is in reality an insignificant speck of dust, an insignificant atom that sooner or later must die.

Such is the Earth, as a physical world. But along with this we know that on this atom live millions of beings whose psyches perceive this boundless world. Each one of these atomistic beings inhabiting the earth is great in itself as the bearer of human thought, penetrating the world. But that is not all; each of these beings can rise still higher, can rise with its super-consciousness above the starry world into the spiritual world, to a height unattainable for our normal consciousness. As explains the doctor of philosophy Carl du Prel, our ordinary mental consciousness, like a vine, can only little by little wind around its trellis—the world. And we people, he continues, "although representing at the present time the highest product of development, with all our organizations, are doomed to relate only with one small corner of the whole world. The transcendental world lying beyond the limits of our senses remains for us, that is our mental consciousness, beyond our comprehension."[24]

———————

After all the foregoing comparisons, after our brief mental contemplation of the world of stars, helping us to *sense* its boundlessness, let us remember the words of St Isaac of Syria about mystical states, when man's consciousness "can touch the depths of the intangible sea." And these words, which are unclear to us about the endless depths of another world begin, by analogy with the world of stars, to take on some sense and meaning.

By analogy we can now, if only remotely, understand the aforesaid saying of St Isaac of Syria, pertaining to the spiritual world, which raises up the soul to a range of impressions immeasurably broader then the astronomical world. Not far from the grandeur and harmony of the physical sphere is the possibility of getting an idea of the greatness of another, higher sphere, the spiritual sphere, a sphere that differs from the physical first of all in that it does not have within itself perishing worlds. William James, in his book *The Varieties of Religious Experience*, has this to say: "The world will perish, as science assures us, will burn or freeze up; but if it is an integral part of a higher harmony, then the purpose of this world (that is, of our earthly world) will not perish and will give sure fruit *in another world*: where God is, tragedy is only temporary and partial, and ruin and destruction can no longer be the real end of all that exists."[25]

As the result of this analogy from the world of boundless physical spheres, maybe our readers' mystical sense will now be capable of feeling to a certain extent what St Isaac of Syria wanted to say with the words about "the depths of the spiritual intangible sea," and from this the reader can already obtain some understanding of the kinds of sensations experienced during the mystical contemplation of divine powers.

———————

We said above that one can perceive first of all in the lives of spiritual athletes two main characteristic paths of this life, the path of contemplation and the path of activity; hence, there are two main types of ascetics—the contemplative type and the active type.

For the contemplative type of ascetic, love of God is first and foremost, and love of people for him is the necessary consequence, an indispensable attribute of his love of God. Of course, during the time when a spiritual striver lives the life of an ascetic—away from the society of men—he is virtually unable to show this love for people in actual deed; nonetheless, this love without a doubt abides in him potentially. The sixth-century ascetic St Isaac of Syria says that a righteous man leading an ascetic life, during those rare periods of his life when he enters into association with people, shows his love for them in deed. During the periods of living in the wilderness, "where it is not possible for man to show love for his neighbor in visible and physical deeds, there, sufficient before God is our love for our neighbor which is accomplished only mentally; especially if the reclusive and silent life and success in it are sufficient in the doing of it [of love]."[26]

The other path to perfection, conforming to the above-mentioned scheme of Abba Dorotheus, as we already said, is when the ascetic proceeds toward his goal first of all through developing within himself love for men—through development that is realized by acts of love; and aspiration toward the Godhead in such an ascetic develops in equal measure. But this love appears not as a contemplative feeling, but as love for God in the feeling of love for one's neighbor. It goes without saying that such a love does not exclude the possibility of divine contemplation, but in this case the ground for the development of striving toward the Godhead is first of all the fervent feeling of the ascetic toward people, growing up in works of love. Such is the active type of ascetic.[27]

The division of spiritual endeavor into two basic types—the contemplative and active types—does not exclude cases of a spiritual athlete combining within himself qualities of both types and, even in full measure, close to perfection.[28]

Such a person was, for example, St Seraphim of Sarov, but it is rare to come across lives of perfect people such as Seraphim. Concerning this, one must note that such a life is made up of alternating periods, one period devoted to asceticism and the other period devoted to active work in the field of public service. The above-mentioned alternation of periods can be accounted for by the fact that no matter how great a person might be by virtue of his spirituality, nevertheless it is necessary to strengthen this spirituality by entering deep within oneself in seclusion from the world. Even the God-man Jesus Christ before the beginning of His great service strove in the wilderness, preparing Himself to be the sacrifice to the world.

But as we already said before, it is relatively rare that one comes across in the world of holy people spiritual athletes similar to St Seraphim of Sarov, close to perfection, containing within themselves the higher qualities of contemplative and active endeavor. Usually we see that the development of a spiritual athlete's life proceeds either in the direction of asceticism or in the direction of Christian activity, manifested in works of love and public service. This can be accounted for in each given case by the most diverse reasons—by the conditions of the environment, by exceptional reversals in the life of an athlete, by the influences of instructors, and so forth. But of course, the main influence here would be the natural predisposition of the saint himself to one or the other type of spiritual endeavor.

In studying the lives of the saints, one can see that some of them already by their very nature possessed a special aptitude for super-consciousness, for sensing the Divinity, for contemplation, that is to say, for divine mysticism. To understand the various degrees of these aptitudes in people, let us make an analogy between mystical aptitude and musical aptitude. Just as there are exceptionally talented people in music, others who are even real geniuses in perceiving musical inspiration, some who have weaker aptitudes, and finally, ordinary people who are by nature less sensitive to music, so in divine mysticism people's natural aptitudes are not identical.[29] As an exception, one comes across people especially gifted mystically, with unusual sensitivity to spiritual influence on themselves, a sensitivity manifested in special spiritual visions. Such exceptional people usually strove toward asceticism, because it developed their mystical aptitudes to the highest limit, to clairvoyance, to unutterable spiritual delight. In the vast majority of cases we come across people mystically ungifted, and we see this not only among unbelievers but also even among sincerely religious people who understand the meaning of mysticism, who understand the meaning of spiritual super-consciousness. Far from all religious people are given the ability to be mystics. Professor Alexander Vedensky says,

> He is still not a mystic who says of himself that he firmly believes in the existence of God. Faith in God, in the church mysteries, still does not constitute mystical perception, no matter how strong and fervent, even though the believer continually feels that he is in the presence of God, [and] approaches the mysteries with the most sincere fear and trembling. Faith is not knowledge.[30]

To supplement these words of Professor Vedensky, we can say that divine mysticism *gives knowledge*, leads to sensations that are more convincing than faith. In this sense, our study of the mystical perceptions of ascetics, fulfilling their lives in the Logos, has for us vital significance. The unanimity of experience of these ascetics determines the bases for the future development and elaboration of Christian philosophy. If man's skeptical mind is inclined to deny constructions based on faith, then it is silent before the strength of fact, before the strength of knowledge. Of course, with the present conditions of our development there are still very few people capable of being mystics, that is, people who sense the higher powers. But this by no means lessens the significance of mystical cognition or the significance of mystical phenomena themselves, as grounds for the substantiating true philosophy. According to the opinion of Vladimir Solovyov, "Mystical phenomena, as the most central and deep, are of paramount and fundamental importance, they are followed by psychological phenomena and, finally, by the most superficial and dependent physical phenomena."[31]

Our other Russian philosopher, N. A. Berdyaev, attaches importance to mysticism in this same regard. He says, "Mysticism is enlightenment, in mysticism there is always illumination, the brilliance of lightning, not darkness or chaos."[32]

Thus, there were saints who did not possess mystical abilities or were very weak mystically, although some of them were at the same time great spiritual athletes in their fervent faith and Christian activity. This is clearly evident from their biographies and the writings that they left. These saints for the most part belonged to the active type. Such, for example, was St John

Chrysostom. He by nature did not possess mystical abilities, and mysticism was weakly manifested in him.

As a graphic example of this difference between saints who were mystics and those who were not, we present here two characteristic episodes taken from the *Menologion*: one from the lives of St John Chrysostom and St Proclus (fifth century), who became patriarch of Constantinople after Chrysostom, and the other from the life of St Gregory, Bishop of Neocaesarea (ascetic of the third century), who possessed mystical gifts (clairvoyance, wonderworking, etc.). These episodes are identical in character and relate to the sphere of the direct influence of the ascetic's higher spiritual power; but the attitudes of the ascetics—Sts Chrysostom and Gregory—to this influence are different. Mystic Gregory of Neocaesarea sensed with his spiritual vision divine powers, contemplated these powers, and was in direct contact with them and in contemplation of them. Yet John Chrysostom, while being under the influence of these same powers and sincerely believing in the influence of God's grace, did not sense them consciously; he was not conscious that he himself manifested not his own, but someone else's, will, that at that time he expressed not his own thoughts, but someone else's, dictated to him by a higher spiritual power.

First we will talk about an incident from the life of St John Chrysostom. The incident from the life of Chrysostom occurred when Proclus was his cleric, cell attendant, and closest disciple. This all took place during the reign of the Byzantine Emperor Arcadius, son of Theodosius the Great (395–408).

At that time—a time of every kind of intrigue at the royal court—a certain noble man of Constantinople was slandered to the emperor by those who envied him.[33] This noble was banished from court and deprived of his high rank. Wishing to appeal to the patriarch for help, he asked permission to visit him at night in order to explain everything, because he was afraid to go during the day when his enemies might see him and slander him even more.

The patriarch summoned Proclus and told him to remind him at night about the nobleman and bring him in.

Night fell. The nobleman came to the patriarch to talk with him and tell him in detail about his misfortune. The noble asked Proclus to announce him to Chrysostom. Arising from bed, Proclus went up to the patriarch's bedroom door, but through the crack of the door saw that he sat writing and that, meanwhile, some venerable old man stood close behind him, bent over his right ear, conversing with him. In appearance this man seemed to Proclus to resemble the prophet Elisha, without hair on the front part of his head and with a large, wide beard. What they discussed was impossible to catch through the door. Moving away from the door, Proclus said to the visitor, "Be patient. Someone else went in to the patriarch before you. Until he leaves, I cannot show you in." In actual fact, Proclus was bewildered and afraid; he could not understand who had come to the patriarch: besides himself, no one else could enter.

The dignitary sat waiting for a long time but, finally, again began asking Proclus to announce him to the patriarch.

"You see, " answered Proclus, "how long I myself am waiting for the man conversing with the patriarch to leave. Nevertheless, I'll go anyway and look through the crack to see if they haven't finished talking."

Proclus went and saw that the conversation still continued. He went a third time to the door, but saw the same thing.

"Father, you shouldn't have let anyone in before me, "said the dignitary, "You knew that I'm in great trouble and that I expect to be killed any day now."

"Believe me, brother," Proclus answered him, "I didn't take anyone in . . . I don't even know who he is. There's no other entrance here by which one could go in. But wait a little longer."

However, at that moment they heard the bell for matins, and Proclus said to the visitor, "Go now in peace; as of this minute the patriarch doesn't speak with anyone. From now on, during the appointed nighttime prayers, he doesn't think about anything extraneous; until daybreak he remains alone, with his whole mind immersed in prayer. Come tomorrow night, no matter what happens, I'll take you in before all others."

The noble got up sadly; with tears in his eyes he went home.

The following night he again appeared at the patriarch's home. As before, Proclus went to announce him and again saw the same thing, the unknown man speaking something in the ear of St John Chrysostom. Proclus again did not dare to interrupt their conversation, and when the bell rang for matins, the dignitary again sorrowfully returned home with nothing.

Proclus was surprised and bewildered about who in fact was coming to the patriarch and when he got through to him. And so he vowed to himself, say the chronicles, not to eat, drink, sleep, or leave the patriarch's door until he succeeded in taking the unfortunate dignitary into John, and find out how this unknown person got in to see the patriarch.

At night the nobleman appeared as usual. Proclus, who was certain that no one was with the patriarch at that moment, said to him, "For your sake, I haven't left this place at all, and now I'll go announce you to the patriarch."

He went at once, but approaching the door he again saw the unknown person, talking into the patriarch's ear. Then Proclus, upon returning, said to the visitor, "Go home, my brother, and pray God to help you, for as I see it, he who is conversing with the patriarch, is sent to him from God and enters invisibly. No one except the patriarch passed through these doors."

The dignitary left in tears, totally despairing of receiving help from the patriarch.

When morning came, John himself finally remembered the dignitary; calling Proclus, he asked him, "Didn't that man come whom I ordered to be brought to me?"

"Yes, Father," answered Proclus, "he did indeed; this is already the third night that he's come here, but you were talking with someone else in private and therefore I didn't dare enter to announce the visitor."

"With whom was I talking?!" objected John. "No one was with me tonight."

Then Proclus described the appearance of the man he saw with the patriarch, and that bending over in back of John, this unknown person spoke with him, whispering something into his ear. Later, Proclus, happening to glance at a picture of the Apostle Paul that was on the wall in John's cell, cried suddenly, "There, that's the same person I saw speaking with you, Father! That's an exact likeness!"[34]

Here we should note that the *Menologion,* in the life of St John Chrysostom, explains that at the time of the above-mentioned vision of St Proclus, Chrysostom was composing his famous commentary of the epistles of the Apostle Paul (to the Colossians, Philippians, Thessalonians, and Hebrews), and that he performed this work with great reverence after having prayed fervently beforehand to receive from above the gift of interpretation.

Having familiarized ourselves with Proclus's interesting vision, poetically and truthfully recounted in the *Menologion* we cannot help but point out the following: In the case described in the *Menologion*, what draws attention to itself is that John Chrysostom did not sense mystically that his work was accomplished *under the real influence of spiritual power in the person of the Apostle Paul, as seen by Proclus, who was mystically more gifted.* Proclus saw this and saw it three nights in a row.

———

Now let us go to the second episode—an event from the life of St Gregory of Neocaesarea.

The time when Gregory lived, namely the third century, was during the early Christian era when the principal dogmas of the religion were not yet explained precisely and formulated, and when they had not yet been elucidated by Church consciousness (by the councils). In this early period, there arose in the minds of Christians contradictory interpretations of the life of Christ. There began to appear among Christians interpreters who even rejected the divinity of the Savior. Christian philosophy, embedded in the concise utterances of St John the Divine, required precise elucidations, and the finest minds of that early Christian era were working on this. These issues also occupied Gregory of Neocaesarea, who had received a solid philosophical education in Alexandria and consciously turned from paganism to Christianity at a mature age. When Gregory had already become a bishop, among the Christians of the Antioch Church there began to spread the teaching of the Antioch bishop Paul of Samosata, maintaining that Christ was an ordinary man, differing from other men only in that he was filled with the Holy Spirit and divine wisdom, which teaching was contrary to the Gospel and the Christian philosophy of St John the Divine. Regarding this, the *Menologion* (taking information on Gregory of Neocaesarea from testimony about his life given by St Gregory of Nyssa) says that the heresy of Paul of Samosato perplexed even Gregory of Neocaesarea himself, and as a deeply religious man, he

> prayed to God and the Mother of God to open to him the true faith. And so, when one night he was praying about this with special fervor, the Most-Pure Virgin Mary appeared to him, shining like the sun, with John the Divine. Pointing with her hand at Gregory, the Most-Pure One commanded John the Divine to teach him the proper way to believe in the mystery of the Holy Trinity.

The words of the revelation said to Gregory of Neocaesarea by John the Divine were the following:

> *God is One*, Father of the Living Word, of the Personal Wisdom, of the Power and eternal Image, Perfect Parent of the Perfect One, Father of the Only-begotten Son. *The Lord is One*, One from One, God from God, the Image and Likeness of the Divinity, Effectual Word, Wisdom, embracing the whole of all that exists, and the creative Power of all creation, True Son of the True Father, Invisible, Incorruptible, the Immortal and Everpresent Son of the Invisible, Incorruptible and Everpresent Father. And the *Holy*

Spirit is One, Who has Its being from the Father and appears to people through the Son, the Perfect Image of the Perfect Son, Life the Cause of all that lives, Holy Fountain, Sacred Thing, giving sanctification, in Whom God the Father reveals Himself, Who is above all and in all, and God the Son, Who is over all, *Perfect Trinity*, by glory, eternity and kingdom, indivisible and inalienable. And so in the Trinity there is nothing created or auxiliary, or introduced, as if not existing before and subsequently entering in. Thus, the Son was in no way deficient before the Father, nor the Holy Spirit before the Son, but is necessarily and invariably always the same Trinity.

After this vision and explanation heard from St John the Divine, Gregory, as told by the chronicles, wrote down in his own hand the words spoken to him by St John the Divine, and this his writing has been kept for many years in the Neocaesarean Church. Gregory of Nyssa, the brother of St Basil the Great, who made known the above-mentioned miraculous origin of the symbol of faith, adds the following: "If someone wishes to be convinced of this, let him listen to the Church in which Gregory of Neocaesarea preached and in which has been preserved up until now the original, written by his blessed hand." Macrina, grandmother of Basil the Great and Gregory of Nyssa, having listened to Gregory of Neocaesarea himself, brought this symbol to Cappadocia and used it to teach her grandchildren, including Basil the Great. Gregory the Theologian was also guided by this symbol.[35]

This written record by Gregory of Neocaesarea is remarkable in that it serves as the basis for our symbol of faith worked out by the councils. Our symbol of faith is set forth more briefly and simply than St Gregory's writing, for it was intended for the understanding and assimilation by the popular masses. However, St Gregory's record is expressed using the philosophical language developed directly from the lofty words of St John the Divine on the Logos.

––––––––––

The incident described by St Gregory of Nyssa is in essence almost identical to the above-mentioned incident from the life of St John Chrysostom. The only difference between them is that Chrysostom, although he even prayed to God before he started working on the commentary of St Paul, and although he also believed deeply in divine grace giving people the light of understanding, he was not consciously aware that he wrote under the influence of a special power. But here, in the case of Gregory of Neocaesarea, the latter showed himself to be not only a believing Christian, but also a mystic. He not only believed in grace, but also, more than that, sensed it directly with his spiritual super-consciousness. He saw St John the Divine and consciously received from him the words of the revelation. The mysticism of St Gregory was stronger than faith, as we are accustomed to understand this latter word; Gregory's perception was already not through faith, but by knowledge. This was direct experience of the divine—experience in a spiritual vision.

Now, concerning St John Chrysostom, he did not belong to the contemplative type of ascetic. He was not a mystic. He was primarily the active type of ascetic.

Independent of the case we have cited from the *Menologion*, Professor I. V. Popov comes to the same conclusion concerning John Chrysostom in his research on him. He says,

> Regardless of his prolonged ascetic endeavors, his four-year stay in a monastery and even his two years as an anchorite, despite his continual respect and sympathy for monastic life, Chrysostom was not a mystic, and in his extensive volumes it is difficult to find mystical elements.... In Chrysostom we will find nothing about contemplation, or about mystical ecstasy, or about the special cultivation of feeling, or about love for God, separate from the active life and love for man. Singing hymns of love, following the example of the Apostle to the gentiles whom he venerated with special love and respect, Chrysostom usually meant by it love for man commanded by Christ, or rather love for God in the person of our neighbor.[36]

But our pointing out the division of ascetics into two basic types—the mystical contemplative type and the active type—does not exclude, as we said above, the possibility of the ascetic combining within himself striking qualities of both types.

St Seraphim of Sarov was such a person. We will cite detailed information about his life in the following chapter.

CHAPTER 2

Seraphim of Sarov

God is a fire that warms and kindles the heart and inward parts. If we feel in our hearts coldness, which is from the devil, for the devil is cold, then let us call upon the Lord, and He will come and warm our hearts with perfect love not only for Him, but for our neighbor as well.

—From the spiritual instructions of St Seraphim of Sarov[1]

Before we talk about the life of St Seraphim, let us say something about the main purpose that he pursued all his life and that constituted the meaning of his ascetic labors.

St Seraphim said that the purpose of life of each person should consist in the *acquisition of the Holy Spirit of God.* To understand the meaning of St Seraphim's words, let us compare what he said with the purpose of life as understood by the greater part of our intelligentsia. For this, let us take a typical definition, namely the definition of the young contemporary philosopher P. D. Uspenskii in his interesting book *Tertium Organum,* in which he says that the meaning of life is in cognition and in knowledge. By this, Uspenskii means *cognition* in a broad sense: "Not only with the mind, but with our whole organism, our whole body, our whole life." Uspenskii explains that, in his opinion, man's strongest emotion is striving toward the unknown. *Even in love,* he says that the strongest attraction to which all else is sacrificed is the attraction to the unknown, *to what is new.*

So the meaning of life for the intellectual philosopher consists first of all in man ceaselessly satisfying his thirst for knowledge, that thirst that constitutes the main life stimulus of man's inquisitive mind: even the most elevated sensations—this is all auxiliary, says Uspenskii's book. The goal of knowledge is always knowledge.[2]

This view is very characteristic and typical of people living in the enjoyment resulting from the satisfying of their inquisitive mind, looking at life from the point of view of interest in the study and knowledge of the new and unknown. Such was not the meaning of life according to Seraphim of Sarov.

Besides cerebral consciousness—consciousness of the inquisitive intellect—an ascetic such as Seraphim had yet another consciousness dominating over the first one. This was the consciousness of the higher reason[3] living in the higher emotions of the heart (emotions of spiritual love and unity). The consciousness of this reason does not concern itself with investigations, as we are accustomed to understand this expression. It lives in the intuitive perception of a higher super-universal power. And the Holy Spirit can illuminate with Its Grace the whole man;[4] this illumination can be accomplished like a streak of lightning that no human mind can keep up with. The power of this illumination is such that for many it even anesthetizes rational analysis, the analysis of the lower reason.[5] And these sensations are so immensely joyful and so extremely intense and absorbing that they constitute the whole life of the ascetic. Even man's most noble emotions appear here only as an instrument; they are converted into a single flame that devours everything. This flame cannot be compared with the pleasure obtained from knowing and knowledge, as we normally understand this word and these pleasures. "This state," says the ascetic Theophan the Recluse, "cannot be compared to any natural delight. It is exceptional and is experienced only by the Lord touching the soul."[6] Such is the acquisition of the Holy Spirit of God.

And subsequently, if from this acquisition knowledge appears, then this does not change the essence of the matter. Knowledge then appears as a result, and not as a purpose. The ascetic does not make a goal of knowledge as we understand the word; he does not test the Divinity. He strives only toward one thing: to be overshadowed by divine grace. He searches for this alone from the Higher Power, and for this alone does he train himself. He has only one goal, and this one goal (all else is auxiliary) is the *acquisition of the Holy Spirit of God,* as Seraphim says.

———————

Seraphim of Sarov (in the world Prochorus Moshnin) was born in 1750 in Kursk of a merchant family. He died in 1833 in the seventy-fourth year of his life.[7]

As a Christian ascetic, he was remarkable in that he combined within himself profound mysticism with the fruit-bearing activity of a spiritual physician, devoting the last years of his life entirely to the service of mankind. Yet the combination and development within him of the contemplative and active types did not proceed simultaneously, but rather they were cultivated consecutively, one type after the other.

The active type made itself known in Seraphim later in life, when he was already sixty years old, when he had already passed through the whole fullness of the contemplative life, when he had attained clairvoyance and penetration into the inmost recesses of man's soul. Up until old age, Seraphim avoided people and gave himself over entirely to working on himself and transforming his passions into lofty feelings, and devoted himself to spiritual endeavor, which bestows on man the gift of higher faith, contemplative faith.[8]

It is interesting to trace, even in a general sense, how Seraphim passed through his consecutive spiritual endeavors, how he "acquired the Holy Spirit of God." We will see that the path of his spiritual striving proceeded as if according to an exact, predetermined plan. Seraphim developed his spiritual powers in consecutive exercises—exercises to us extraordinary, very difficult—such exercises against which our reason is inclined to protest, for no voluntary physical tortures are in accord with the requirements of our reason, which first of all protects the life of form.[9]

Seraphim's harsh life did not at all have the effect of diminishing his joy of life, which was the most important trait of his character. According to reliable sources, Seraphim was so filled with spiritual joy that he was never seen to be sad or despondent, and he tried to transmit to others this joyful frame of mind.

We have little information about the childhood years of Prochorus Moshnin. We know only that by nature Prochorus was in general disposed to mysticism, that he had inclinations to the development to superconsciousness. So when Prochorus was only ten years old, already at that time he had miraculous dreams. During a serious illness that befell him at this age, while asleep he was overshadowed by an extraordinary vision—the Mother of God appeared to him and promised to visit him and heal him of his infirmity. This dream came true: It happened that soon after this that a procession of the cross was carrying an icon of the Mother of God close by the house where he lay sick. Prochorus's mother carried her ailing son out to kiss the icon; the boy recovered. This event left a profound impression on Prochorus's soul.

It is further known that over the years Prochorus's piety increased. Prochorus was not attracted to commercial trade, for which his close ones wanted to train him. Soon his strong striving toward the church began to make itself known. Finally, at seventeen years of age Prochorus's intention to dedicate himself to monastic life took form. His relatives did not hinder him in this. Prochorus's mother even blessed her son in this endeavor with a copper cross that Prochorus later always wore on his breast.[10]

Concerning the extent of Prochorus's education, it was the same as for all merchant children of that time. His studies were elementary, using the book of hours and the psalter.

Prochorus Moshnin entered the Sarov monastery as a novice at age nineteen. There he was entrusted into the guidance of a certain elder (Joseph) with whom he embarked on the path of spiritual endeavor.

While a novice, Prochorus passed through a whole series of obediences. He worked in the bread bakery, in the *prosphora* bakery, and in the joiner's shop. Finally, he was made sacristan. But while fulfilling all this, Prochorus devoted himself with fervor to inner spiritual endeavor. Under the guidance of his elder, he developed within himself a striving toward the life of contemplation. In his free time outside of church services and obediences for the brotherhood, he left the monastery and withdrew into the forest to pray in solitude.

At twenty-one years of age, the novice Prochorus became ill with dropsy, which caused him to be bedridden for three years. Prochorus bore this sickness with patience. The termination of his illness was marked by a special vision. Again the Holy Virgin Mary came to him. After this vision Prochorus's health began to improve, and soon he recovered completely.[11]

From this second vision of the Holy Virgin, it is apparent how Prochorus's mysticism had progressed. When he was a ten-year-old boy, the Mother of God appeared to him in a dream; now the vision of the Mother of God occurred when he was awake.

At age twenty-seven, the novice Prochorus was tonsured a monk and was given the name Seraphim. To all those around him the newly tonsured monk gave the impression of possessing special abilities: Seraphim had a good memory, a sharp imagination, and a natural gift for words. Although, as we said, his studies were limited, yet during the period of his novitiate in the monastery Seraphim's spiritual knowledge was broadened. He studied intently the works of the ascetics, Basil the Great, Macarius of Egypt, John of the Ladder, St Isaac of Syria, and others;[12] these works were part of the collection the *Philokalia,* first printed in Slavonic in 1793 when Seraphim was thirty-four years old.

Seraphim was also gifted physically. Tall in stature, he possessed considerable strength. In spite of his strict abstinence, he had a healthy appearance. His face was white, framed by a broad and thick beard, his eyes were expressive, his look intent and penetrating.

In the year he was tonsured a monk, Seraphim was ordained a deacon. He fulfilled his diaconate with fervor, as he had his novitiate in general. He sensed the significance of the throne of the altar, before which he served. During the church service, he devoted himself to higher contemplative prayer, and with his spiritual vision he began to sense another world.

And then, at this time of his life, one day during liturgy, namely, on Great Thursday of Passion Week, he fell into an unusual state: When in deacon's vestments he was performing the service, after the words "O Lord, save the God fearing," he pronounced the liturgical exclamation, "And to the ages of ages," and turning around, while holding the stole in his right hand, toward the western doors (to the doors of the entrance into the church temple) suddenly, in front of everyone, he stopped short and froze on the spot, as if struck by something extraordinary. The impression of what he experienced was so powerful that he could not say anything; he could not even move from his place. Then two of his fellow deacons approached Seraphim and led him into the altar. The service continued, but Seraphim could not serve. He stood motionless in the altar for about two hours.

Seeing this, the monks in the altar did not disturb Seraphim. They attributed Seraphim's condition to physical exhaustion, thinking that the young deacon's stopping in the middle of the service occurred as the result of prolonged fasting to which he subjected himself. But when Seraphim came to himself and when the monastery elders Pachomius and Joseph began questioning him about the reasons for what happened, then Seraphim had to tell them what happened to him and what he experienced.

As he revealed to Pachomius and Joseph, the following is what happened to him: When after his last exclamation Seraphim turned to face the western doors, he was suddenly struck by an extraordinary light, "as if from the rays of the sun." As the chronicle says, Seraphim saw in this light, "the Son of Man in glory shining with an unutterable light brighter than the sun and surrounded like a swarm of bees by the heavenly powers. From the western church doors, He passed through the air, stopped opposite the ambo and, raising His hand, blessed those serving and praying. After this He entered through the royal doors next to His icon."[13]

According to our subjective impression, the picture of this vision is singularly sublime. Seraphim undoubtedly saw Him, about whom he told the elders. And he saw, as he said, "like a swarm of bees" that which surrounded the Son of Man, but he saw this with his spiritual vision through his heart.

Here it is interesting to mention a saying of St Isaac of Syria that is closely related to a similar vision. "If you are pure," he says, "then heaven is within you and you will see within yourself angels, and with them and I them the Lord of angels."[14] Concerning how the pure in heart are able to see angels and the Lord of angels, St Isaac of Syria in another place of his works[15] explains that the soul having attained purity, sees them "not with the physical eyes," but rather "spiritually, with the eye of insight, that is, as we understand it, through the inner vision, locked in the heart—in the organ of higher spirituality."[16]

This vision strengthened Seraphim even more in his spiritual endeavor. He sensed with his inner vision the power of the greatness and care for mankind of the Son of Man, and from this time the young spiritual athlete devoted himself to the main purpose of "acquiring the Holy Spirit of God" with extraordinary fervor. He sought solitude more often and withdrew, when he could, into the Sarov forest to pray.

In general regarding similar experiences such as those experienced by Seraphim of Sarov, a psychologist of our [nineteenth] century, William James, says that "mystical states attaining their full development are absolutely authoritative for those people who experience them."[17] Higher mystical contemplation, according to James, carries with it such a full awareness of the reality of its object and leaves such an indelible impression, that in the eyes of the mystic the sensation of all other reality pales before it.

Finally, in the thirty-sixth year of his life, after Seraphim had been consecrated a priest, he decided to give himself up fully to the feat of anchoritism, withdrawing himself completely from the world. He even left the monastery confines and went to live in the dense forest six versts from the Sarov cloister. There, away from the impressions of the world, he could concentrate deeply in prayer and struggle ceaselessly with his passions. There is evidence that in this forest he led a harsh life and, as they say, did not spare himself, taking upon himself voluntary sufferings. He explained the necessity for these sufferings thus: "Passions are destroyed by suffering and sorrow—either voluntary or sent by Providence." The young ascetic's nature was strong and healthy; he had no sorrows. He then feared that passions would flare up in him, a man full of vital strength and energy, that physical desires would flare up and take from him all that was spiritual and terribly dear to him, that he had been able to acquire during the time of his first steps in spiritual endeavor. And he had acquired quite a lot. He was haunted by the sweet memory of the vision of the Son of Man in glory. All of life appeared to Seraphim in a new light.

The chronicles say that in every object, in every action, Seraphim saw a hidden relationship to spiritual life.[18] Undoubtedly, Seraphim had already attained much at this comparatively young age. While he was passing his life in spiritual endeavor, he read a great deal, intently studying the Gospel and religious books. He would often say, "It is very helpful to study the word of God in solitude; for this practice alone, aside from other good deeds, the Lord grants a person the *gift of understanding.*" And this gift of understanding, illuminated by the Logos, this gift of the higher reason, was most certainly possessed by Seraphim. Having come to know all forms and levels of prayer, he rose to the highest levels of prayerful contemplation.[19]

We should mention here that Seraphim's mystical path was that path that was indicated by the ascetics of the *Philokalia*—St Isaac of Syria, John of the Ladder, and others—whose collections of sayings are cited in our book *Super-Consciousness.*[20] The main bases of this mysticism are in the *pure, deep emotions of the heart and first of all in the emotions of repentance and humility.*[21]

Then it is in this mysticism, as we also explained in detail, that the so-called Jesus Prayer has its essential meaning.[22] Seraphim thought highly of this prayerful endeavor; subsequently, when he devoted himself to the duty of teaching others, he advised everyone to turn to this prayer.[23] The above-mentioned prayer, consisting of the words "Lord Jesus Christ, Son of God, have mercy on me, a sinner," is in essence a paraphrase of that cry that, according to the Savior's parable, was uttered by the sinful publican crying, "God, be merciful to me a sinner." As we read in the Gospel (Luke 18:13), the Savior thought more highly of this sinner–publican than the virtuous man who was self-satisfied and self-righteous (the Pharisee).

Grieving for sins in a heart crying to God was this ceaseless spiritual struggle in which Seraphim's mysticism developed. His super-consciousness grew in his humble heart. There, within himself he found the Grace of Christ. His lower reason[24] was completely absorbed by the higher reason, the root of which was in the lofty emotions of love, in this great burning of the spirit and heart.[25] Seraphim understood profoundly the meaning of this flame of the heart. Teachings left by him begin with the following words:

> God is a fire that warms and kindles the heart and inward parts. If we feel in our hearts coldness, which is from the devil—for the devil is cold—then let us call upon the Lord, and He will come and warm our heart with perfect love, not only for Him, but for our neighbor as well. And from the presence of warmth the coldness of the hater of good will be driven away.[26]

To supplement the above, it would be interesting here to mention that Seraphim's ascetic life at that time was accompanied at times by astonishing occurrences, amazing those who came into contact with them. Seraphim's hermitage was in the wilderness, and at that time in the Sarov forest there were many wild beasts.

According to the testimony of many eyewitnesses,[27] it was found that a bear often came to Seraphim in the depths of the forest, which he fed and which obeyed him. He was also visited by wolves, foxes, and rabbits, and even lizards and snakes, big and small, crawled up to him. The ascetic was not afraid of them and "without interrupting his hourly doing of the Jesus prayer," brought out to them a basket of bread.[28]

Here we consider it helpful to cite the words of a certain ascetic who is able to explain Seraphim's free intercourse with wild animals. Says this spiritual athlete,

> When I began to pray with the heart, everything around me presented itself to me in a heavenly appearance: trees, grasses, birds . . . as if everything said to me that it exists for man, testifying God's love for man and everything prays and sings glory to God. And I understood from this what is called in the *Philokalia* "knowledge of the words of creatures," and saw the means by which it is possible to converse with God's creatures.[29]

———

Rumors of Seraphim's life of spiritual labor began to spread throughout the region. Visitors began coming to him in great numbers. But Seraphim was burdened by these visits. It was especially difficult for him when women came to him. Seraphim feared temptation; his physical powers had still not been subdued. He did not yet consider himself completely delivered from the influence of feminine charms. In the teachings left by Seraphim for monastics, he expresses his view on the danger of feminine charm for the monk. Here is what he says: "One should especially keep oneself away from the society of the feminine sex, for just as a wax candle, even though unlit, will melt when placed amongst burning candles, so the heart of a monk will imperceptibly weaken from conversation with women."[30]

All this led Seraphim to the decision to beg permission of the igumen of the monastery to forbid women to come to his wilderness hillock. Finally, he himself rushed to block with logs the path to his hermitage and from this time on the path was closed, not only to women but also to all outsiders in general.

Still Seraphim was not satisfied with this. The harder he strove to protect himself from all that interfered with "the acquisition of the Holy Sprit of God," all that hampered the development of his spirituality, the more violent were the temptations of the power that attacked him.[31]

Then Seraphim decided to undertake an extraordinary heroic ascetic labor (spiritual struggle): *For a thousand days and a thousand nights he stood on a rock.* Such a mighty spiritual struggle was characteristic of such a mighty nature as Seraphim possessed. During the day, he stood in the forest where he had found for this purpose a tall granite boulder, and at night he stood in his hut where he had put a smaller rock. Seraphim performed this spiritual struggle when he was forty years old.

Standing on the rock, Seraphim prayed, and his prayer to God consisted in consciousness of his sinfulness; like the publican he cried, "God, be merciful to me a sinner."

In the *Menologion*, it says that after this spiritual struggle, "the enemy was conquered once and for all and the mental warfare ceased."[32] If one follows Seraphim's life to its end, then this spiritual struggle proves itself to be profoundly meaningful. One must keep in mind that Seraphim with all the powers of his soul wished to be delivered from that side of his nature that attracted him to personal selfish interests, darkening spiritual life. And his ascetic endeavors brought him to the point that he was delivered from this. At the same time, having passed through these spiritual struggles, he became clairvoyant and performed miracles, and these gifts he later devoted to the work of serving his fellow man. In the subsequent period of his elderhood, he was a true succorer to the grief-stricken Russian people.

We already said above that in general our rational mind (ratio) is inclined to protest against spiritual feats such as Seraphim's last feat. Right now we can cite a very typical example of such a protest expressed in a commentary on Seraphim by a certain Russian publicist. The point of the matter was that Seraphim gave himself up to stylitism at the end of the eighteenth century, during an era of large-scale religious movements in the West, and the publicist on this account hurls at Seraphim the following reproach: "The Spirit of God and the spirit of darkness collided, like two hurricanes in the spinning whirlwind of revolution, and kingdoms fell, peoples perished, but he (Seraphim) stood for 1,000 days on a rock in silent prayer. Men fought with men for the future of the world, but he fought with devils for himself alone."[33]

Of course, if one evaluates people from the standpoint of their aptitude for revolutionary struggle for formal law, striving to establish in the world *external truth,* in which many see the only cure from all evil, then Seraphim, as such a revolutionary, was a negative phenomenon. But one should not judge Seraphim with this yardstick. He had his own bases for seeking other means to heal people, and for this he strove first of all to understand the inner spiritual life of a man, to find *inner truth in the inner conscience.*[34] For this, he strove to cleanse himself of base passions, and later to help other people in this same direction. And the results of Seraphim's life justified his spiritual endeavors. Seraphim in his time accomplished not a small amount for suffering mankind; he zealously served people with his moral strength. Thousands of sufferers came to the elder for spiritual help—not illusory help, but real, healing people—there came those worn out by a life that many of them passed in the fruitless struggle in the sphere of that same formal law in which man's lower reason sees the only panacea for all evils.

After the spiritual struggle of standing on the rock, fate sent Seraphim a trial, and as the reader will see later on, Seraphim's spiritual strength during this trial revealed itself to the fullest.

Robbers attacked Seraphim in the forest and demanded money. Seraphim answered that he had not received money from anyone. The robbers did not believe him. Seraphim had an ax in his hand. He possessed physical strength and could have defended himself with the ax, but he lowered the ax, crossed his arms on his chest, and said, "Do what you have to do."

The robbers did not waste any time; they mutilated Seraphim. After they left, he barely crawled to his cell. The Sarov brethren were horrified when they saw Seraphim: his head was perforated, his ribs were broken, and his chest was crushed. It is amazing that he even survived after this.

For us people of this world, it is of course difficult to understand his indifference to his own personal danger that Seraphim revealed on this occasion. Seraphim was above entering into a fight with robbers to defend himself. Looking at these people, he thought not of himself, but of them.

Here one should mention that Christian ascetics recognize as correct nonresistance to evil only *when someone is personally subjected by another to offenses*. Such offenses a Christian ascetic must endure without murmuring. But this same Christian ascetic, according to the views set forth in the *Philokalia,* "flares up with zeal against those *who attack the poor or who speak falsehood about God,*"[35] and such zeal is recognized as a positive quality of the Christian ascetic.

Concerning the question of nonresistance to evil, we cite here what William James says about it in his book *The Varieties of Religious Experience.* In his opinion,

> a man who does not attempt to lead his life in non-resistance to evil, as did the saints, does not have the right to judge the value of this kind of behavior. And when obvious results appear, we see that here the success is much more complete than the successes achieved by force or reasoning. Force destroys our enemies. Reasoning helps to preserve what we have. Nonresistance to evil, when it achieves success, turns enemies into friends.[36]

The attack by robbers experienced by Seraphim affected perceptibly his physical condition. After this occurrence, we described Seraphim's appearance as changed from what it had been before. Instead of a vigorous monk, as everyone was accustomed to seeing him, now one saw an old man, bent to the ground, who when he walked, leaned on an ax handle or cane. Seraphim's bodily forces were shaken. But his moral power remained invincible. On the contrary, it continued to grow, and until he was sixty years old Seraphim did not relax his ascetic labors. With the same fervor during this time he passed through the spiritual struggles of reclusion and silence.[37]

Finally, being forced as the result of a leg infirmity to live within the monastery compound (in order to partake of the Holy Mysteries), Seraphim was able to create a hermitage for himself in his monastery cell. He locked himself in his cell, avoiding intercourse with people, giving himself completely to prayer and withdrawal within himself. Here is how the monastery chronicler described his life at that time:

> The *staretz* did not have anything in his cell, not even the most necessary things. An icon of the Mother of God before which a lampada burned and a cut-off stump for a chair comprised everything.... On his shoulders under his shirt Seraphim wore on a cord a large 9-inch iron cross for the

mortification of the flesh. But chains or a hair shirt he did not wear. "Whoever insults us in word or deed," he said, "and if we endure the offense according to the Gospel, these are our chains and our hair shirt; these spiritual chains and hair shirts are higher than iron ones."[38]

Only in old age, when he was past seventy, did Seraphim end his life of reclusion; he began to allow visitors into his cell. Only then did he feel that he was mature for teaching.

As we see, Seraphim had to work on himself for a long time and with great effort before he decided to enter the path of elderhood. Seraphim attained much during this period of life that was preparing him for elderhood. He not only possessed the rare ability of insight and penetration into men's souls, but he gained something even higher than this ability, namely, the *gift of clairvoyance* about which we will talk further on. Now concerning Seraphim's insight, it appeared as the result of his knowledge of the human soul within himself. Only a man who knows his own passions and conquers them, knows their actual strength, can perceive them intuitively in another person from the slightest indications. And so it is precisely that ascetics enter the path of teaching only after they have passed through all the trials of their own inner struggle.

The ascetics of the Eastern Church say very definitely that a Christian ascetic should not strive prematurely to public service (teaching, preaching, etc.). Symeon the New Theologian expresses his opinion regarding this in the following characteristic, saying,

> It is right for us to bow our necks to the yoke of Christ's commandments, not turning to the side ... renewing ourselves, until the Son with the Father, through the Holy Spirit enters within us and begins to dwell in us. And already when in this way we obtain Him for ourselves as a dweller and teacher ... to that one is entrusted service, and may he perform it in a way pleasing to God. But before its time one should not seek this service, one should not even accept it when given by people.[39]

And so after long and persistent work on himself, Seraphim began, finally, his service to the Russian people as a spiritual physician and helpmeet in everything he could do to help poor people. By his activity, Seraphim exerted enormous influence on people's morals. Everyone left him with an enlightened soul and softened heart. And people valued him. Those hungering for his help flocked to him in great multitudes, especially during the last ten years of his life. Sometimes more than a thousand people would come to him in a day.[40]

Seraphim's solicitude toward people was figuratively expressed in the following words, which he said to a certain monk: "Sow the wheat given to you," said Seraphim to the hieromonk. "Sow it on good ground, sow it on sand, on rock, and in weeds. May it all take root somewhere, grow and bring forth fruit, even if not right away."[41]

At this time of his life, that is, in November 1825, seven years before his death and by then already physically infirm, Seraphim decided finally to relax somewhat the severity of his life. He allowed himself during the summer to spend days in the forest near the monastery. Here on a hill, next to a spring by the name of Theologian, a small log hut was built for Seraphim that had no windows or doors, with a side entrance through the earth under the wall. On weekdays Seraphim spent his time at the Theologian spring, returning to the monastery in the evening.[42]

What Seraphim looked like in his old age can be seen in prints that have been distributed everywhere. In these pictures, we see Seraphim as a white-haired elder, bent over, leaning on a walking stick, with an ax in his hand, in a rumpled monastic cap, in a white sackcloth smock, with a sack over his shoulders.[43]

The strength of spirit in Seraphim manifested itself toward the end of his life in a special gift of clairvoyance, enabling Seraphim to grant moral healing to those seeking his help. The human soul was open to Seraphim, like a face in a mirror. Several of his visitors, because of false shame fearing to acknowledge their sins, Seraphim brought to repentance by beginning to tell them what was tormenting them, as if these sins had been committed in his presence.[44]

There is an interesting account by the founder of Visokogorsky *pustyn'*,[45] Antony, of his conversation with Seraphim concerning his clairvoyance. It happened that Antony had to be present at the conversation of Seraphim with a certain merchant whom Seraphim earlier did not know at all. Meanwhile, Antony witnessed how Seraphim from his very first words began exposing the merchant's vices. When the merchant, after Seraphim's soul-piercing words, left his cell all in tears, the amazed Antony said to Seraphim: "Batiushka, how did you tell the merchant everything he needed without having asked him anything?"

We cite word for word Seraphim's answer to this question, as it was written down by Antony. Seraphim said,

> He (the merchant) came to me, like others, just as you came as to God's servant. I, sinful Seraphim (and that is what I think, that I am a sinful servant of God), what the Lord commands me, as his slave, that I pass on.... The first thought that appears in my soul I consider an indication by God, and speak, not knowing what the person conversing with me has in his soul, but just having faith that what the will of God directs is for his welfare. As iron to the smith, so I give myself and my will to the Lord God. What is pleasing to Him, so do I act; *I do not have my own will,* but rather, what is pleasing to God, that I pass on.[46]

We quoted these words of Seraphim in full because they give the key to explaining the psychology of clairvoyance—of that special aptitude of man's higher reason to super-consciousness.

To understand this aptitude, we cite here as a parallel to the above-mentioned answer of Seraphim a quote on the very same subject that we have taken from the writings of another famous Christian mystic, living in another country and growing up under completely different conditions than did Seraphim.

The Christian mystic about whom we are now talking is the famous mystic of the seventeenth century, Jakob Boehme. Here is a quote taken from Boehme that determines the relationship between man's lower and higher consciousness, that is, between what we call the lower and higher reasons, and that explains how man, in renouncing himself, becomes the organ of the Holy Spirit. Boehme says,

> When one neither thinks for oneself nor desires for oneself, when one's mind and will begin to surrender calmly and passively to perceiving the expressions of the eternal Word and Spirit... and when with abstract thought one locks up the imagination and outer senses, then eternal hearing, vision and speech open in you, and God will hear and see through you, because now you will be the organ of His Spirit, and God will speak in you and whisper to your soul, and your spirit will hear His voice.[47]

From these closely analogous words of Seraphim and Jakob Boehme, we see that their higher reason began to become active in their super-consciousness from the moment they completely renounced their rational will ("I do not have my own will," said Seraphim; "When one neither thinks for oneself nor desires for oneself," said Boehme). Concerning Seraphim, at the moment of his clairvoyance his whole soul no longer belonged to him, but to a higher origin—the Logos, creating in man the light of true understanding. "As iron to the smith, so I give myself and my will to the Lord God," said Seraphim.

If looking at the depicted process of Seraphim's clairvoyance in order to define this phenomenon, proceeding from the conditions in which human consciousness generally works, then this phenomenon must, of course, be ranked with those phenomena that are unconscious to the intellect. But one should note here that Seraphim's unconscious was in this case altogether special. Seraphim felt with his heart, whence arose his penetrating words.[48]

This, by the way, explains why Seraphim was never carried away by the fruits of his works. He attributed nothing to himself: "Not to us, O Lord, not to us, but to Thy name give glory of Thy mercy," he constantly repeated.[49]

In Seraphim's biographies composed by his contemporaries and in accounts about him, many examples of Seraphim's clairvoyance are cited, recorded from the words of people who experienced it.[50]

Owing to Seraphim's clairvoyance, sometimes episodes with visitors occurred that had a comical side. For example, in Seraphim's biography there is a narrative about how a certain General L. happened to come to Sarov. This was a rather arrogant man who was successful in his service and who, like many others like him, had formed a solid awareness of his own superiority as compared with those around him. A landowner by the name of Prokudin dragged this general to Elder Seraphim.

Here is a description of the general's visit with the elder: Just as soon as they, that is, Prokudin and the general, went into the elder, Seraphim went up to meet him and unexpectedly for the general bowed down to his feet. By Prokudin's account, this astonished the general. Prokudin went out of the cell, leaving the general to converse with the elder. According to Prokudin, after a few minutes something completely unexpected happened—weeping was heard coming from Seraphim's cell; surprisingly, it was the general who was weeping. After half an hour, the door opened, and Seraphim led the general by the hand out of the cell. The general continued to weep, covering his face with his hands. He forgot his decorations and service cap in Seraphim's cell. Later, Seraphim brought them out to the general.[51]

It is interesting to note that when during the general's heated conversation with Seraphim these decorations fell off, Seraphim said to him, "This is because you received them undeservedly."

In the chronicle from the *Menologion,* it also says that Seraphim's conversation, besides its clairvoyance, was striking for its *simplicity.*[52] Let us quote some characteristic simple sayings of Seraphim; they give a certain understanding of his conversation. "Do everything slowly, little by little, not suddenly," he said to people carried away beyond measure on the first step of spiritual endeavor. "Virtue is not a pear, you can't eat it all at once"; "One must love everyone, and most of all God"; "Get to know good and evil in oneself; blessed is the man who knows this"; "Judge yourself; that way God will not judge you"; "Many have perished for making concessions to the world"; "The true purpose of our lives consists in the acquisition of the Holy Spirit of God.... For this, great is the power of prayer"; and so on.

It is interesting to mention how Seraphim also made a distinction between theoretical faith and religious experience to which he attached importance. He said, "To teach others is just as easy as throwing stones to the ground from the top of a cathedral, but to master in deed that which you teach is the same as if you yourself were to carry these stones to the top of the cathedral."

We should mention here that although Seraphim devoted himself to monastic life and preferred the life of a monk to life in the world, and encouraged in monasticism those who were so inclined, yet he regarded Christian marriage with respect. "Virginity is glorious and marriage is blessed by the Lord," he said to laypeople, and "God blessed them, and said: Be fruitful and multiply."[53]

In reports by contemporaries about Seraphim, we have quite a bit of information regarding the fact that, besides his clairvoyance, there were still other states of spiritual super-consciousness to which he had access.

From these accounts, of particular interest is a description of a certain instance of Seraphim's special enlightenment, which was witnessed by a local landowner, N. A. Motovilov. Information on this has reached us because Motovilov left notes about his relationship with Seraphim that were printed in a periodical.[54]

We should mention here that Motovilov was greatly devoted to Seraphim and that Seraphim loved him as his pupil and as a deeply religious man. Their close relationship began after Seraphim healed Motovilov of a grave illness. We will give a detailed account of this healing in a later section.

Motovilov tells about Seraphim being inspired by a special spiritual enlightenment in the following notes: "It was Thursday. The day was overcast. There was half a foot of snow on the ground and the snow was coming down fairly hard." Motovilov and Seraphim were then in the forest at his near hermitage. Seraphim seated Motovilov on a felled tree stump, and he stood next to him. They got into an interesting conversation about the true purpose of Christian life consisting in the acquisition of the Holy Spirit of God. Seraphim talked much about this and with great animation; the subject of their conversation inspired him. Seraphim spoke about the power of prayer, saying that through God and the Grace of the Holy Spirit, people "saw not in dreams or in reverie or in the frenzy of a deranged imagination, but rather truly in reality.... We do not seek the Grace of God, because of the pride of our mind we do not allow it to come dwell in our souls, and that is why we do not have true enlightenment from the Lord. The trouble is that we, prospering in age, do not prosper in Grace or in God's reason."[55]

It is here that Seraphim also talks about the case of the descent of the Holy Spirit on the apostles and about other unusual cases of the Holy Spirit's manifestations.

At the height of this animated conversation, Motovilov asked him, "How am I to know that I am in the grace of the Holy Spirit?" Seraphim began to speak spiritedly to Motovilov about this, that it was very simple, and began to cite examples from the lives of the apostles, but Motovilov was not convinced by this. "I still do not understand how I can be absolutely sure that I am in the Spirit of God," continued Motovilov. "How can I discern within myself His true appearance?"

Seraphim answered, "Your Excellency, I already told you that this is very simple and recounted to you in detail how people are present in the Spirit of God and how we should understand His appearance in us.... Now what more do you need, Batiushka?"

"What I need," said Motovilov, "is to understand this well!"

Then Seraphim took him very firmly by the shoulders and said to him, "Batiushka, the two of us together are now in the Spirit of God! ... Why do you not look at me?"

Motovilov answered, *"Batiushka, I cannot look because lightning is flashing from your eyes. Your face has become brighter than the sun, and my eyes are racked with pain!"*

Seraphim said, "Do not be frightened, your Excellency, for you yourself have become just as bright as I am. You yourself are now in the fullness of the Spirit of God, *otherwise you would not be able* to see me like this."

And inclining his head to Motovilov, he said quietly in his ear,

Now give thanks to the Lord God for His unutterable mercy to us. You saw that I did not even cross myself, but only prayed mentally in my heart to God and said within myself: O Lord! vouchsafe him clearly and with his bodily eyes to see that descent of Thy Spirit with which Thou dost favor Thy slaves when Thou in Thy goodness dost will to appear in the light of Thy magnificent glory. And here, batiushka, in an instant the Lord fulfilled the humble request of wretched Seraphim."

After these words, Motovilov looked into Seraphim's face and an even greater reverential fear came over him.

Imagine to yourself that in the middle of the sun, in the most brilliant brightness of its midday rays, there is the face of a man conversing with you. You see the movement of his lips, the changing expression of his eyes, you hear his voice, you feel that someone is holding you by the shoulders, but not only do you not see these hands—you do not even see yourself or his figure, but only a blinding light, spreading far off, several yards around us, and illuminating with its striking brilliance the carpet of snow covering the glade and the snowflakes settling on me and the great *staretz*. Writes Motovilov, Can you imagine the position I was in at that moment?

"How do you feel right now?" Seraphim asked Motovilov.

"Unusually well!" he said.

"Well in what way? What exactly?"

Motovilov answered, "I feel such calm and peace in my soul that I cannot express it in words!"

"This, your Excellency, "said Seraphim, "is that peace about which the Lord spoke to His disciples: 'My peace I give you.'"

And here is another account of one of the eyewitnesses—an account of another higher contemplative state that Seraphim experienced, a state of so-called spiritual ecstasy, when a man's thoughts are stilled and he is powerless to communicate clearly what he is experiencing in the ecstasy. An account of such a state of Seraphim is set forth in the *Menologion* from the words of the monk John, who was close to Seraphim and happened to be present at the time of the ecstasy.

One day, Seraphim revealed to John that he had knowledge of *other worlds*: he had been there. "Only I do not know," said Seraphim, "whether in the body or out of it, God knows—this is incomprehensible.... And of the joy and heavenly sweetness which I tasted these it is impossible to tell you."[56]

According to the words of the monk John who heard this, Seraphim, having said this, bowed his head and was silent. His eyes closed; with his extended right hand, the elder rhythmically and gently stroked his heart in an upward direction. John saw that Seraphim's face "was changed in a marvelous way and gave off such an unusual light that it was impossible even to look at him."

After a half-hour of silence, Seraphim finally began to speak.

"If you knew what joy awaits a righteous man in heaven, you would be determined to endure sorrows with thanksgiving during this temporary life."[57]

Apropos of this spiritual ecstasy overshadowing Seraphim, we will cite some general characteristics typical of similar ecstasies—information derived from the teachings expressed by the church fathers St Gregory of Nyssa and Dionysius the Aereopagite.

Gregory of Nyssa defines these states thus: having left everything visible, not only that which the senses perceive, but also that which the reason (the lower reason) sees, the mind (the higher reason) unceasingly goes farther within, until it penetrates the invisible and incomprehensible and there sees God.[55] Speaking of similar states, Dionysius the Aereopagite notes that during such a state the mind does not exist either for itself or for others, but rather exists solely for Him Who is above all.[59]

So from these words of Gregory of Nyssa and Dionysius the Aereopagite we see that man, striving toward the Divinity, can during spiritual ecstasy rise above in its sensations not only the perceptions of the five organs of sense, but also above the consciousness of its own reason. During such a state, carried to the point of boundlessness, a man's life sensations are transformed; they pass over entirely into the realm of the Logos. Man casts off all bonds of the physical sensations and the lower reason. According to the accurate definition of Prof. I. V. Popov, this state of ecstasy is psychologically typified by the loss of consciousness of not only the sense perceptions, but also of abstract ideas.[60] In other words, the lower reason (ratio) is completely anesthetized.

It was this state that Seraphim experienced in the above-described case of his spiritual ecstasy.

———

Seraphim also performed miracles of healing. Of interest is the description of the healing experienced by this same Motovilov whose story about Seraphim we cited above. It was from this miracle of Seraphim that the acquaintance between Motovilov and Seraphim began. During the course of three years, Motovilov suffered, as he said, from "severe rheumatic and other illnesses combined with weakness of the whole body and paralysis of the legs, twisted and swollen at the knees and with sores on his back and side." He was a man of substance and spared nothing on his cure, but the doctors could not help him.

Finally, on the 5th of September, 1831, he was brought paralyzed to Seraphim in his near hermitage, and he began to beg Seraphim to heal him. Seraphim was touched by his entreaties, but first of all asked Motovilov if he believed in the Lord Jesus and the Mother of God; he answered that he believed.

Then Seraphim asked Motovilov if he believed that the Lord Jesus Christ could even now, as described in the Gospels, instantly heal him through the intercession of the Mother of God. The sick one said firmly that he believed this also.

And the healing took place. We have extracted the process of this healing from Motovilov's notes.[61]

"So if you believe, "concluded Seraphim, "then you are already well."

"How can I be well," I asked, "when my people and you are holding me in your arms?"

"No!" said Seraphim. "You are now in your whole body already completely well."

And he ordered those who were carrying me to leave me, and he himself, taking me by the shoulders, lifted me from the ground and placed me on my feet, saying to me, "Stand more firmly, get a better foothold on the ground, that's it, don't be timid, you are now completely healthy." And then he added, looking at me joyfully: "Don't you see how well you are standing now?"

I answered, "I am standing well in spite of myself, because you are holding me so firmly and well."

And, taking his hands away from me, he said: "So now I am not holding you any more, but rather you are standing very firmly even without me; now walk bravely, my batiushka. The Lord has healed you, now start walking and moving around."

Taking my hand in one of his, and with the other pushing my shoulders, he led me over the grass and uneven ground next to a large pine tree, saying: "See, your Eminence, how well you were walking."

I answered, "Yes, because you are leading me so kindly."

"No," he said to me, taking his hand away from me: "The Lord Himself was pleased to heal you completely, and the Mother of God Herself entreated Him concerning this; now, even without me, you will walk and will always walk well; go on, . . ." and he began to push me so that I would walk.

"But I will fall and hurt myself," I said.

"No," he contradicted me, "you will not hurt yourself, just walk firmly."

And here when I felt in myself a certain power overshadowing me from above, and I took courage a bit and proceeded to walk firmly, then he suddenly stopped me and said, "Enough for now," and asked: "So, are you convinced now that the Lord has truly healed you completely in every way? . . . Hope in Him and thank the Queen of Heaven for Her great mercy toward us. But as your three-year suffering has gravely exhausted you, now you must not walk a lot all at once, but gradually, little by little, get used to walking and take care of your health, as a valuable gift from God."

And so, a miracle was performed. Further on in his notes, Motovilov says that after having lain motionless for three years, he sat himself down in his carriage and drove from the hermitage into the monastery and startled everyone with his healing.

And here is yet another of the many healings performed by Seraphim, as taken from the *Menologion*.

The wife of a certain Vorotilov was on the verge of death. Her husband rushed to Seraphim for help; but the elder informed him that his wife must die. Then in a flood of tears, Vorotilov fell at Seraphim's feet, imploring him to pray for her return to life and health. Seraphim submerged himself in "mental prayer"[62] for about ten minutes, then opened his eyes, raised Vorotilov to his feet, and said to him joyfully, "So, my joy, the Lord is granting your wife life. Go in peace to your home."

Vorotilov went home and found out his wife felt relief precisely at that moment when Seraphim was praying so fervently. According to the words of the chronicler, she soon regained her health completely.[63]

So passed the life of this ascetic, devoting the last period of his spiritual endeavors to the work of helping people who came to him. He strove to be truly helpful to everyone, and all who had contact with Seraphim, says the chronicle, felt his great love with its grace-giving power.[64]

Apropos of Seraphim's activity, it is interesting to mention how William James, a well-known psychologist of our day, describes the lives of saints similar to Seraphim. "Saints," he says, "with their over-abundance of mercy, are great standard-bearers of the faith, rays of light cutting through the darkness. They are individual blazing sprays of a great torrent on the sun, fore-runners of a new life."[65]

––––––––––

Now let us turn to the death of Seraphim. Here is how his death occurred, judging by the chronicle in the *Menologion*.

On the 1st of January, 1903, Brother Paul, who lived next to Elder Seraphim and usually brought him food, noticed that Seraphim went out three times to the place he had prepared for his burial, where he stayed quite a long time looking at the ground.[66] In the evening, that same monk heard how Seraphim sang in his cell the paschal hymns, glorifying the resurrection of Christ.

The next day, January 2, at six o'clock in the morning, Paul left his cell to go to early liturgy and in the passageway smelled smoke and something burning. In Seraphim's cell candles always burned that he never extinguished. To all warnings by others concerning the possibility of a fire, Seraphim usually answered, "While I am alive, there will be no fire, but when I die, my death will be discovered because of a fire." And that is how it was, says the chronicle.[67]

Paul knocked at the elder's door, but it proved to be locked. Then he informed the others about this, assuming that the elder had gone to his hermitage and that something was burning in the cell.

When the door was torn from the inner latch, they saw that there were no flames, but in the disorder of books lying around and likewise assorted pieces of cloth that people diligently brought to him were smoldering. They extinguished the smoldering things, lit a candle, and saw Seraphim in his usual white overblouse in his customary place of prayer, on his knees before the analogian with a copper crucifix on his neck. His hands, folded in the form of a cross on his chest, lay on a book on the lectern. Seraphim's eyes were closed. His face was as if animated by his last prayer in this world. His body was still warm. But the monks could not wake Seraphim up. He had reposed.

In concluding our account about Seraphim, we quote the following profoundly meaningful words that during his life he often repeated to his spiritual children.

When I die, you come to me at my grave. When you have the time, you come—and the more often, the better. Everything that weighs on your soul, whatever may have happened to you, whatever you may be grieving about, come to me, and all your sorrows bring with you to my grave. Fall to the ground, as to a living person, tell me everything and I will hear you; all your sorrow will fly off and pass away. As you always spoke with a living person, it is the same here. For you I am alive and will be forever![68]

CHAPTER 3

Francis of Assissi

Praise to Thee, Lord, praise to Thy creations, But first of all, let us glorify our brother—the sun, Who gives the day and shows Thy light. He is so brilliant in great radiance, And is Thy prototype, Most High.

> —From the hymn "To the Sun" by Francis of Assisi

Mystical phenomena, being the most central and profound, are of paramount and basic importance, says Vladimir Soloviev.[1] This thesis of Soloviev is in full agreement with the words of James, that the spontaneous intuitive conviction of each human being is *hidden in the depths of his spirit.*[2] On the basis of these propositions, one could say that the character and direction of mystical feeling, implanted in the hearts of men, influence their religious worldview as well. In this sense, one can say that human religion itself is first of all derived from mysticism, or rather, derived from the level of mystical development at which stand the spiritual leaders of humanity.

Although mystical feeling is indeed the basic principle of religious belief, by itself this feeling, its growth and development, can fluctuate depending not only on the powers of the mystical genius, but also on well-known historical conditions. It can happen that the mystical leaders of mankind, influencing the masses, go by different paths in their mystical development, losing unity with one another, which unavoidably reflects on the masses; the masses of people will then follow their leaders by different paths, and the religious worldview of these masses will begin to separate people and estrange them from one another.

By far the most striking case of such a separation and estrangement of people from one another in the history of Christian mysticism we see in the division into Eastern and Western mysticism—a division running parallel with the gradual estrangement from one another of the Eastern and Western

Churches, concluding with the final division of these churches into the Catholic Church and the Eastern Church.

To show most clearly the very character of this division of Christian mysticism in two directions (in the direction of Western mysticism and in the direction of Eastern mysticism), let us liken the development of Christian mysticism to the growth of a light-loving plant.

The growth of such a plant, as we know, depends not only on the conditions in which the plant's roots grow, but also mainly on the influx of light to this plant. The same can also be said about Christian light-loving mysticism, illuminated by the grace of its great sun the Logos. The growth of this mysticism and its most perfect development depend first of all on whether or not on this plant shines unhindered the Light of the Sun, which is its main source of life.

And it was precisely amid these favorable conditions that the mysticism of the East was placed. As the result of the correct laying down of the foundations of the Eastern Church, the mysticism of the East grew freely in its striving toward the great spiritual sun–Logos, and it developed more freely than the mysticism of the West, fettered by the prejudices of the earthly desires of the Catholic Church, fettered by the ways of papism and the spiritual prerogatives of the clergy.[3]

From the books of the *Philokalia*,[4] and also from the life of the Orthodox St Seraphim of Sarov that we have just studied—we see that Eastern mysticism has one main goal: it strives toward the acquisition of the Holy Spirit and proceeding firmly toward this acquisition, and it senses in advance the future fullness of the kingdom of God's Spirit in eternal life. Meanwhile, the leaders of the Western Church, and after them the whole Catholic Church, in their conceit have already appointed themselves the realization of God's city on earth, and besides, a city governed by earthly power. Because of particular historical conditions, Catholicism tolerated within itself the following abnormalities: It placed between Christian mysticism—a light-loving plant—and the Logos, the sun of this plant, an opaque partition. It placed between God and people an earthly sovereign—the pope—and by this obscured the attainment by Catholics of direct spirituality in the realm of the Logos. According to Catholics' historically established prejudice, inculcated in them by their religion, the pope is Christ's vice regent on earth, a person infallible, divine. In the very era of the flourishing of the earthly power of Catholicism in the thirteenth century (in the era of Francis's spiritual endeavor), the pope was even in effect a ruler of earthly kingdoms and peoples. Such an organization of religion, its being reduced to earthly sovereignty, the atmosphere in which

Catholics were raised, was the main cause hindering the correct development of Catholic mysticism; here mysticism developed under abnormal conditions. It was allured not so much by the elements of the life of the spirit as
by the elements of the life of form,[5] it was attracted away from the true Light
by mental and sensual elements. And this leavening of the Catholic world
estranged it from the Eastern world.

Thus, the main reasons for the religious separation of the East and West
consists not in the dogma of the *Filioque,*[6] not in ritualistic and formalistic
arguments, but chiefly in papism and in those mystical directions that manifested themselves so differently in the spiritual endeavors of both churches.
Powerful mystical leaders of the Western Church, such as, for example, Ignatius Loyola, set as their purpose service to the pope, the earthly Christ. Their
ideal of spirituality was obscured by striving to realize the earthly power of
Christ, whereas the spiritual athletes of the Eastern Church always remained
faithful to the pure service of the heavenly Logos, and received the spiritual
Christ within themselves. As a result, it turned out that Western mysticism,
bound by the burden of papism and along with it the striving toward human
power, could never rise to the heights of Eastern mysticism, although among
the saints of the Catholic world there were great spiritual strivers, in their
lofty impulses and innate mystical ability. Even a Catholic saint such as the
amazingly gifted Francis of Assisi, not even he, as we will see later, could
renounce mentalism and sensuality in his mysticism. Besides this, we will see
further on that the reason for this lay in his lack of humility, although Francis
did talk a great deal about the significance of humility in his words and ver-
bal teachings.[7] True humility was foreign to the Catholic spiritual world, and
this true humility could not exist in such a church where its head, the pope,
declared himself to be the infallible ruler.

To elucidate all this accurately, we will present the mystical life of
St Francis of Assisi parallel to the life of St Seraphim of Sarov. We chose for
such a comparison the life of the aforementioned Catholic saint because it
sharply points out Catholic mystical traits formed in Francis's era (thirteenth
century)—traits that in the sixteenth century were carried to the extreme
by his follower, another Catholic saint, Ignatius Loyola. The mysticism of
Francis of Assisi, if we compare it with the mysticism of Seraphim of Sarov,
vividly sets off for us the essence of Orthodox mysticism. In this way, we
will understand the true significance and loftiness of the mysticism of the
Eastern Church.

In this chapter, we give an account of Francis's life. And in the next chapter we will attempt to compare the religion and mysticism of Francis of Assisi

and Seraphim of Sarov. Although the conditions and eras in which Francis and Seraphim lived (the thirteenth and eighteenth centuries) are like two different worlds, yet this will not interfere with our work because we will be concerned not so much with the external activity of these saints as with their inner psychology.

And so let us talk about the life of Francis of Assisi.[8] First of all, we should say a few words about the epoch in which he was active.

This era, the beginning of the thirteenth century, was the time when the secular authority of the pope reached the height of its power, when the kings of England and Aragon acknowledged themselves to be vassals of the vice regent of St Peter and when the Hohenstaufen Empire, hostile to the papacy, collapsed. In addition, this era was a time of the moral decline of the Catholic clergy. Describing the breakdown in morals within the clergy at that time, a researcher of Francis's life, P. Sabatier, says that at that time the finest hearts of the Catholic world turned to the East, asking themselves mentally whether the Greek Church would not come and cleanse all this evil and take over the inheritance of its sister.[9]

It was in this era that Francis appeared. This remarkable man, by his spiritual endeavors, strove to recall the apostolic times; by his example, he strove to revive the extinct Christianity of the West.

First of all, we feel we should mention that the external circumstances of Francis's life differed sharply from the path by which Seraphim of Sarov traveled, of which we spoke in the previous chapter. The latter, as we already know, appeared as a public figure in his later years. The energy of all his life up to the age of sixty Seraphim used in the work of struggling with himself, in the work of accomplishing his own moral perfection. Francis's life took shape differently. In his early years, Francis abandoned himself with enthusiasm to the joys of worldly pleasures. His life of spiritual endeavor began at the age of twenty-three. Francis's spiritual development was accomplished unusually fast; already after four years of spiritual striving, he felt that he was fully developed for apostolic preaching, which was highly active and left a vivid impression.

Beside this, one must say that there was a great difference in the very character of the public activity of these two saints. Seraphim's public service manifested itself in the broad but modest activity of elderhood, in energy spent on the spiritual healing of people. Although Seraphim did much for the Christian concept, being himself by today's standards a rare example of a man of holy life, he did not play any particular sociopolitical role. But Francis, on the contrary, had to play a big sociopolitical role. The force of events resulted in his creating a mighty monastic corporation—the Franciscan order—the pope himself and the Roman conclave reckoned with this corporation. Owing to the fact that Catholicism in the era of Francis was very influential in the Western world, acting like a nerve connecting Western nations, Francis's ideas seized not only Italy, where Francis was active, but other countries as well.

Francis was born in 1182 in Italy, in the city of Assisi; his family was one of the richest in the city. Francis's father, whose name was Bernadone, was a prosperous textile merchant. In his early years Francis was not noted for his religiosity, although by nature he was a pensive youth. He was not raised on the Psalter but on the tales of chivalry of that time; he dreamed of knighthood, of its glory and great exploits. The end of the twelfth century was a time of enthusiasm for chivalry in western Europe. Knights were then being celebrated by the famous troubadours of that time. This was an epoch of songs about King Arthur and the knights of the Round Table.

One should mention that Francis was not devoid of practical abilities. Early on, he began to help his father in his trade, and not without success. But if he was useful to his father in acquiring material means, then he also had another, completely opposite trait—he had the urge for extravagance. He squandered his money on luxury and pleasure.[10]

Francis liked to make merry. He willingly attended the carousals of his contemporaries; he had a passion for music. One chronicler of Francis's life says that in the days of his youth, the streets of Assisi often resounded with the songs of young people accompanying Francis. At these feasts, Francis was chosen master of ceremonies or "king" of festivities, and with a scepter in his hands, he led the young people. Francis's first biographer, his contemporary Thomas of Celano, in speaking of these revels, notes that for the participants, for Francis's drinking companions, Christianity was just a word. The ambition of these youths was even aimed at seeming worse than they were in actual fact.[11]

Francis's parents did not see anything wrong in their son's way of life; according to Thomas's words, they encouraged Francis in this, taking pride in his brilliance and worldly successes.

Of course, such conditions of Francis's youth did not portend any particular success in the path to moral perfection. Even less could one expect from this ambitious minion of fortune future religious endeavors.

However, we see further on that Francis was made into a man of real spiritual strength, and this strength, as we will realize, came from his amazing heart, which possessed an innate goodness—an exceptional goodness that by its very nature was imbued with such energy of altruism that no kind of bad conditions could extinguish this energy. If nature bestows on human beings musical or some other kind of genius, then there are also exceptional cases of people born into the world who are gifted with the genius of a heart sensitive to goodness.

And here—despite a life full of luxury and vanity, despite proud, ambitious dreams, which escaped Francis in such phrases as "Do you know that the day will come when the whole world will bow down before me?"[12]— despite all this, there were times when he was overcome by unusual bursts of kindness and sacrifice that startled everyone. Seeing a beggar who touched his heart, if his money had been given away, he would not stop until he had taken off his clothes and given them to the beggar. Francis's pity for the poor and unfortunate knew no bounds.

And it was this instinctively good heart that protected Francis from being overly captivated by the pitfalls that young people are generally inclined to abandon themselves to.

In his research on Francis, Johannes Jørgensen speaks of Francis's trait—during his frivolous life, during all these uproarious feasts with his contemporaries—not to abandon himself completely to base passions, not to abandon himself to disrespect of women.

All Francis's friends knew well that in Francis's presence they should avoid frivolous talk about women common among youths, and if someone decided to risk voicing indecent double entendres in Francis's presence, then he momentarily saw that Francis's face took on not only a serious but almost a severe expression.[13]

One of the general attributes of human nature is that people with strong impulses of the heart, capable at times of surrendering themselves to external impressions, are also inclined to reverse movements—movements toward entering deeply within themselves, toward impulses critical of external, vain things incapable of satisfying natures seeking reality, and not the illusive upsurges of their souls. In the movements of heart of such people, as with the swinging of a pendulum, the more it swings to one side, the greater will be its swing to the opposite side.

In Francis also there was a wide sweep in these impulses. It is interesting to note that Francis's movements of heart toward entering deep within himself came awake usually after suffering illnesses. And that is under-standable. Every serious illness, as any sorrow, forces a person to tear himself away from seething life, forces him to look at himself and be concentrated.

At the same time, it is remarkable that after a serious illness in Fran-cis awoke his instinctive super-consciousness, of which he had an abun-dance because of his mystical nature. Regarding this, sometimes strange things happened: for example, there were times that he heard mysterious voices. He then would hear as if the voice of the Logos Himself, calling him to Himself.

But Francis did not obey this voice at once, although the time of vic-tory of the higher power over Francis' frivolity did not tarry for long. The moral overturn in Francis took place in the twenty-fourth year of his life. This radical change gave a push to the quick development of his moral powers. From this time, his life moved at a quick tempo. Soon he was com-pletely transformed; everything external and illusory he rejected. He gave himself over entirely to another life—to a life of spiritual endeavors for the good of men. Unfortunately, these works, though fraught with major con-sequences, were not long-lasting. Death struck Francis down in the forty-fourth year of his life. We will see further on that one of the main reasons for his early death consisted generally in the weakness and frailness of his physical nature.

As we have seen, such was not the nature of Seraphim of Sarov. Seraphim of Sarov endured during his life physical trials that were very difficult. He suffered extremely cruel maiming by robbers, and he died in old age in the seventy-fourth year of his life.

It would be apropos to mention here that the outward appearances of Seraphim and Francis differed greatly from one another. Seraphim, as we know, was by nature of powerful build and tall stature, with a face on which lay the imprint of health, despite his ascetic life of fasting. Concerning Fran-cis, according to the testimony of those who knew him, he was of frail build. The delicate, refined features of his face were animated by brilliant eyes. He had the appearance of a nervous, highly impressionable person.

Francis was representative of a passionately enthusiastic romantic type, fired up to do good. But he was no stranger to a keenness for outward effect, was no stranger to induced exultation and even to a certain amount of theatricalism.[14]

Now Seraphim, on the contrary, was a man capable of spiritual feats without a shadow of anything ostentatious; and besides, spiritual feats of extraordinary, titanic power. This was a true representative of the Russian people, of that people which gave birth to saints such as Sergei of Radonezh or Alexei, Metropolitan of Moscow.[15]

———————

Susceptible to illnesses, Francis was subject to attacks of fever—a sickness even till now prevalent in Italy. However, bouts of this infirmity were still rare during this seething period of his life about which we are now speaking. At this time, such attacks passed away quickly for him. His youthfulness held sway, and after these short-lived trials Francis again gave himself over to pleasures and ambitious dreams. And his dreams were expansive; he dreamed of attaining glory by feats of chivalry, enticingly drawn in his imagination.

And so one fine day, it seemed these dreams were to be fulfilled. Francis was then past twenty years of age. It happened at that time that the political situation in Italy and the lucky chance of Francis's close friendship with a certain knight from his hometown gave the youth the opportunity to enter the field of military life and take part in the battle of the Guelphs and Ghibellines. The knight took Francis on his military expedition to Apulia and promised to introduce Francis to the famous Count Gauthier de Brienne, the chief military commander of the kingdom of Sicily, warring at that time with the Germans, who had seized power in Italy and who were hated by the Italians. Francis decided to take advantage of this lucky opportunity. He was already dreaming that he would quickly attain his goal. The Count Gauthier de Brienne would of course make no delay in initiating him into the knighthood.[16]

Francis's parents were in sympathy with their son's dream. They spared no money in equipping the young soldier magnificently; they dressed him in the splendid military armor of that time.

Before his departure for Apulia, Francis had an unusual dream, personifying his fantasies. He dreamed that someone invited him to a spacious and wonderful palace, the walls of which were hung with a multitude of magnificent weapons. To Francis's question of whose splendid weaponry and palace this was, he heard a voice which said to him, "All this will belong to you and your soldiers."[17] This dream made an impression on Francis. He believed in his fate.

But side by side with these ambitious dreams, under no circumstances did Francis's innate qualities abandon him. Let us point out the following typical case. A few days before his departure to Apulia, Francis happened to meet one of his military friends. He learned from his friend that because of his poverty, he was obliged to clothe himself very frugally and that he felt oppressed by this. Then Francis, not giving it much thought, gave his comrade his expensive clothing in exchange for the scanty equipment of the poor man. So this is how Francis began his new career, this magnificent knight-to-be. At the first impulse of his heart he forgot his striving for brilliance.[18]

But, finally, all the preparations for departure were finished. Francis set out on the way to Apulia (where the whole detachment was supposed to assemble), the road from Assisi to Apulia going through the town of Spoleto. Here in Spoleto, however, something totally unexpected happened to Francis, which forced him to abandon everything and return home.

Writing a detailed analysis of Francis's life, Johannes Jørgensen tells of this event: "In Spoleto, Francis' path was halted by that same hand that had already once sent illness down upon Francis, forcing him at that time to take thought and enter deep within himself."[19]

From the moment of arrival in Spoleto, Francis was again overcome by an attack of fever; again this illness confined Francis to his bed. And when he lay prostrate in a state of unconsciousness, he suddenly heard a voice that asked him where he was directing his path. "To Apulia in order to become a knight," answered Francis. "Then tell me," continued the invisible voice, "who can do more good for you, a Master or his slave?" "The Master, of course!" answered the astonished Francis. "Then why," the voice continued, "have you cast off the Master for the slave, the Prince for the vassal?"

After these words, Francis, of course, understood whence came this oracular voice. Struck by this mysterious call, as the Apostle Paul before Damascus in days of old, Francis suddenly cried, "Lord, what wilt Thou have me to do!"

To this, the voice said, "Return home; there you will be shown what to do. The dream you had should be understood differently from the way you understood it." And the voice fell silent. Francis awoke.

He did not sleep the whole time of this memorable night. All his plans changed. At the crack of dawn, he saddled his horse. He had decided to abandon his romanticized military adventure and returned home.[20]

Even after the abortive expedition to Apulia, the former carefree life again took over, and again it caught Francis up with its vain interests. Yet Francis began to change noticeably: sometimes he would appear pensive; his contemporaries noticed that at times he revealed a need for solitude. New, overwhelming thoughts began to oppress him.

One day (in the summer of 1205), at the very time of this inner battle blazing up in Francis's soul, he took it into his head to make merry with his friends again. He decided to arrange for them one of his magnificent festivals at which he was usually chosen "king." Everything was provided for splendid merriment.

The gala was a glorious success. At the end of the feast, a group of young people, as it always happened before, set out to stroll the streets of the town, singing merry songs.

As can be seen from Jørgensen's book from which we take the following account—an account based on the closest sources—Francis, who was taking an active part in this night outing, was soon overcome by a mood unharmonious with the general gaiety. He began to fall behind the noisy crowd, purposely began slowing down, to let the group move off. His friends did not notice this, being carried away by their own merrymaking. They went farther and farther away from him. He heard their songs more and more faintly. Finally, the sounds died out in the distance. Francis felt completely alone in the total quiet of the night, on the lonely street.

And then once more that mysterious power, whose words had awakened Francis's soul in Spoleto, again overshadowed him. All of a sudden, Francis's heart, this heart of a youth tired of the world and its emptiness, was filled, as Francis himself later recounted, with such a delightful sensation that he almost lost consciousness. He could not move or speak; and as he later confessed, if he had then been cut to pieces, he would not have felt it.

How long Francis spent in this state, he never found out, but he came to himself only when he finally heard the voice of one of his friends who had returned to look for him. His friend tried in every way to drive Francis out of his wits, shouting to him, "Eh, Francis! What are you standing like that for ... why are you lost in thought, are you planning to get married?"

"Yes, I'm thinking of getting married," Francis answered finally, having awakened from his ecstasy, "and my bride is richer, more beautiful and more pure and chaste than any you have ever known."

Jørgensen further says that in this moment all his fruitless life, disordered and full of emptiness, in glaring illumination passed before Francis; he clearly saw himself in his pathetic reality. And in contrast with this life, he felt the possibility of a different life for himself. He conceived of another life, not with illusory pleasures, but rather full of other sensations, true goodness, radiant beauty—a life in Jesus Christ, in great spiritual striving. From this time began Francis's deep repentance.[21]

We took this scene from Jørgensen to show the reader how Francis's moral change came about. And we now see how during this turbulent time in his life his passions burned out, his soul was cleansed, and he was led out on the road by his golden heart, in which his higher reason awoke and quickly started to grow. After this break, Francis's life of spiritual endeavor commenced.

One should mention here that Francis's subsequent work on perfecting himself was of very short duration. We will see further that the time of Francis's internal spiritual striving embraces only two brief periods. The first lasted only four years, from 1205 to 1209, that is, from the day of Francis' above-described change to his entering on the path of apostolic activity; and the second period lasted the three final years of Francis's life, from 1223 to 1226, that is, from the time that Francis freed himself from preaching.

The time in between these two periods (about fourteen years) was totally taken up by Francis's social and religious activity, which although very interesting in itself, still contained little information proper regarding the development of Francis's mysticism, which constitutes the main subject of our research.

Further on in our account we will cite in full detail mystical scenes from the second period of Francis's spiritual activity, for these scenes are very characteristic illustrations for understanding his super-consciousness. As regards the first period of the saint's spiritual striving, in speaking of this period, we will only touch generally on Francis's characteristic features, for information relating to this period gives negligible material about Francis's mystical perceptions in this first stage of his spiritual striving.

Turning to the first period of Francis's spiritual endeavor, that is, to the time of his working on himself, beginning at twenty-three years of age up to the moment of his commencing the work of preaching, we will see that this four-year period was full of manifestations of Francis's diverse lofty impulses to self-sacrifice for his fellow man and for the glory of Christianity. These were ecstatic, spontaneous impulses.

Soon after his emotional upheaval, having departed for Rome to the sepulcher of St Peter, Francis started by giving away everything he owned, and taking all his money from his pouch, he placed it on the sepulcher.[22]

Then Francis was again overshadowed by a mysterious vision that showed him his future path.

From the testimony of his contemporaries, the next day, while Francis was long in prayer, he again heard a voice that said to him, "All that which up to this time you loved with earthly love and desired to have, you should despise and hate, if you want to know My will. If you begin to fulfill it, then everything that now seems sweet and pleasant to you, will become bitter and unbearable."[23]

And here, a striking example of the reforging of Francis's instincts revealed itself in his relationship to a leper. At that time in Italy, there were quite a few of them. These were sick people whom everyone avoided, for touching them transmitted a terrible incurable disease.

For Francis, a home for lepers was a place about which he earlier could not even think without experiencing a feeling of horror. Before, when he sent alms to a home for lepers, he himself usually tried to avoid this terrible place. But now Francis decided to make himself over. Meeting a leper one day, he got down from his horse, gave the sick one alms, and even kissed his hand; Francis soon became a frequent visitor of these unfortunate souls.

We already know Francis's earlier relationship to the poor. Even before the beginning of his spiritual striving, he always felt pity for them, but now there appeared in him a special relationship to the spiritual struggle of almsgiving. Poverty now acquired for him a more profound meaning: Francis became possessed by the idea that the true follower of Christ not only was called to give alms, but also should himself become poor, and he himself in renunciation should "for the sake of Christ" beg for the holy bread of alms.

We should mention here that after the moral change in Francis, his life in the home of his parents with every day became more and more difficult. Because Francis had turned down a brilliant career, the self-love of Francis's father was dealt a blow.

Although the elder Bernardone gave Francis unlimited sums of money for luxury and extravagance, allowing the youth to maintain himself on a level with the young nobles, he could not look on indifferently when his son gave away his money by the handful to the unfortunate people he met.[24]

But Francis did not pay attention to this and was not content with his bursts of self-sacrifice for his fellow men. Besides this, he had a constant striving to serve Christ, for whom he "felt compassion" with his whole being. (As we will see later, in Francis's mind the concept of Christ's sufferings was one of the chief stimuli developing toward the end of his life of mysticism). And he fulfilled his striving to serve Christ in every way he could.

Francis began wholeheartedly to assist in the restoration of chapels and churches. First of all, he undertook the restoration of church of St Damian, standing alone outside of Assisi, deserted and rundown from age. At this church, there lived a poor priest whom Francis grew fond of. One day, having given this priest money for oil for the ever-burning votive lamp, Francis promised to bring him more money for other needs.

We will see here that the fulfillment of this promise was the beginning of Francis's abrupt break with his father and with the world. Here is how it all happened.

Wishing to help the church of St Damian, Francis, one day when his father was absent, sold several pieces of cloth from his shop and, besides this, even sold the horse on which he rode to the neighboring village for this purpose. The money Francis got for all this, he brought to the above-mentioned priest, asking his permission to stay at the church. After long entreaties, the priest agreed to let Francis stay with him but did not accept the money from him, knowing that Francis received it for goods that had belonged to his father.

Then Francis, wishing no matter what the consequences to give this money to the church, threw the purse with the money onto the church windowsill.[25]

Having received permission to live by the church, Francis decided once and for all to make his home there and begin the life of a hermit. Close by the priest's house, hidden from view, was a small stone cave. Francis settled there, spending his days and nights in this refuge in fervent, zealous prayer.[26]

When Francis's father returned from his travels and heard what Francis had done, he became very indignant. Finding out where his son was hiding, he set out to search for him, accompanied by relatives and neighbors. But Francis hid himself in his cave, and they could not find him; only one servant from his father's house knew about this cave, and this servant took to Francis the food he needed.

After a while, Francis himself came to his father in town. But the humble appearance of his son did not disarm his parent. Beside himself from anger, he beat his son unmercifully and locked him up. In his father's absence, his mother for a long time tried to talk Francis into giving up his capricious whims. Becoming convinced of the futility of her admonitions, she quietly, unbeknownst to his father, set Francis free. Then Francis left his parents' home forever. He sent off to his father all that he had left, even his clothes. Later on, when his father met Francis and scolded and cursed him, Francis took as his father an old beggar so that he would make up for his father's blessing. This took place in 1207, when Francis was twenty-five years old.[27]

Settling by the church of St Damian, Francis collected alms for its rebuilding and carried on his shoulders the rocks needed for building. Francis fed himself on handouts. At mealtime, he walked through the town with a bowl in his hands, gathering into it leftovers of various foods. At first, this mixture was repugnant to him, but he soon overcame his revulsion to such food.

When the church of St Damian was repaired, Francis took up the building of another church, namely, the chapel of St Mary. He settled in a hut near the church, clothed in a felt caftan that had been given to him by a certain peasant. He went around at this time with his caftan belted and with sandals on his feet. On those days when he went out to gather alms, he took a bag and staff with him. Meanwhile, as his biographers recount, he always maintained an expression of satisfaction and joy on his face. So passed two years.

———————

We are now approaching that turning point in Francis's life, when suddenly, even surprising himself, he finally found his true vocation, the vocation of preaching, when he took his first steps toward founding the famous Franciscan order.

On February 24, 1209, during mass in the chapel (close by which Francis lived in a hut), he heard the priest reading the following words from the Gospel—the words spoken by Christ to His disciples, when He sent them to preach the Kingdom of Heaven: "Provide neither gold nor silver nor copper in your money belts, nor bag for your journey, nor two tunics, nor sandals, nor yet staffs," and so forth.[28]

Francis's biographers say that after these words and after the priest explained their meaning in detail, Francis, filled with enthusiasm, suddenly exclaimed, "This is what I need! This is what I want to devote all my strength to!"

Under the inspiration of this revelation, Francis, as it seemed to him, understood his real calling—the calling to become an apostle. Francis decided that Christ's true disciples should become His apostles. Liberated from everything vain, and feeling deeply inspired, they should go into the world to proclaim anew to people the great word: "Repent, for the kingdom of heaven is at hand."[29]

And so Francis felt he had discovered his true vocation—the vocation to be an apostle and carry out in deed all that the Savior Himself required of his disciples. He decided to begin with the literal fulfillment of this requirement.

Leaving the small church, he took off his sandals, threw away his staff, cast off his cloak with which he protected himself from the cold, and replaced his belt with a cord. Clothed in a gray tunic commonly worn by the local poor peasants, barefoot, with a hood over his head, he felt as if he were transformed. The outward change was negligible, says V. Ger'e concerning this event, but it contained within it what for Francis was a great idea: to follow Christ.[30]

The day in which all the above took place was significant in Francis's life. On this day, the preparatory period of his spiritual striving came to an end. It was from this time that Francis's service began. Having now become an apostle, he began his service in the work of revitalizing Christianity within the Catholic Church.

———

The development of Francis's preaching went unusually quickly and successfully. We should mention that at that time the soil prepared for preaching was rich; the official representatives of Christ were then famous for their negative qualities, and the world of the Middle Ages in its striving toward religion did not find proper support in its pastors.

On May 16th of that year when Francis began his preaching, he was joined by two followers.[31] Their number gradually grew and, when there were already seven, Francis sent them all out on the work of preaching to the people. Finally, in that same year of 1209, Francis and his followers, already numbering twenty-four people, set out for Rome to Pope Innocent III with a petition for a blessing on their undertaking.

It turned out that circumstances in Rome proved favorable for Francis. According to the words of the researcher of Francis's life, V. Ger'e, it was not easy for the head of the church at that time to give permission to preach to such volunteers as Francis (people knowing little about theology). It was also not easy to legitimize "evangelistic life" in absolute poverty, in an era when not only the clergy but also even Catholic monasticism plumed itself in the vastness of its estates, with worldly honor and temporal power. Nevertheless, Innocent III still decided to legalize the new brotherhood. V. Ger'e explains Pope Innocent's decision thus: At that time, there was coming to light the very unsuccessful result of Pope Alexander III's (Innocent III's predecessor) refusal to legalize a similar petition submitted earlier by the followers of another preacher, a certain Peter Valdes of Lyons. With this harsh refusal, Pope Alexander III turned these "poor of Lyons," as they were called, into heretics and later had to destroy them with fire and sword, if only by these means to bolster the waning authority of the Catholic Church.[32]

However, having decided to bless Francis and his brotherhood on the path of preaching, the Pope set one chief and indispensable condition—their total subordination to the authority of the Catholic Church, and their total subordination to the representative of Christ on earth, the infallible Pope.

At this point, it is interesting to note that the curia was not content with Francis's oath of loyalty; it wanted to place the church's stamp on all the Franciscans. Cardinal de St Paul was charged with tonsuring them. From that time, all Franciscans entered into the very bosom of the Catholic Church. Speaking of this, the biographer of Francis's life, P. Sabatier, notes that Francis's creation, the Franciscan order, was compelled in this way to degenerate in the future into a purely clerical institution.[33]

We will not expatiate here on the troubles through which the new brotherhood had to pass; we will not concern ourselves about Francis's administrative and organizational activity in the institution he formed, nor will we give an account of his subsequent travels to Egypt as a missionary. What interests us in Francis's biography is something else. What interests us chiefly is the development of his mystical feeling, the development of his inner life of spiritual striving. Yet Francis devoted himself again totally to this life only in 1223 (three years before his death), when the Franciscan order was already consolidated and his work had spread in the Catholic world, when Francis could transfer his power into other hands. And it is about this last period of Francis's spiritual striving that we will give the reader as much detailed information as possible.

———————

In this last period of Francis's spiritual activity, as V. Ger'e says, we see the saint in remote villages and wilderness hermitages of his native Umbria, where he was able to pray in solitude and devote himself to his religious meditations.[34] It is to this time that Francis's chief written works pertain: his epistles "to all the faithful," "to all the brotherhood," and others.

Unfortunately, Francis's strength in this period of his life began to weaken. His health in general had never been strong. We already know that from his childhood, he had been tormented by attacks of fever. Then the exhausting and severe fasts to which he subjected himself undermined his organism. Also he slept very little, and that was either in a sitting position or with a stone or piece of wood under his head, instead of a pillow. Besides this, he had a diseased liver, and during his last years he suffered from prolonged hemorrhaging. To this was added a sickness of the eyes that he contracted during his trip to Egypt.

In spite of all these physical infirmities, in this last period of his life there was an increase in his mystical feeling, revealing itself in the visions that overshadowed him. All this took place under the following circumstances.

In the beginning of August 1224, Francis decided to spend the autumn fast (before Dormition) on the wilderness mountain of Alverna. This mountain was given to Francis by one of his admirers, Count Roland de Cattani.

Francis set out for this mountain with five of his disciples, including the Franciscan Leo, who was closest of anyone to Francis in his love and unusual devotion to him. The mountain was vast, very high, and climbing to the top was not easy.

A little below the crest of the mountain on the landing of one of the cliffs, the Franciscan brothers built for Francis and his closest disciples a hermitage of huts; and there Count Roland built a small chapel.

While already approaching this place, Francis began to feel that his physical powers were leaving him. Then the brothers entered a peasant's hut by the road and asked him to give them a donkey for Francis. Guessing that before him among these wanderers stood Francis himself (whose fame at that time was already great), the peasant with joy gave them the donkey. Turning to Francis, he said, "Be truly as good as people speak of you, because there are many who believe in you."[35]

Francis was deeply touched by these simple sincere words of the peasant. In a fervent impulse, he expressed his feeling to the peasant by kneeling down before him and kissing his feet.

———————

Finally, the wanderers arrived at their hermitage and settled down there. But Francis soon decided to leave them, wishing to seclude himself. He at first settled in a cell not far away, in the shadow of an oak tree. But later he completely departed from them to a ravine between two cliffs. This new place that he chose for himself was very remote, and to get through to it one had to pass a precipice over which a bridge was formed from a large tree that had fallen in that place.

According to Francis's wish, only one brother, Leo, was permitted to approach this place where Francis had settled, and that was only two times a day; once during the day to bring Francis bread and water, and the second time at night before daybreak. To this end, the two of them had agreed upon a prayer by which Leo received permission to cross the bridge, and only then could he come close to his dear teacher. The chronicle explains Francis's decision to seclude himself completely from everyone in that he was experiencing lofty contemplations at that time.[36]

For several days, Brother Leo carried out everything exactly as his teacher had instructed, and all went according to Francis's will. But then one night before dawn, Francis did not answer the agreed-upon call by Leo. This was during a moonlit autumn night, one of those bright fresh nights that are so frequent in the Apennine Mountains. Leo stood for a long time before the bridge in indecision; should he go to Francis or not? Finally, he decided to cross to the other side of the bridge.

Having crossed the precipice and silently approaching Francis's hut, Leo heard the saint's voice like a distant echo coming from afar. This was Francis saying his prayers. Going a few steps further, Leo saw Francis on his knees with his gaze directed toward heaven. Leo stopped motionless; he could make out the following words of Francis's prayer: "O Lord, what am I before Thee? What significance do I have in comparison with Thy power, an insignificant worm of the earth, Thy worthless servant!" And Francis repeated these cries continually until Leo betrayed his presence with a careless rustle.

Hearing the noise and seeing the figure of an unrecognized stranger, Francis, startled by this, began shouting to Leo, "In the name of the Lord God, whoever you are, stop—where are you from?" And he quickly went up to Leo.

The latter, as he himself later recounted, felt at that moment so cold from fear that if the earth had opened up, he, it seems, would have cast himself into the chasm in order to hide. He was terribly afraid of losing his dear teacher.

But here Francis finally recognized Leo and began to reprimand him meekly for his disobedience in crossing the bridge without special permission. Leo begged Francis to forgive him and, under the impression of the scene of Francis praying, he could not resist asking Francis to explain to him the meaning of his prayer.

"O little lamb of the pastor Jesus," said Francis, "O my beloved and dear Leo! During this prayer which you heard—before me appeared two great lights [*deux grandes lumieres m'ont été montrés*]. One, in which I recognized the Creator, and another, in which I recognized myself. And at that time as I was beseeching the Lord to show me *what* I was in comparison with Him, I was plunged into contemplation, in which I saw the infinite depths of His divine mercy and the sad abyss of my worthlessness."[37]

This vision was very typical. We will return to it in the next chapter when we talk in detail about Francis's mysticism.

Thus on Mt Alverna the days and nights passed for Francis in uninterrupted prayer. But here the holy day of the Elevation of the Cross of the Lord on September 14 was approaching. For Francis, this day had special significance. The idea of the cross and of Him crucified on it always aroused in Francis strong religious feeling. Francis was always especially touched by memories of Jesus's sufferings.

Before daybreak on September 14, Francis was praying on his knees next to his cell, with his face turned to the east, his hands raised to heaven.

We are copying out this prayer of Francis and all of the subsequent account of the vision that overshadowed him from the ancient legend about this, cited word for word by Jørgensen in his research.[38]

"O Lord Jesus!" the kneeling Francis cried in prayer, "I beg of Thee only two mercies: send them down to me before my death. The first is that I might, as much as this is within my strength, experience in soul and body all those sufferings which Thou, sweetest Jesus, endured in Thy torment- ing passions. And the second mercy for which I thirst, is that I might, as much as possible, feel with all my being that boundless love with which Thou didst burn, Son of God, and which forced Thee to endure so many torments for us despicable sinners!"

And at that time, as Francis prayed thus for a long time, he came to the firm belief that the Lord heeded his supplications, that he experienced both one and the other for which he had asked, experienced it within the limits possible for God's creature. And as soon as he realized that this was happening, he gave himself up to contemplation of the Savior's sufferings, contemplation leading to the highest degree of concentration (contempla- tion[39] *avec un grand recueillement*). Then the flame of Francis's religious energy flared up in him so strongly that in the overabundance of his feel- ings of love and compassion, *"he felt himself completely transformed into Jesus [il se sentil change, tout à fait en Jésus]."*[40]

And at that time, while Francis was prostrate on his knees before the Lord, at that time, as he burned with an enveloping flame, he suddenly in these morning hours saw a six-winged seraphim descending to him from heaven.

And this seraphim came so close to the saint that Francis could clearly and distinctly see on the seraphim the image of the Crucified One, and along with this could see how the wings of the seraphim were positioned. Two wings were raised above the head, two were spread for flying, and the last two enveloped its body.

And as soon as Francis saw this vision, it aroused in him fear and trem- bling. At the same time, he felt both a fullness of joy and a sense of sadness and rapture because he was experiencing great happiness in the knowl- edge that the Savior Himself favored him with His friendly appearance

[*Jésus daignait se révéler à lui si familièrement*], favored him with His gaze, full of tenderness. But at the same time the sight of the Lord nailed to the cross caused Francis unutterable sorrow. After a while, the wonderful appearance disappeared.

From that time a mighty flame was strengthened forever in Francis's heart, a fervent love for the Savior was strengthened.

And on the saint's body, this appearance left the image and miraculously imprinted marks of Christ's sufferings, for at that very moment it was as if nails began to appear on Francis's hands and feet; it appeared that the centers of his hands and feet were as if pierced by these nails. On the right side of his chest an imprint from the stab of the spear, similar to a scar, became visible—inflamed and oozing blood that soaked through his clothing.

The saint concealed this from the brothers; he even hid his hands, but walking on the ground with his wounded feet became impossible for him. It soon became clear to the brothers, especially when they had to wash the saint's bloody clothing, that Francis bore on his chest, on his hands, and on his feet the image and bodily resemblance of the Savior.[41]

The description of this vision of St Francis during prayer on Mt Alverna we have cited here from the original source which, as Jørgensen supposes, transmits the event according to the reports of those brothers who were then close to the saint, the Franciscans.

Concerning these amazing phenomena, namely, Francis's wounds on his hands and feet resulting from his mystical ecstasies, about this we will speak in the following chapter of our work. We will only say here that these phenomena provoked a multitude of imitations in the Catholic world. These phenomena later even received their own special name—*stigmatization*. And the very wounds on the body forming during these phenomena began from that time to be called by Catholics *stigmata*.

———————

After these visions, a period of most terrible trials set in for Francis, his most painful suffering. To his many illnesses, of which we spoke earlier, were added also a heart ailment and gastric attacks brought on apparently by cancer;[42] but especially agonizing sufferings were caused by an infirmity of the eyes, which at that time was completely incurable.

For a time, Francis even lost his sight altogether. But precisely under these grievous conditions, when God's world grew dark for him, poetic inspiration awakened in him. He composed then his famous hymn in which along with

"brother sun" and "sister moon" and other creations of the world he glorified
the Creator—composed a hymn in which he expressed his striking poetic talent. Here is an excerpt from this hymn that we have taken from Jørgensen's
translation:

Lord, my God and All-mighty,
To Thee we send our praises,
We bless and glorify Thee.
Praise to Thee Lord, praise by thy creatures,
But above all we glorify the brother sun,
Who gives the day and shows Thy light.
He is so radiant in great brilliance
And is Thy prototype, Most-High.
We also thank Thee for the sisters given to us,
Sparkling in the heavens, the stars and moon;
Thou didst create them in such beauty.
Praise to Thee for our mother earth,
By whom we live, who nourishes us,
She gives us wonderful fruits,
Gives us beautiful flowers....
For everything, Lord, we thank Thee,
For everything we send up praise to Thee.

In 1226, two years after the visions we described, Francis's illness began
to progress quickly to its end. It is interesting to note how Francis, sensing
the approach of death, expressed his admiration of poverty. He ordered that
he be stripped naked and laid on the bare ground. "This was the final tribute
he paid to lady poverty," says Ger'e, "poverty which Francis served in faith
and truth all his life—this was a symbolic rite, expressing that he was leaving life without any possessions." To this eloquent fact of Francis's biography, Thomas of Celano adds that when the guardian[43] brought clothing to
Francis and ordered him to put it on, the dying man was gladdened by the
appearance of the guardian, that the clothing he was giving him was not to
be his own, but was rather a loan.[44]

These days before his death, Francis ordered that the Gospel according
to St John be brought and read to him beginning from the place where it says
that Christ knew "that his hour had come."[45]

After this, Francis commanded that bread be brought to him; he blessed
it and ordered that it be broken and a piece be given to each of the brothers

standing there. "He was remembering," says the chronicler, "that holy supper which the Lord celebrated with his disciples for the last time."[46]

On their knees and in tears, the brothers surrounded the deathbed of their teacher; the monks read prayers in a low voice.

"God is now calling me," said the dying man, "and I forgive all my brothers, both present and absent, all their offences and their errors, and absolve them their sins as far as this is in my power."[47]

Finally, Francis's last words were "I have fulfilled that which I was supposed to fulfill. Christ will teach you how to act further. Farewell, children . . . I am returning to God; may He have mercy upon you."[48]

On Saturday, October 3, 1228, Francis's life quietly blew out. Two years after his death, Francis was canonized a saint by the Roman Church.

CHAPTER 4

The Mysticism of St Seraphim
and St Francis

During my prayer before me appeared two great lights [*deux grandes lumières m'ont été montrés*], one in which I recognized the Creator, and another in which I recognized myself.

—St Francis's own words about his prayer

He [Fr Sergius] thought that he was a burning lamp and the more he felt this the more he felt a weakening, the extinguishing of the divine light of truth, burning within him.

—From L. N. Tolstoy's story "Father Sergius"

True righteous men always think to themselves that they are unworthy of God.

—Words of St Isaac of Syria

Of the information from Francis's biography, by far the most interesting fact of his life—a fact extremely characteristic of this saint's mysticism— is Francis's stigmatization, that striking phenomenon in which Catholics see the seal of the Holy Spirit, leaving on Francis's body the marks of Christ's suffering. It must be said that this fact is characteristic not only of Francis's mysticism, but also of Catholic mysticism in general. Francis's stigmatization was not any exclusive phenomenon among ascetics of the Catholic world. It had its predecessors and many imitators after Francis. In the works of Catholic writers living before Francis, one comes across indications of cases of stigmatization occurring earlier. Peter Damini tells of a certain monk who bore on his body a representation of a cross. Caesar Heisterbachsky mentions a novice on whose brow a cross was imprinted.[1] But besides, there is a multitude of information testifying that after Francis's death there occurred a series of stigmatizations. Stigmatizations most recent to us in time have been thoroughly studied by various researchers. These phenomena, as V. Ger'e says, throw light on their original source. Many of them were subjected to careful observation and were documented in detail; for example, the case of Veronica Juliani (1660–1727), who was under the observation of doctors. And there were modern cases of stigmatization, for example, Louisa Lato (1850–1883), described by Dr Varleman,[2] and Madelaine N., described by Pierre Janet in 1901.[3]

Along with this we should note that the Catholic world regarded the fact of Francis's stigmatization with great reverence, it regarded this fact as a manifestation of a great miracle in the saint. Francis was canonized two years after his death, and one of the chief motives for his canonization was the fact of the miraculous marks on the saint's body. These marks were raised as a direct indication of sanctity. For us, this seems very characteristic because we meet nothing of the kind in the mysticism of the Eastern Church, of which St Seraphim of Sarov, as we already said before, was a striking representative.

We should also mention here that the historical information about Francis's stigmatization does not at this time arouse doubts within the scientific world. In this regard, we make reference to the researcher of Francis's life, Sabatier, who thoroughly worked out the question of Francis's stigmatization. Sabatier comes to the conclusion of their undoubted reality; only he looks for the explanations of Francis's stigmatization in the unknown spheres of mental pathology within the bounds of psychology and physiology.[4]

Although we are mainly interested in the explanation of stigmatization from the mystical standpoint, yet without question the explanation of stigmata as physiological phenomenona is also of great interest. Therefore, before we speak about the mystical side of the question, we consider it necessary to touch on investigations of the physiological process of stigmatization. This research will also give us information for judging the mysticism of the Catholic saint.

We will report here information on the results of the work of the French scientist, G. Dumas, that sheds light on the process of stigmatization from the psychological and physiological point of view.[5] Here are the main conclusions to which Dumas came concerning stigmatics:

1. We must acknowledge the sincerity of stigmatics and their spontaneous [*spontanéité*] manifestation of stigmata, ruling out the possibility of the wounds being self-inflicted while in a state of unconsciousness.

2. The wounds forming during stigmatization, examined as phenomena relating to the life of blood vessels, are explained by mental suggestion that is not powerless in phenomena of nourishment, blood circulation, and secretions, and might easily give rise to skin damage.[6]

3. The wounds of stigmatics are evoked by a certain ecstasy, when conscious life is swallowed up by some sort of all-powerful image, granting this image full predominance.

4. Stigmata do not become manifest as the result only of a passive representation in one's imagination of a wound on the body, but according to the testimony of stigmatics, this representation is accompanied by another active representation or image—namely, the image of a fiery ray or spear issuing from the contemplated wound (afflicting the body of the stigmatic). Often this result did not come about during the first visions, but was achieved gradually according to the extent to which the image represented in ecstasy took final possession of the contemplating subject.

Finally, Dumas established the following general indicator of those who are stigmatized. All stigmatics, regardless of what their sign consists of—be it the imprint of a cross on a shoulder, the marks of the crown of thorns on the head, or, as with Francis, hands and feet being stricken and a wound in the side—all of them felt unbearable pain in the stricken part of the body and, at the same time, a lofty delight in the thought that they proved worthy of suffering with Jesus, and atoning, like Him, for sins of which they were not guilty.[7]

The summarized analyses of Dumas concerning stigmatics are highly interesting. They lead to the conclusion that in the process of stigmatization, irrespective of the passionate emotion of feeling (emotional ecstasy of the heart), a large role is played by the mental element, namely, mental imagination, vividly representing the suffering image. Besides, mental suggestion also plays a role here, that is, a series of mental volitional impulses, seeking to transfer the sufferings of the imagined image to the physical sensations of the stigmatic's body, which under the influence of these forces does begin to feel real pain and even reproduces on itself the marks of these sufferings. Therefore, if one is to acknowledge that stigmatization is a mystical manifestation at all, then into this mysticism enters not only emotional movements (which Williams James recognized as the source of mysticism) but also, besides emotions, into this process of stigmatization enters, in equal degree if not more, the strained working of cerebral imagination and suggestion, as well as feelings of a purely sensual nature.

―――――――

After this general conclusion regarding stigmatics, we are going to talk strictly about the mystical condition of Francis that led him to stigmata. Cited in *Fioretti* is Francis's ecstatic prayer before the actual vision.[8] This prayer is very typical. Francis prays that he might experience *"with his soul and body"* the sufferings of Christ. In this prayer, Francis thirsted for divine inspiration to such an experience, thirsted for the sensation of this experience not only with the soul, but also with the body.

Thus, Francis, in giving himself up to ecstatic prayer, did not renounce the body, but on the contrary, he strove for earthly sensations; he asked God that even his body react to the sufferings of Jesus.

At this moment, we find it necessary to make a slight digression. As a contrast with Francis's prayer, let us recall how higher mystical (spiritual) prayer is understood by the ascetics of the Eastern Church (according to the *Philokalia*). According to their understanding, this is prayer that separates man not only from all that is physical and sensual, but also from rational thought. This is a direct spiritual lifting up of man to God, when the Spirit Itself, from the words of the Apostle Paul, make intercession for us with groanings that cannot be uttered.[9]

Now let us return to our investigation. Francis's ecstatic prayer was heard. The suggestion became reality. The chronicler says that *"Francis felt himself completely changed into Jesus,"* changed not only in soul, but in body as well; that is, in sensations not only spiritual and psychological, but also physical.

Fully allowing that during the described state Francis was raised up spiritually to the Logos, at the same time we cannot attribute the emergence of his particular physical sensations to the action of spiritual power. We cannot explain his bodily sensations otherwise than as merely the working of his own mental imagination, moving parallel with his spiritual ecstasy. Of course, it is hard to say what predominated most in Francis in the given case, his spirituality or his mentalism (mental imagination); but at any rate, we can say that mentalism was quite powerful here. This is supported by the following important circumstance—by the unusual complexity of the vision that came to Francis after he felt that he was completely changed into Jesus.

Let us recall how in fact this vision occurred. First of all, Francis, totally unexpected for himself, saw something miraculous; namely, he saw descending to him from heaven a six-winged seraphim, like the one described by the prophet Ilias [*sic*]. And that was the first stage of his vision. Then after this, as the seraphim was approaching, Francis (thirsting for Jesus and feeling himself "changed into Christ") began to see the seraphim also nailed to the cross.

Here are the words of the chronicler about this second stage of the vision: "And this seraphim came so close to the saint that Francis could clearly and distinctly see on the seraphim the image of the Crucified One."

Upon seeing such a representation on the seraphim, Francis then recognized in the image of this seraphim Christ Himself coming down to him. And then his craving to sense Christ was satisfied; he felt His sufferings with his own body (for which he had so striven and for which he had so fervently prayed). Then began Francis's stigmatization.

It is impossible not to be struck by the incredible complexity of Francis's vision. On the one vision of the seraphim suddenly descending to Francis from the heavens was laid the image of another vision, that vision for which Francis thirsted most of all, the image of the crucified Christ. The process of the emergence of these visions gives the impression that the first vision of the seraphim, as unexpected and sudden, was outside of Francis's autosuggestion. But then on this real vision was placed another image, and it was placed by the power of Francis's own imagination. Only in this way can we explain why there remained in Francis's consciousness such a complex idea that had room for two visions, two images: both the vision of the seraphim and the vision of Christ.

Thus, to the real vision of the six-winged seraphim Francis's imagination joined another image—the image of the crucified Savior.

———

The exaggeratedness in St Francis's exultation as evidenced in the above-described vision is revealed in particular boldness if we compare this vision with the sublime vision of Christ that descended upon St Seraphim of Sarov when he was serving as a deacon on Great Thursday of Passion week. We spoke in detail concerning this in the second chapter of this book.[10] All of this came over Seraphim totally unexpectedly. In his prayers and spiritual endeavors he did not beg, as Francis did, to "feel himself changed into Jesus."

He prayed simply and deeply and repented of his sins. Meanwhile, mystical grace-filled power grew in him, and it grew on account of his spiritual endeavors; yet he himself did not even feel or recognize this. And here this power, at the moment of his standing before the altar in church, when Seraphim's heart was burning, when, as expressed in the inspired words of a certain ascetic, "the soul, having emptied itself of everything external, unites itself with prayer and this prayer, like a flame, surrounds it as fire does iron, making it all fiery,"[11] in this great moment the mysterious Divine Power, breaking through all human shells, unexpectedly for Seraphim, utterly startled him with its vision.

So that this will be absolutely clear to the reader, we will remind him how all this took place.

Seraphim of Sarov, vested as a deacon during the liturgy, after he pronounced before the royal gates the liturgically prescribed exclamation, "O Lord, save the God fearing and hear us," experienced something totally unexpected, something he had never dreamed of or imagined, *from which he could not come to his senses for two hours.* Concerning this vision that had overshadowed him, he thus recounted later on. At first he was struck by an unusual light, as if from rays of sun. Then he saw the Son of Man in glory shining with an ineffable light brighter than the sun surrounded by the heavenly powers, "like a swarm of bees." Proceeding from the western gates, He stopped opposite the ambo and, raising His hands, blessed the servers and those praying. Then the vision vanished.

Now let us attempt to explain how this vision took place. We have already explained in the book *Super-Consciousness* that pure spiritual contemplation, attained in the way indicated by the ascetics of the *Philokalia*, develops in a man's heart, outside the mental and sensory spheres and consequently outside the sphere of mental imagination. Therefore, the experiences of this super-consciousness, springing from the mysterious feeling of man's union with God, are usually difficult to communicate using our weak language. So it happens that upon people who have developed within themselves sensations of spiritual super-consciousness *visions* descend, imprinted on a man's consciousness. But these visions, in the majority of cases, are sudden and unexpected, and they overshadow a man's inner being, as if coming from within. St Isaac of Syria says, "If you are pure, then *heaven is within you, and you will see within yourself angels, and with them the Lord of angels.*[12] According to the teachings of the fathers of the Eastern Church, all these sensations and visions appear to a humble man above all expectation, for in his humility, the ascetic does not feel himself worthy of it. This same St Isaac of Syria explains that "the contemplation of supernatural knowledge granted by Divine Power the soul received ... within itself immaterially, gratis, quickly and *beyond expectation*, it comes to light and is revealed from the *very innermost parts*, for according to the words of Christ—the kingdom of heaven is within us." This contemplation "of the image within, imprinted upon the innermost mind (the higher reason), is *revealed by itself* without thinking about it."[13]

As a result of the previously stated comparison of these two visions and of what Seraphim and Francis experienced during these visions, we see here a sharp difference between the mysticism of these two saints. St Seraphim's mysticism appears to us as a purely spiritual ecstasy, as the descending of spiritual sight upon the ascetic, as the enlightenment of his higher reason,[14] while Francis's super-consciousness appears as a mysticism darkened by his own imagination and sensuality.

A typical difference between the mysticism of Francis and Seraphim we see also in the different relationship of both of them to Christ proper. Compared with Seraphim, who sensed in his heart the spiritual power of Christ and received Christ *within himself*, Francis, in his conception of Christ, perceived first of all an impression from the *earthly life of Christ*, was absorbed in His *external suffering image*. This impression upon Francis came as if from without, and Francis strove with all the powers of his soul to imitate Christ. For him, Christ was an external object, and Francis's mysticism developed as proceeding from the image of Christ and His suffering.

We must say that this imitation of Christ reached the point with Francis of his directly copying the Savior's life. For example, in the beginning when seven disciples had gathered around Francis, he too, like the Savior sending His apostles to preach, sent his apostles and gave them almost the same instructions, saying, "Go forth in twos to different parts of the earth, preaching peace to men and repentance for the remission of sins."[15] The Savior, as we know from the Gospel, "called the twelve to Himself, and began to send them out two by two.... So they went out and preached that people should repent."[16]

Also of interest is the following case of Francis's direct copying of Christ. Not long before his death, in his enthusiasm to imitate the Savior wherever possible, he repeated before his disciples something even resembling the great Last Supper itself. We already spoke in the last chapter how before his death he ordered that bread be brought, blessed it, ordered that it be broken up, and gave a piece to each of the disciples standing there. "He remembered," says Francis's biographer, "that holy meal which the Lord celebrated with His disciples for the last time."[17]

In his great humility, Seraphim of Sarov never ventured anything of the kind.

––––––––––

The difference between Francis and Seraphim we see in Francis's unusual rapture and his idealization of the spiritual endeavor itself to which he had abandoned himself. This rapture contrasts with the simplicity with which Seraphim worked on himself, although the inner burning of Seraphim's spirit and his spiritual endeavors were strong and deep.

Simplicity of feeling and Seraphim's unostentatious work on himself were strikingly evident in his spiritual struggle of standing a thousand days on a rock, when struggling with his passions he cried to God, "O God, be merciful to me, a sinner."

Parallel with Seraphim's repentance, we cite an example of how Francis repented of his sins.

It happened one day that because of illness, Francis abandoned the established rule of strict fasting. This slackening of the rule tormented the ascetic's conscience. He decided to repent and punish himself. Francis expressed this repentance in the following manner. The chronicle states that

[Francis] ordered that people be gathered on the street in Assisi for a sermon. Finishing his sermon, he told the people not to disperse until he returned, then went himself into the cathedral with many of the brethren and Peter de Catani and told Peter under a vow of obedience and without contradiction to fulfill what he would tell him. The other answered that he neither could nor should desire or do anything against his *will,* neither with him nor with himself. *Then Francis took off his tunic and ordered Peter to tie a rope around his neck and pull him half-naked into public to the same place where he had been preaching.* Francis ordered another brother to fill a cup with ashes and, ascending the elevated place from which he preached, poured these ashes on his head. The brother, however, did not obey him because in his compassion and devotion to Francis he was too grieved by this order. So Brother Peter, taking the rope in his hands, dragged Francis behind him as he had ordered. Meanwhile, he himself wept bitterly and the other brothers shed tears of pity and sorrow. While Francis was thus being dragged half-naked before the people to the place where he had been preaching, he said: "You and all those who by my example abandoned the world and lead the life of brotherhood *consider me a holy man*, but before the Lord and before you I repent that during my illness I ate meat and meat broth.[18]

Of course, Francis's sin was not that great and hardly deserved such a dramatic form of repentance in which he clothed his repentance; but such was the general feature of Francis's religiosity. He strove to idealize all that an ascetic should fulfill, strove to idealize the very spiritual struggle of repentance.

Francis's idealization of Christian endeavors can be observed in the spiritual struggle of compassion. This is seen in how Francis related to the poor. In Francis's eyes, poor people were beings standing far above other people. In the Catholic saint's opinion, a poor man was the bearer of a holy mission, as the image of the poor sojourning Christ. Hence, in his instructions Francis even obliged his disciples to beg alms.[19]

Concerning Seraphim of Sarov, while relating to the poor with Christian love, he did not glorify poverty itself as a spiritual struggle of imitating Christ. In his teachings, he simply said that "one must be merciful to the poor and homeless—great luminaries and fathers of the church gave much care to this,"[20] and nowhere in his instructions is there a hint that monks be required to go begging for alms.

Finally, Francis's idealized exaltation is especially revealed in his recollections of the earthly sufferings of Christ. It says in Francis's biographies that *"drunk with love and compassion for Christ*, blessed Francis would sometimes pick up a piece of wood from the ground and, taking it in his left hand, would move his right hand as if with a bow on a violin, singing the Franciscan hymn of the Lord Jesus Christ." This singing would end with tears of pity for Christ's suffering and heavy sighs, and falling into a reverie, Francis rested his eyes on heaven.[21]

There were traits that Francis shared in common with Seraphim, in their character as well as in their religiosity. This latter is explained by their both being fervent Christians; they both strove toward good, and both were sincere spiritual strivers. Regarding the traits they had in common, we will also say a few words that are essential for the most exact description of both saints' character.

First of all, one should point out that both saints displayed the following trait in common: their joy for life. According to the testimony of all who knew Seraphim of Sarov, he was so imbued with spiritual joy that no one ever saw him sorrowful or despondent, and this joyful mood he tried to transmit to others.

We see the same thing in Francis. Ger'e, the researcher of Francis's life, in his book about the saint writes that "Francis' inherent joy for life which was in full vigor during his youth, never left him, *transfiguring* spiritually even amidst the most difficult monastic ascetic labors." The chronicle says that "outside the hours of prayer and church services Francis always tried in particular to display an outward look of *joy* and to experience it inwardly. This same thing he loved exceedingly in the brothers, and he often reproached anyone for displaying sorrow and grief.[22]

Both Seraphim and Francis treated their physical body with great severity, subjecting themselves to privations and burdens of all kinds. Not to mention strict fasts, Francis generally did not spare his health. One of his comrades recounted that "although Francis suffered from illnesses for many years, still he was so devout and zealous in prayer and church services that when he prayed or read the canonical hours, he never leaned against the wall, but rather stood straight with his head uncovered." Francis gave his own body a very characteristic name. He called it *brother donkey*, which had to be weighed down with a heavy burden, poorly fed, and beaten often with a whip.[23] Seraphim of Sarov acted similarly to this. For example, he was always seen with a sack on his back where he had a book of the Gospels and a load of rocks and sand to mortify his flesh. To questions of why he did this, the elder answered, "I am tormenting him who torments me."[24]

Both of them, Seraphim and Francis, were equally strict in regard to fulfilling the necessary Christian mysteries. Thus Seraphim, when his legs became enfeebled and therefore could no longer walk from his hermitage to church for communion of the Holy Mysteries, because of this was forced to leave even his cherished hermitage and move back again to the monastery, where he arranged for himself an anchoretic life in his cell, about which we spoke before.[25]

We see that Francis was also strict in regard to fulfilling the sacrament of communion. Ger'e says that although Francis valued highly seclusion and solitary prayer, he did not value any less church services and the real manifestations of man's bond with the Godhead in the sacrament of communion. For this reason Francis was happy, writes Ger'e, when he was able to get permission from the monks of the Benedictine monastery on Mt Subazio to use their chapel and settle nearby.[26]

Like Seraphim, Francis was very strict in relation to the spiritual labors of renouncing one's will (obedience) and chastity. In his instructions, he demanded of the brethren immediate obedience. "Dear brothers," he said, "fulfill an order at the first word and do not wait for it to be repeated, do not tolerate the thought that what you are ordered to do is impossible to fulfill, for if I were to command something above your strength, holy obedience would not be found powerless."[27] No less than any of the ascetics of the East, Francis in exactly the same way valued the purity of chastity.[28] Finally, Francis devoted himself to the endeavor of prayer with no less zeal than Seraphim.

Seraphim's and Francis's common traits can be observed even in some less important details of their lives. Such an example was both saints' nearly identical loving relationship to animals. We spoke before how Seraphim treated animals and, specifically, how he behaved with the bear that sometimes came to visit him.[29]

Francis displayed a very similar relationship in general to animals. True, in Italy in the location where he lived there were no bears that Seraphim tamed, but instead there were many others of God's creatures with which Francis knew how to live a touching communal life. Francis treated animals with the very same compassion and love as he did people, considering them to be man's younger brothers and calling them together with man to serve the Creator.[30] The chronicle says that one day a rabbit that had been caught in a net was brought to Francis. The little animal straightway hid in his bosom; Francis set him free, and the rabbit followed in his footsteps like a dog to the nearby forest.

A grasshopper, chirring in a fig tree near his cell, responded to his call and came down onto his hand. "Sing, my brother," said the saint, "praise the Lord with thy joyful cry."[31]

From the information we have drawn from the biographies of Francis and Seraphim, highly significant for our research are the actual reports of miraculous manifestations of spiritual super-consciousness in both saints.

Let us elucidate as accurately as possible this side of spiritual life:

1. We have already said that if one were to compare Seraphim's vision of the Son of Man in glory with Francis's vision on Mt Alverna (stigmatization), the first vision gives the impression of an unusually sublime, purely spiritual vision, which cannot be said of St Francis's vision—a vision darkened by his own imagination and sensuality. Here we should mention that such was Francis's super-consciousness at the end of his

life. The vision described on Mt Alverna was the highest degree of mystical perception that Francis attained before his death.

2. Meanwhile, this same Francis, during the years of his youth when he had not yet become famous for his apostleship (when his spirituality was not darkened by the consciousness of his great works), he still had occasions of revelation other than a kind of artificial exultation; for by nature Francis was profoundly mystical and he had in addition to this a heart of genius for good. Let us merely recall his vision in Spoleto or the revelation on the street in Assisi at night that transformed him from a light-minded youth into a zealous Christian ascetic. But at that time, Francis was a completely different person: as yet, he did not consider himself a great light (*grande lumière*), as he called himself later on Mt Alverna.

3. Concerning Seraphim of Sarov, on the contrary, his spiritual super-consciousness *progressed* in its development to the end of his life. We have seen that during Seraphim's last years he had perceptions of an extraordinary spiritual power and also ecstasies of direct communion with the Godhead. Let us recall Seraphim's shining with light during his conversation with the landowner Motovilov and Seraphim's ecstasy during his conversation with the Sarov monk John, when Seraphim's face shone with an unusual light. The state of this last ecstasy Seraphim could not even express in words. This ecstasy of Seraphim we will judge at greater length according to information on similar ecstasies left us by another mystic of the Eastern Church, Symeon the New Theologian.

4. Seraphim, as we saw, possessed a high degree of clairvoyance. The hearts of the people he met were an open book for him. This clairvoyance appeared as the result of his spiritual enlightenment. Yet in the material on the life of Francis, nowhere is it mentioned that he ever manifested a similar ability.

So in general, on the basis of research information, it is possible to come to the indubitable conclusion that compared with Seraphim's mysticism, Francis's mysticism proved to be far from perfect. If this is so, then why is it that Francis did not acquire for himself the Holy Spirit of God in a degree equal to that of Seraphim of Sarov?

Readers will see further that this can be explained by a closer study of the psychology of both saints. They will see that this question is resolved on the basis of the information we have from the saints' biographies, if we compare some of the most striking facts and the opinions of the Christian ascetics themselves, and elucidate them from the point of view of the philosophy of the Christian ascetics of the Eastern Church—the philosophy we became acquainted with in the *Philokalia*.[32]

This question is resolved, as we will see, when comparing the character of humility of both saints.

And so before everything else, we will ascertain what exactly constitutes the difference in their humility. We cited before an interesting episode from Francis's life, when before his death, in his enthusiasm to imitate Christ, he as it were took on before his disciples the role of Christ Himself; namely, he reproduced the scene of the Last Supper, giving the broken bread to his disciples who had gathered at his deathbed. Pointing out this fact, we then noted that St Seraphim, in his deep humility, did not manifest anything of the kind.

In this scene performed before his death, Francis likened himself in the eyes of his disciples to the Savior of the world Himself. Having gone through the spiritual path of apostleship and created his mighty Franciscan order, renewing Catholicism, Francis in his final days felt that he had accomplished a great mission for the salvation of people. Therefore, conscious of having accomplished his work of teaching, he, in the symbolic form we described, copied from the Last Supper, also expressed to his disciples, or rather to his apostles, his testament for their inviolate brotherhood and his parting words for their service in the future. Francis's inner humility was not an obstacle to such a self-awareness.

But meanwhile, it is this humility of Francis, as we know, that one day led to him repenting, half-naked with a rope around his neck, in the square of Assisi before a gathering of people. How does one reconcile all this; how is one to understand Francis's humility?

Much is revealed to us if we compare Francis's humility with the humility of Seraphim of Sarov, whose humility was an emotion deeply penetrating his soul, an emotion that never ceased.[33] One can conceive of the awesome strength of Seraphim's humility in his standing on a rock for a thousand days, crying unceasingly, "O God, be merciful to me a sinner."

Although Francis, as we know from his biography, also worked much on himself, and he often expressed the necessity of humility and gave to the Franciscan brothers instructions helpful in this regard, yet he himself for all his life was far from cultivating in himself Seraphim's deep humility, with which we became acquainted in the biography of the Russian saint. Francis's humility came over him only in isolated surges, albeit exceedingly strong;

it came over him in transports not free of exaggeration and even, one could say, theatricalism. This humility of Francis did not become an inseparable quality of his nature. Often, completely different moods would burst into his nature. So, from his biography we learn about such speeches of Francis to his disciples: "I am not conscious of any sins I am guilty of which I have not atoned for by confession and repentance. For the Lord in His mercy granted me the gift of clearly recognizing during prayer in what way I was pleasing or unpleasing to Him."[34] These words, of course, are far from real humility. They sooner remind us of the speech of that self-satisfied man (the Pharisee) who in the parable of the Great Teacher stood in the temple in front of the publican who was calling in deep humility to God, "God, be merciful to me a sinner." These words of Francis, spoken by him consciously, that he had atoned for his sins and was pleasing to God, do not at all meet the requirements that are demanded of a humble person by the Christian ascetics of the *Philokalia*, in whose footsteps Seraphim of Sarov followed. Thus, St Isaac of Syria says,[35] "Truly righteous men *always think of themselves as being unworthy of God*. And that they are truly righteous is ascertained in that they consider themselves cursed and unworthy of God's care and confess this secretly and openly and are taught this by the Holy Spirit so as not to be left without proper carefulness and labor while they are in this life."[36]

Along with this, we should mention that Francis's emotional movements toward humility, like the burst of repentance in the square in Assisi, of which we spoke, were on the whole rare occurrences. Usually, Francis's humility manifested itself not as an emotion, but as a mental consciousness of his weak powers as compared with what the divine power of Christ represents. No matter how much Francis got carried away in his imitation of Christ, no matter how he acknowledged that he was a great apostle of love sent into the world for the salvation of men, he nevertheless did not lose the awareness of his smallness before the limitless power of the Godhead. This very awareness of Francis was his humility. It clearly bespoke itself in our description in the last chapter of Francis's first vision on Mt Alverna, when as the chronicle says, before Francis appeared *"two great lights"*—one in which he recognized the Creator, and the other in which he recognized himself. And while he was seeing this, how Francis prayed with the words "Lord! What am I before Thee? Of what consequence am I in comparison with Thy power, an insignificant worm of the earth, Thine insignificant servant?" At the same time, Francis, by his own acknowledgment, was immersed in contemplation in which he saw the endless depth of divine mercy and the sad abyss of his own insignificance. Thus Francis, in comparing himself mentally with the Godhead, was conscious of his imperfection and insignificance, and this was his humility.

Such was not the humility of Seraphim of Sarov; his was not so much the mental consciousness of his sin as a constant emotion, and an emotion very deeply felt, as well. In Seraphim's instructions, both spoken and written, nowhere is it said that he compared himself with the Godhead and mentally assessed his true worth. His humility he always bore in his heart, without any such comparisons.

Instead of these comparisons, he continuously gave himself over to only one emotional movement: the feeling of his sin (imperfection) and contrition of heart for this sin. "Lord Jesus Christ, Son of God, have mercy on me a sinner" was the constant prayer he raised to God.

As the result of all the above, if one were to judge the humility of Francis as compared with the humility of Seraphim of Sarov—proceeding from the requirements that the Christian ascetics of the *Philokalia* established for humble monks—then the humility of the Catholic saint appears before us not as a pure ideal of Christian humility. To Francis's humility was added not a small dose of consciousness of his own righteousness, the consciousness of his pleasing God, and this already darkened Francis's path. One can apply to Francis's given state the words full of profound analysis of Count Tolstoy, who in one place in his story "Father Sergius" told of the stage of Fr Sergius's mental condition analogous with Francis. Tolstoy says, "He [the Christian ascetic Sergius] thought that he was a burning lamp, and the more he felt this, *the more he felt a weakening* of the divine light of truth burning within him."[37] And so with Francis, his consciousness that he also was a "light," that he was pleasing God, and so forth was that obstacle that prevented him from attaining the higher degrees of spirituality that, as we know, overshadowed St Seraphim of Sarov.

The father of Eastern mysticism, St Anthony the Great, says firmly that if a man does not have extreme humility, humility with all his heart, soul, and body, then he will not inherit the kingdom of God.[38] This statement of St Anthony is explained in that *only deep humility can uproot in man the evil mental force contained in self-assertiveness, the self-gratification of a man who considers himself righteous. And only such humility, entering into the flesh and blood of a Christian ascetic, can, according to the meaning of the teaching of the Eastern Christian ascetics, save him from the importunate associations of proud human thought.*

Humility is that essential power that curbs the lower reason with its mental passions,[39] creating in man's soul ground for the unobstructed development of the higher reason and for the lifting up of man to the highest stage of contemplative life. In this regard we refer once again to the authoritative word of the Christian ascetic of the *Philokalia*, St Isaac of Syria. He maintains that only "humility is the source of the mysteries of the new age."[40]

After all that has been recounted here, after we explained the difference between the humility of Francis of Assisi and Seraphim of Sarov, and also after we explained why the absence of real, true humility darkens the path of the Christian ascetic in his attaining higher spiritual super-consciousness—there appears yet another question of what causes prevented Francis from following the true path of attaining true humility, of attaining this emotion in its pure form, as attained by Seraphim of Sarov. After all, Francis, as we were convinced, had a heart of genius for good. Why did it not lead him out onto the continuous road, onto that road of which the fourth-century Christian ascetic St Anthony the Great speaks in his words that "if a man does not have extreme humility with all his heart, soul and body; then he will not inherit the Kingdom of God."

The chief and basic cause darkening the aforesaid ascetic path of Francis, we see in the fundamental conditions of the Catholic Church in which Francis was raised and grew up. In Francis's era, there was no true humility at all in the Catholic Church. Even if there was so-called humility within the clergy of this church, then it was only for show or in general it was very far from that ideal of which Anthony spoke. And finally, according to the conditions of that time and the conditions of the Catholic Church itself, this true humility could not even be created among the Catholics. The very vicar of Christ on earth, with his pretensions to power, not only spiritual but political as well, was a representative not of humility but of spiritual pride, for one cannot even conceive of greater spiritual pride than the belief in one's infallibility. This poison, contaminating the Catholic world, was bound to have an effect on Francis. Despite all his apparent humility, Francis, just like the pope himself, was sick with the infirmity of spiritual pride.

This was most strikingly evidenced as he was dying, in his farewell words addressed to the Franciscans: "Here God is calling me," said the dying man, "and I forgive all my brothers, present as well as absent, their offenses and their errors and absolve them their sins as far as this is within my power."[41]

Judging from these words, Francis in his dying minutes felt that he was empowered, just like the pope himself, to absolve sins.[42] And of course, we will say, if Francis spoke thus, if he considered himself to have the right to accomplish all this, then only in the conviction of his own holiness, in the awareness of which he departed from his earthly life.

Eastern Christian ascetics did not die like this. For all that we have studied the *Menologion*, not one of them allowed himself to appropriate the right of similarly absolving the sins of his neighbor. On the contrary, all of them died in the *awareness of their imperfection*, in the hope of forgiveness of their own sins from the merciful Lord. So for example, in contrast to the aforesaid words of Francis on his deathbed, we cite here, as a standard, the dying words of the fifth-century Thebaid Christian ascetic Sisoes the Great. Surrounded at the time of his death by the brethren, at that moment when he was apparently conversing (says the chronicle) with invisible beings, to the brothers' question "Father, tell us with whom thou art conversing?" Sisoes answered, "They are angels come to take me, but I am imploring them to leave me for a short time *in order to repent*." And when the brothers, knowing that Sisoes was perfect in virtues, contradicted him, "Thou hast no need of repentance, Father," then Sisoes answered thus: "Truly I do not know whether I have even begun my repentance."[43] Many saints of the Eastern Church died in a similar awareness of their imperfection.

Irrespective of this, it must be acknowledged that, given the conditions in which the Catholic Church existed in the thirteenth century, Francis's thoughts regarding his beneficial effect on the people of this time and his righteousness found justification in actual facts. If one were to compare Francis's activity in renewing Catholicism with the activity of the papacy at that time, then of course it was natural for Francis to see and feel his own significance, and to acknowledge himself as pleasing to God. The contrast of darkness was already so terribly great in that troubled time of the whole Catholic world.

CHAPTER 5

Mysticism of the East and Mysticism of the West

A conversation [*colloque*] takes place when man *imagines* before him Jesus Christ, crucified on the cross.

—From the teaching of St Ignatius Loyola on contemplation

Of thyself *do not form imaginings*, and do not pay attention to those that form of themselves, and do not allow the mind to imprint them on itself. For all that is imprinted and imagined from without serves to entice the soul.

—From the teachings of the ascetics of the Eastern Church

May the reader not think that having titled this chapter "Mysticism of the East and Mysticism of the West," we have taken upon ourselves to research in detail the comparative mysticism of the Eastern and Western Churches in all their characteristic manifestations and in various eras. We must say that such a task would go far beyond the scope of the present work, which concerns the lives of the saints of the Eastern Church proper and the manifestations of their spiritual contemplation. Such a comparative account of Eastern and Western mysticism would be an undertaking so broad that it would require a great deal of specialized research. It would have to contain an accurate study of the lives of notable Catholic mystics, parallel with a study of the lives of Orthodox clairvoyants and contemplative ascetics. We are not taking upon ourselves such a task. In this chapter we will dwell only upon some striking manifestations of Western mysticism, manifestations appearing in the Catholic world after Francis, so that by comparing these manifestations with the mysticism of the *Philokalia* we can understand the significance of Eastern mysticism, the most perfect mysticism of all that humanity has attained in this direction for its long life on earth.

Therefore, we will not talk about the many notable Catholic saints showing forth in the mysticism of the West. We will not, for example, touch on the life of such a famous Catholic saint as the Franciscan monk Bonaventure[1] (thirteenth century). We will likewise only slightly touch on the mysticism of such Catholic ascetics as Thomas à Kempis (fifteenth century) and St Teresa of Avila (sixteenth century). However, we will dwell at length on the mysticism of the Catholic spiritual striver, St Ignatius, for this mysticism is interesting to us in that Ignatius broadly developed Francis's mysticism in the direction of mentalism. This trait of Ignatius's mysticism especially characterizes Catholic mysticism and distinguishes it most from the mysticism of the Eastern Church.

———————

Thus, the mysticism of Francis was developed, as we said, by another prominent representative of the Catholic world—St Ignatius. This is the same Ignatius Loyola who (three centuries after the death of Francis) founded the famous Catholic order of the Jesuits, the main difference between the statutes of this order and the statutes of the Franciscans being the fact that in the rule of the Jesuit order, it was clearly and definitely stated concerning the vow of each Jesuit to continually and faithfully serve the vicar of Christ on earth— the Roman pope. And the chief means of attaining this goal in the aforesaid order was by preaching and educating youth.

Ignatius Loyola left the Catholic world a vivid memory of his mysticism. Among his other works, he wrote a remarkable guide to attaining states of ecstasy. This guide is called *Spiritual Exercises* (*Exercitia spiritualia*). We consider it necessary to expatiate on this guide because it very distinctly defines that direction toward mentalism and sensuality that contaminated the Catholic spiritual world.

But before all this, let us say a few words about the author of this guide— Ignatius himself. Ignatius Loyola was born in 1491 in Spain of an aristocratic family. He spent his early years at the court of the Spanish king, and in his youth, just like Francis, was fascinated by novels of the Middle Ages. He was ambitious. At the age of thirty, he took part in a battle with the French defending Pamplona, and was severely wounded. During his illness, he began to read the lives of the saints, whose endeavors—especially those of Francis of Assisi—took on in his eyes the very same value as earlier did the endeavors of the knights and heroes. The example of Francis fascinated Loyola. The greatness of the apostolic vocation was pictured in his imagination, and he decided to devote himself to preaching. At first he gave himself over to the ascetic life (in the small town of Catalonia, Manresa). He acknowledged later that at that time he was overshadowed by various visions. Subsequently, in 1528 he went to Paris to receive a theological education. In Paris, he formed a circle of friends who were very interested in preaching. The forming of this circle was finalized in 1534. In 1537, Loyola left for Rome; he obtained from the pope a blessing on the organization of the Society of Jesus. The rule of this order was established in 1540. Loyola was able to soundly organize and develop this institution, making of it a powerful instrument for Catholic propaganda. Undoubtedly, Loyola possessed an enormous talent for organizing. Loyola died in 1556 in Rome. Almost seventy years after his death, the Catholic Church canonized him.

———————

At first acquaintance with Loyola's treatise *Spiritual Exercises* and with how these exercises are practiced in the Catholic world,[2] one comes away with the general impression that Loyola's method of spiritual exercises has in many ways bases similar to the method of exercises in the Hindu Raja yoga, of which we spoke in detail in our book, *Super-Consciousness*. There we pointed out that, according to the explanation of A. Besant, the method of Raja yoga is always a method of thinking and requires concentrated thought and contemplation.[3] And so as we said, these mental exercises begin with meditation, that is, with devoting oneself for several minutes to deep reflection on some noble thought,[4] after which this meditation passes over into a more concentrated form of mental contemplation, and in these contemplative states the chief role belongs to the power of cerebral imagination.

Similar meditations and contemplative exercises are recommended by Loyola as well, and the chief role in these exercises, just as in Raja yoga, belongs also to *mental imagination*. But Loyola's mentalism is not as pure as in Raja yoga. A. Besant says that the method of Raja yoga is *always* a method of thinking.

With Loyola, it is united also with religious emotions, inflamed by the work of the imagination, the main subject of contemplation most often being a vivid scene from the life of Christ.

Now passing on to a closer examination of Loyola's *Spiritual Exercises*, we see that after the first steps of the exercises, acknowledged to be very important, namely the exercises of a recluse in examining his conscience (examen) and in repentance of sins,[5] the next most important exercises are defined by Loyola using the terms *mediter* [meditation] and *contempler* [contemplation]. By the word *meditation* is understood the exercise in abstract contemplations (by abstract thought), "when a man calls to mind a memory of some Christian dogmatic or moral truth, when along with this thought he begins to strive to penetrate it, while the will of the Christian ascetic is directed toward submission to the truth, toward suggesting to oneself the desire to become attached to it."[6] By the word *contemplation* is understood contemplation not of something abstract, but rather contemplation of the truth, incarnate in the life of the Savior, the soul of man training itself in its imagination to see and hear the Word made flesh, merging with the God-man, contemplating Him.[7]

Finally, besides these contemplative states, with Loyola there is still a higher state—*"application des sens."* This is "when the effort of the working imagination has already ceased, when the mystery from the life of the Savior appears freely before the soul of the contemplative, when it takes place before his eyes and makes an impression on all his bodily senses."[8]

The method of leading a man into all of these contemplative states is as follows:

The object or subject of contemplation, according to Loyola, should be envisioned in advance and arranged *into two or three points* (*en deux ou trois points*), which rivet the memory and which contain within themselves circumstances worthy of note. Then the ascetic approaches the beginning of the exercises, called *entrance* (prelude). He seizes control of his memory, his imagination, and his will. "The memory provides the *points* fixed in advance in the brain. The imagination forms in it a kind of picture, the heart in fervent prayer asks for knowledge and love, and all this is done, as it were, in the presence of Christ Himself."[9]

According to the words of the Catholic book, *Manrese*, St Ignatius proposes with the help of these exercises and, above all, the exercises in examining one's conscience (examen) and repentance of sins, to give man the possibility of attaining the following: Even if a man starting out in spiritual striving is sinful, yet if he is armed with good intentions, if he is reasonable, and if he is free for spiritual striving (is master of his own time and future), then of such a man, although he be a "wretched sinner," St Ignatius hopes to make a saintly man, and even a great saint.[10]

Let us cite from Ignatius Loyola's book, *Spiritual Exercises*, examples of his contemplative exercises. We have said that, according to Loyola's directions, the object or subject of contemplation should be envisioned in advance and arranged *into two or three points* that rivet the memory and that contain within themselves circumstances worthy of note.

We will first take examples of such points and indicate the rather interesting points that Loyola advises the one doing the exercises to fix in his brain before the contemplation of hell. (The purpose of this contemplation is to bring the recluse to a sincere repentance of sins.)

The first point is that the one doing the exercises see with "the help of the imagination" the terrible flames of hell. Loyola says, "I will see there, will look attentively at the souls of people imprisoned in their burning bodies, as if in eternal dungeons."

The second point is "also *with the help of the imagination* to hear the groans, complaints, heart-rending cries resounding in this ruinous place, hear the curses constantly being spewed out against Jesus and His saints."

The third point is *again to imagine* that one smells the smoke, brimstone, pitch, in a word, that foul smell that is emitted by the den of all sorts of putrefaction.

The fourth point is to "experience all that is most bitter in the world. In this way, try to make oneself sensitive to the tears continually being shed by those who are excommunicated; try to suffer pangs of conscience—the worm gnawing in sinners."[11]

Now we will cite an example of the exercises called *entrance (prelude)*. The entrance that we are now taking pertains to contemplation of the "first day of the incarnation of God the Word." The first prelude of this contemplation is

> *to imagine to oneself, as if this were before one's eyes*, the whole historical course of the mystery of the incarnation, namely, how the three Divine Persons of the Holy Trinity look down upon this earth, populated with people who in great crowds are rushing into hell; how the Holy Trinity, touched with compassion, decides to send down the Word to be incarnate of man in order to save the human race; how, as the result of this decision, on a foreordained day the Archangel Gabriel appears as a messenger to the blessed Virgin Mary.

The second prelude consists in "*a vivid imagining* of a place which they see as if before their own eyes. Here they represent to themselves at first the earth, populated by various tribes, and in one corner of this world, in Galilee, in Nazareth, a small house in which the Holy Virgin lives."

The third prelude is described this way: "This is a supplication that I, the supplicant, may know the mystery of the incarnation of the Word for my sake, a supplication that this knowledge kindle more and more my love for Him and compel me to serve Him exclusively."[12]

And here is an example of a contemplation presented already in the form of a conversation (*colloque*) between the recluse and the crucified Christ, Whom he sees in his contemplative state. We take this conversation word for word as it is set forth in *Spiritual Exercises*.

This conversation takes place when the person *imagines before himself* Jesus Christ crucified on the cross.... At that time, when this striking picture appears before the person's eyes, he begins to ask himself, to ponder, weigh what exactly inclined the Creator to become man and take on the form of a creature and slave. How did it happen that, possessing by His very essence an eternal nature, He willed to come down to a state of death, to true mortal sufferings.

———————

Moreover, one should blame oneself, reproach one's conscience, asking: what have I done so far for Jesus Christ? Can I say that I have really done anything for him? And at the least, what will I do from now on? What should I do?

———————

Directing in such a way my gaze on the crucified Jesus, I will tell Him all that my mind and heart prompt me to say.... The present conversation can be compared to a conversation between two friends or a conversation of a servant with his master.[13]

Here one must not ignore the close similarity of this contemplative conversation of Loyola with how St Francis prayed on Mt Alverna, when he pictured to himself "two great lights," in one of which he recognized the Savior, and in the other *himself*.

Along with this, we consider it interesting here to mention some purely external methods that Loyola advises the one doing these exercises to employ. Thus, for example, Loyola says that "during the exercises in contemplation of hell and repentance, the one exercising should deprive himself of daylight as much as possible. For this he should keep the doors and windows closed all the time while he is occupied with this endeavor, and he will admit to himself daylight only as much as needed in order to read or in extreme necessity."[14]

From all these excerpts taken from Loyola, one can see that his mysticism leads almost to pure mentalism, that it is close to Raja yoga, in which cerebral imagination plays a large role. For this, it is enough to recall, for example, this exercise in yoga that Vivekananda advises to carry out: "*Picture to yourself*," he says, "some place in your heart and in the center a flame; *imagine* that this flame is your own soul, that within this flame there is a radiant space and that this space is the soul of your soul—God—contemplate this is your heart," and so forth.[15]

———————

Yet if St Ignatius Loyola developed St Francis's mysticism in the direction of pure mentalism, in this regard taking it to the extreme, still one must say that in the Catholic world there were also deviations from such enthusiasms; that there were spiritual strivers who did not attempt in their mystical states to give themselves over solely to the impulses of their cerebral imagination, but rather strove for spiritual super-consciousness. We number among such Catholic saints the famous Thomas à Kempis (died 1471) whose ideas were not far from those of the ascetics of the Eastern Church, which is why Thomas à Kempis' main work, *The Imitation of Christ,* was translated many times into the Slavonic and Russian languages. (The first translation into Slavonic was made in 1647.)

Thomas à Kempis understood well the higher stages of spiritual super-consciousness. This is evident, for example, in the following statement in his composition, "De nativitate Christi" ["On the Birth of Christ"]. He says that

> there are such holidays of the soul, in which the sweet rapture of the inner feeling is so strong that the weakness of human nature can barely endure it; no signs or words can possibly express what the soul feels within itself at such visitations.... When the soul, forgetting itself and all else, remembers God alone, when *freeing itself from all corporeal imagination* and contemplating only eternity, plunging itself into the abyss of divine light, when illuminated by the rays of the eternal Sun, it soars higher than all creation, then it accomplishes this great and mysterious celebration, a celebration that belongs more to the glory of eternal blessedness than to the grievous state of our present life.[16]

If one were to compare this description of a mystical state with the description by St Isaac of Syria (see Chapter 1, note 19), many common traits would be found.

Speaking of typical manifestations of Western mysticism, neither can we be silent about St Teresa of Avila, recounting her mystical experiences in her autobiography written in 1561–1562. To define the mysticism of this saint, it is sufficient that we refer to the authoritative opinion of William James, who studied the writings of St Teresa.

In his book *The Varieties of Religious Experience*, James says that the piety of St Teresa does not give the impression of great depth and in general "her presentation of religion amounts to, if one can express it like this, *an endless amorous flirtation between a suitor and his Divinity.*"[17]

The mystical rapture of Teresa aroused her physical nature; she tells of a feeling of delight as of something that is difficult to endure and almost bordering on physical pain. Of the part played by the body in heavenly joys, she says that the feeling of joy "pierces it (the body) to the marrow of the bone, while earthly delights act only superficially. This is only an approximate description," she adds, "but I am unable to express myself more clearly."[18]

From this information it is evident that a sensual element also entered into the super-consciousness of St Teresa; and this quality of her mysticism she has in common with the sensual mysticism of St Francis, expressing itself, as we already know, even in such physiological phenomenon as stigmatization.

Now we will turn to Eastern mysticism and remind the reader of its principal foundations. We said that the super-consciousness of St Seraphim, developed according to the way of the Christian ascetics of the *Philokalia*, was concentrated in Seraphim's heart. There, within himself he sensed the fire of Divinity; he sensed Christ. This feeling of unity with God descended upon him naturally and freely, as the direct result of his spiritual growth, as the result of his enormous work on himself *in the path of humility and repentance*. Spiritual consciousness descended upon St Seraphim just as St Isaac of Syria said of it—Seraphim's soul perceived this super-consciousness within itself *immaterially and unexpectedly, without thinking about it* (i.e., without deliberately searching for it). This realization of super-consciousness in Seraphim was the same realization of that pure spirituality overshadowing the heart of man, spoken of by the Christian ascetics of the *Philokalia*, which we discussed in detail in the last four chapters of our book, *Super-Consciousness*.

Therefore, now that we have acquainted ourselves with Western mysticism, as it differs from Eastern mysticism, it would be interesting to learn how the Eastern ascetics regarded the kind of mysticism we see in St Francis and St Ignatius; namely, to ascertain whether or not there were any indications in the *Philokalia* on the possibility of similar ecstatic manifestations as we saw in Francis and about which Loyola speaks in his writing, and what opinions concerning such states of ecstasy were expressed by Eastern Christian ascetics.

After a close study of the works of the ascetics in the *Philokalia,* it turns out there are such indications. Although the mysticism of the Catholic saints,

Francis and Ignatius, took root and became established considerably later than the time of the lives of the Eastern Christian ascetics, as for example, St Isaac of Syria, Nilus of Sinai, and Symeon the New Theologian, nevertheless, it seems that directions in mysticism similar to Loyola's arose in their era. Therefore, in the aforementioned Eastern ascetics we found writings defining their views on such mysticism. We also found typical instructions on such mysticism in saints of a later era, namely, Gregory of Sinai and Gregory Palamas.

We will quote the writings of these Eastern Christian ascetics as they pertain to the question of interest to us. We will begin with the fifth-century Christian ascetic, Nilus of Sinai. Nilus of Sinai, addressing monks with his instructions on prayer, says,

> When you pray, do not attach to the Godhead some sort of appearance and do not allow your mind to become transformed into some kind of image (or conceive oneself in the form of some image, or that any kind of image become impressed in your mind); but *immaterially* approach the Immaterial One and come together with Him.[19]

Further, he says, "Do not think that the Godhead is qualitative (takes up space, is extended, has parts); as the Divinity has neither quantity nor form."[20] Besides this, Nilus of Sinai says definitely, "Do not desire *to see sensorially Angels or Powers or Christ,* so as not to go out of one's mind, accepting the wolf for the pastor and worshipping the enemy demons."[21] He adds, "If you wish to pray in the spirit, borrow nothing from the flesh."[22]

And here is what St Isaac of Syria says: "As long as man uses force so that spirituality come down to him, it does not submit. And if he is boldly puffed up and raises up his gaze to the spiritual, and approaches it in his mind before the time (before acquiring true holiness), then soon his vision will become dulled and instead of reality he will perceive phantoms and shapes."[23]

Also of interest are the following words of St Symeon the New Theologian on the state of one praying, close to what Ignatius Loyola is striving after in his spiritual exercises. Symeon the New Theologian says,

> When someone standing in prayer and raising to heaven his hands, eyes and mind, keeps in his mind divine thoughts, *imagines heavenly blessings, the ranks of angels, the abodes of the saints* ... and sometimes even elicits tears and weeps, then during this type of prayer, he little by little begins to be conceited in his heart, he himself not understanding this: it seems to him that what he is doing is from the Grace of God.... But this is a sign of prelest [delusion].

In the opinion of Symeon the New Theologian, such a state can be very dangerous for a Christian ascetic, and "if it turns out that he does not go out of his mind, yet still it will be impossible for him to acquire virtue or passionlessness" (higher spiritual super-consciousness). Symeon says further, "Those standing in this path are in prelest who see light with their bodily eyes, smell fragrances with their sense of smell, hear voices with their ears, and so on."[24]

The fourteenth-century ascetic Gregory of Sinai has this to say about the same thing: "*From yourself do not form imaginations* and do not pay attention to those that form by themselves and do not allow them to be imprinted upon yourself. For all this which *from without* is imprinted and imagined serves for the captivation of the soul."[25] "The mind (the lower reason) in itself has the natural power to dream and can easily build illusory images of what it desires.... Then the one experiencing this is now a dreamer, and not a keeper of silence."[26] "May he who approaches contemplation without the light of Grace know that he is forming fantasies and does not have contemplation, is in a dreaming spirit, being entangled in fantasies and deceiving himself."[27]

Finally, Gregory Palamas, also a Christian ascetic of the fourteenth century, says concerning contemplative states,

> In this case, man rises up not on *fantastical wings of the imagination,* which like a blind man wanders around everything and does not receive a true and certain understanding of either sensory or mental subjects; but here man rises up to truth by the ineffable power of the Spirit, and with his spiritual ear hears ineffable words and sees the invisible, and all this is a miracle.[28]

These views of the Christian ascetics of the *Philokalia* passed on, along with the spreading of religious enlightenment, into Russian Orthodox mysticism as well.[29]

Here, in conclusion, we cite one very characteristic opinion of a Russian Orthodox writer close to us in time—the ascetic, Bishop Theophan the Recluse (who died in 1894)—on mysticism based on the ecstasies of an exulted imagination. Thus he writes to one of his students, who was carried away by rapturous prayers,

> May the Lord deliver you from rapturous prayers. Raptures, strong movements with excitement are simply the sanguine mental movements of an inflamed imagination. For them Ignatius Loyola wrote many instructions. Men reach these ecstasies and think that they have reached high degrees, but meanwhile all this is *soap bubbles*. Real prayer is quiet, peaceful and it is such in all its degrees.[30]

In another of his letters, Theophan says,

The imagination—the ability to form and retain images—is an unskilled labor ability . . . the very lowest! So therefore it is not proper to allow it to appear with its images in a higher realm such as prayer . . . mental/contemplative activity is lofty, but spiritual activity as manifested in prayer is still loftier . . . . *If one admits images, then there is the danger of praying to a dream.* There is one path—heartfelt prayer (prayer of pure feeling). . . . It comes to mind what was said of a *staretz* [elder] who always imagined God in a form. When it was explained to him that this should not be done, he said: you have taken God from me . . . . But they did not take God from him, but rather his dream."[31]

And so we see that the kind of mysticism for which Francis laid the foundation and which Ignatius Loyola subsequently developed was disapproved of by the Eastern ascetics, and they even considered the path of this mysticism unsafe for the soul of a Christian ascetic.[32]

There is one aspect that we have still not touched upon in this comparison of Eastern and Western mysticism—this is the aspect of special manifestations of mystical power in both forms of mysticism, manifestations expressed in the performance of so-called miracles, namely, those of healing. We did not have to concern ourselves with this in comparing the lives of St Seraphim and St Francis because of the number of books from which we studied the life of St Francis (the works of Jørgensen, Ger'e, Sabatier, and Jebar); Francis's miracles of healing are only briefly mentioned in the research of Sabatier and Ger'e, and this information was not sufficient for judging the process of these miracles. It is to be supposed that these researchers did not find in the original sources on Francis trustworthy information regarding this side of the saint. And this explains why in Jørgensen also nothing is said of such miracles by Francis. In his extensive research Jørgensen expatiates only on one, as he says, big miracle (*le grand miracle*) of Francis, his stigmatization. In our opinion, it would be most probable to assume that in general Francis did not perform miracles of healing. Such an assumption concurs with Francis's spiritual super-consciousness (which generally gives the power to perform healings) being darkened by the impulses of his mentalism.

Francis could not perform those mentalistic miracles *which yogis perform by their conscious will*[33] because the path of Francis's mysticism was still the

Christian path in which faith in the power of God comes first; and in this faith can be manifested the action of a great super-universal power, called divine grace, which is immeasurably more powerful than man's will. In any case, for a believing Christian *one's own will* cannot receive that tension attained by yogis, who believe first of all in *their own mental power and will* and with this power create phenomena that from the outside resemble miracles performed by holy people.

But if in the information on Francis's life we do not have material for judging his miracles of healing, still this does not exclude the possibility of such miracles occurring in the Catholic world. Undoubtedly, these miracles are performed in the Catholic world even up to this time. Therefore, it would be extremely interesting for us to touch on the matter of the character of these miracles (as compared with miracles performed in the Orthodox world). Miracles in the Catholic world are performed, for example, in Lourdes, a small town in France famous for its miracle-working statue of the Mother of God in a grotto. Every year, thousands of sick people stream into Lourdes to the holy statue, and some of them, before the eyes of everyone, are healed in a miraculous fashion.

This practice of Lourdes healings gives valuable material for studying the character of Catholic miracles, and we will use this material in comparing, for example, a Catholic miracle in Lourdes performed on a person afflicted with neurotic paralysis, with a miracle of St Seraphim that he performed on a similarly afflicted landowner, N. A. Motovilov. The reader remembers Motovilov's original account of his healing; we reproduced this account in detail in the second chapter of this book.[34]

———

Material on the mystical states experienced during miracles performed in Lourdes we have in the vivid and truthful descriptions of the manifestations of these states given by the famous representative of the French school of naturalism, Émile Zola. These descriptions appear in his book *Lourdes*. The plot of the story in this book does not in the least interfere with their veracity; it merely outwardly intertwines with the previously mentioned descriptions that have by themselves independent meaning as true pictures of reality. In the foreword to his novel *Lourdes*, Zola says,

> I followed after the pilgrims and unassumingly described the history of one of these pilgrimages, dividing it into five days. I attempted to reproduce the noisy, motley crowd of believers—representing all possible classes, sick and

healthy, priests, nuns—spending several days in prayer and returning from Lourdes with an enlightened soul … or with a still more despondent heart.[35]

In this book *Lourdes*, in the chapter describing the fourth day of the pilgrimage, there is a scene of the mystical states of the Catholic crowd, entering into ecstasy in the square before the grotto where stands the famous statue of the Mother of God, illuminated by the flames of candles. In this same chapter are portrayed the experiences of the sick, of whom some were healed before everyone's eyes. Finally, and this for us is the most interesting, the author has clearly recounted the methods used by the Catholic clergy for exciting the crowd into ecstasy.

Let us take some scenes from these descriptions. On the fourth day of the pilgrimage, writes Zola, the crowd was made up mainly of sick people.

All of the vast space, partitioned off by ropes, was overflowing with sick people, joining the national pilgrimage, numbering from 1000 to 1200 people. In the brilliance of a sunlit day, under the azure dome of the sky, humanity bared all its sores. Three hospitals unloaded here their frightful population….[36]

In front, right by the grotto, lay the critically ill; the flagstones of the square were covered with sufferers. Carts, stretchers, and mattresses were all entangled; some of the sick sat up in their boxes which resembled coffins—the majority were lying on the ground. Some were brought in dressed, on mattresses upholstered in colored ticking. Others in their underclothes were covered with blankets, from under which could be seen only their heads and pale hands….[37]

All illnesses were represented…. But the sicknesses and suffering retreated into the background once everyone had gathered there and lain down, fixing their eyes on the grotto. Pitiful, emaciated faces, with skin the color of earth, were transformed, lit up with a ray of hope. Sick hands were folded in prayer, heavy lids found the strength to open, weak voices became louder at the exclamations of the priest.

"Mary, having conceived without sin, pray for us!" cried the priest in a loud voice. The sick and the pilgrims repeated with each appeal more loudly, "Mary, having conceived without sin, pray for us!"[38] "Queen of Heaven, may the breath of Thy lips touch our sores—and our sores will heal!…"[39]

Fr Massias rises to the pulpit. This is a holy man, a righteous one. The people know Fr Massias; no sooner does he appear than the hearts of the pilgrims immediately light up with hope. Many were convinced that *his religious ardor would help in the accomplishment of miracles.* The Virgin willingly heeds his impetuous and tender appeals.[40]

Entering the pulpit, Fr Massias did not start speaking right away. He seemed very tall, thin, and pale, and the already drawn face of the ascetic was made even longer by a colorless beard. His eyes were burning, his lips moved from a rush of oratorical inspiration.

"O Lord, save us, we are perishing!" he cried.

The crowd repeated, with each moment becoming more carried away, "O Lord, save us, we are perishing!"

Raising his hands, Fr Massias broke out with fiery exclamations, just as if pouring out the surplus of a heart overflowing with passionate faith.

"O Lord, if Thou so desirest, Thou canst save me!"

"O Lord, if Thou so desirest, Thou canst save me!"[41]

Fr Massias voiced his cries still louder, with extraordinary passion, combining his cries with sobs.

"Jesus, son of David, I am perishing, save me!"

The crowd of pilgrims sobbed after him: "Jesus, son of David, I am perishing, save me!"

The appeals increased, raising to the heavens a complaint on the sorrows of the whole world.

"Jesus, son of David, have mercy on Thy sick children!"

"Jesus, son of David, have mercy on Thy sick children!"

The excitement of the crowd reached extreme limits. Another priest, Fr Furkad, at the steps of the pulpit, carried away by the passionate impulse of ecstatic hearts, raised his hands, likewise crying in a loud voice in order to force miracles from heaven. The mass ecstasy spread all the while, passed on infectiously from person to person, compelling everyone to bow their heads prayerfully. Even young ladies, who simply out of curiosity were sitting at the railing of the Gave riverfront, grew pale from agitation under their parasols....[42]

Suffering humanity cried from the abyss of its despair, as if dying and struggling with death, wanting to force God to grant as its lot eternal life.

"Lord, son of David, heal our sick ones!"

"Lord, son of David, heal our sick ones! ..."[43]

At four o'clock in the afternoon a large Catholic procession was supposed to come to the grotto, triumphantly bearing the Holy Gifts. The crowd met it with noisy rejoicing, with an irrepressible surge.

Fr Massias again entered the pulpit;[44] this time he had devised another method. After flaming appeals, breathing with faith, hope, and love, he commanded the crowd to plunge themselves into absolute silence—so that every pilgrim without opening his mouth could be secretly submerged for two or there minutes in prayer to God. The reverential silence, suddenly reigning over the multitudinous crowd, was striking in it trembling grandeur. The solemnity of these moments shook the soul, over the people blew a breath of passionate, irrepressible striving for life.

Then after several minutes the appeals began again. Fr Massias did not allow the surge of enthusiasm to cool, urging on with his cries the frantic crowd. And Fr Furkad, standing on one of the steps of the pulpit, wept, his face washed with tears turned toward the heavens, as if imploring God to come down to earth.

Meanwhile, the procession with the Holy Gifts approached, delegations and clergy stopped on the right and left. When the canopy entered the square allotted for the sick and stopped before the grotto, when the sick people saw the sanctuary shining like the sun, born on hands, they became unusually agitated. No one observed any order, voices flowed together, the crowd was becoming frenzied. Cries, appeals, prayers mingled together with loud weeping. Emaciated bodies rose up from the sick bed, trembling hands stretched toward the shrine, fingers cramped with convulsions wanted, as it were, to grasp hold of a miracle passing by.

"Lord Jesus Christ, save us, we are perishing! Lord Jesus Christ, we bow down to Thee, heal us!... Lord Jesus Christ, Thou art our Savior, Son of the Living God, heal us!"[45]

Finally, one of the sick ones lying in the square began crying out with boundless rejoicing, "I have been healed, I have been healed!"[46]

This was a young girl, Maria, who for several years had lain motionless and who was carried on a stretcher. Her immobility had encouraged her neurotic–pathological condition. Her organic injury had brought with it nervous exhaustion. The doctors could not heal her of her sickness.[47]

Zola describes the mental state the sick girl was going through before the moment of healing in the following way: "When the Holy Gifts were brought and she suddenly looked at the blindingly shining sanctuary, *she was overshadowed*: It seemed to the young girl that *she had been struck by lightning*. Her eyes lit up, finally, with a lively spark; they glowed like stars. Under the influence of the saving excitement of blood, her face became rosy, shone with health, with a rejoicing smile.... All her virginal organism shuddered, as if being reborn from the sudden shock. First to be freed from fetters were her legs, then she shuddered and some sort of heavy weight rose to her throat.[48] Through this weight from her parted lips broke out a cry of boundless rejoicing: "I have been healed.... I have been healed!" Zola also says that right there in the crowd several more healings took place. A woman suddenly rose up who had previously been lying on her mattress; she was wrapped in a sheet, as if in a shroud. A blind woman suddenly saw the shining grotto. A dumb woman fell on her knees and with a loud, resounding voice began to thank the Most Holy Virgin.[49]

However, enough of these scenes of Lourdes ecstasies and healings. The external manifestations of the mystical states during the described miracles are too vivid to judge their internal character.

Let us leave Lourdes and travel mentally to another place of great miracles—Sarov hermitage. Let us recall a healing analogous to the healing of Maria—the healing of the landowner Motovilov by Seraphim of Sarov. Let us recall under what conditions Motovilov's sudden recovery took place.

Motovilov was also brought to Seraphim as an immobile paralytic. Seraphim was touched by Motovilov's supplications to be healed and before the act of healing asked the sick one—did he believe in the power of God to accomplish this? He answered firmly that he believed. To this St Seraphim told him simply that he, Motovilov, *was already healthy*. However, Motovilov began to argue with Seraphim, assuming that this could not occur so quickly and simply. Then Seraphim took Motovilov's hand in one of his, and with the other hand began pushing his shoulders a little and *led him, a paralytic*, over the grass and uneven ground, saying, "There, your grace, how well you are walking!" To this Motovilov answered, "But this is because you are pleased to lead me well." "No," said Seraphim, taking his hand away from Motovilov, "the Lord Himself was pleased to heal you completely ... now, walk!" "*I felt within myself,*" says Motovilov further, "*a kind of power overshadowing me here from above, I gained a little courage and began to walk firmly.*"

Thus, Motovilov noted down the chief moments of his healing. After this startling miracle, Motovilov already had the strength to climb into his carriage.

Here it is interesting to note a common characteristic in the feelings before the moment of Maria's healing in Lourdes and Motovilov's healing in Sarov. That is, Maria, at the moment of her healing, felt that she was *overshadowed*, that she was *struck by lightning*. Motovilov says that before he began to walk firmly, he *felt within himself a kind of power overshadowing him from above*.

The word *overshadow* in both places is used in one sense, namely, in the sense of the inspiration of power. There it *is lightning*, here it is *power overshadowing from above*. The sensations during the healings in both places are the same.

Now the question arises, where did this power appear from?

To the young girl, during the healing it seemed that it descended upon her at the moment the Holy Gifts were being carried close by her, at the time she fixed her gaze on the holy sanctuary. Motovilov was healed when Seraphim took him by the hand and as if forcibly led him over the grass. Concerning the girl, a skeptical mind might suppose that the power of healing originated within herself, as the result of her deep faith in the Holy Gifts—a faith reaching the point of ecstasy, giving a nervous shock to her organism. Now concerning Motovilov, here one cannot explain that healing as an outburst of faith shocking Motovilov's organism, because Motovilov, as can be seen in his testimony, was not in ecstasy before the moment of healing and even manifested not a little discretion, starting to argue with Seraphim and expressing doubt in the miracle. Obviously, Motovilov was healed not by an outburst of his own ecstasy, but rather by power *overshadowing him from outside*, and the conductor of this power was St Seraphim of Sarov.

It is worthwhile mentioning here that Seraphim performed all this very simply.[50] He did not lead Motovilov into a state of ecstasy and did not use any kind of methods to inflame Motovilov's imagination to ecstasy. Before the miracle, he only asked the sick one if he believed in the power of God and when the sick one answered that he believed, Seraphim performed the miracle of healing. Seraphim's miracle is distinctive in that its character directly reminds us of the miracles of the Great Teacher Himself, who just as simply said to the paralytic, "Rise, take thy bed and go to thy home," and he rose up and went. Of course, for this, one word was enough because this was the source of spiritual power, this was the sun itself; but here in Seraphim we see only a conductor of this great spiritual power.

After all that has been stated, another question arises: Were those Catholic priests and Catholic spiritual strivers (Frs Massias and Furkad) conductors of this spiritual power—those who in Lourdes excited the sick and those praying into ecstasies, who for this deliberately employed various methods of prayer to jolt the imagination, first striking the nerves of the sick with their ecstatic appeals, then leading the crowd into absolute silence, into quiet, silent contemplation, next breaking out into tears and weeping? Were they real conductors of this spiritual power?

Healings take place in Lourdes—undoubtedly. But they are accomplished according to our deep conviction, and not through Catholic ascetics carried away by the mental mysticism of Loyola, striking at an inflamed imagination; rather, these miracles are accomplished solely thanks to the profound faith of the sick ones themselves. This faith breaks through all covers and layers, including the layers of mentalism and sensuality of Catholic mysticism. Undoubtedly, in some of the sick people at Lourdes a pure spiritual super-consciousness penetrated by deep religious feeling could have developed. It could have developed by itself from the constant self-absorption of the sick one and his sincere unceasing prayers. And this super-consciousness could, in the religious atmosphere of Lourdes, flare up so strongly that when the Holy Gifts were being carried past the sick person, then, indeed, he was struck by the lightning of healing.

From information gleaned from the comparison of St Francis's mysticism and the mysticism of Seraphim of Sarov, and likewise from the comparison of the basic views of the Christian ascetics of the *Philokalia* with the fundamentals of the *Spiritual Exercises* of Ignatius Loyola, one can already judge the characteristic differences between mysticism of the East and mysticism of the West. These comparisons that we have made in a general way just the same give us enough material to characterize both kinds of mysticism. And here are the chief conclusions we have reached concerning the substance of the present subject.

First, in the mysticism of the East in the person of St Seraphim of Sarov, we see an example of the complete rebirth of a man, going the way indicated by the Eastern Christian ascetics. We see here an example, in an ascetic, of the total absorption of the lower human reason by the higher reason (logos).[51] Inherent to human beings, this lower reason, with its characteristics of egocentricity and self-assertion (the result of which pride usually appears), is changed completely in an Eastern Christian ascetic into divine reason, revitalized in man's heart. In other words, the lower reason of such an ascetic acquires all the characteristics of the higher reason—simplicity, sincere deep humility, striving to prove itself in sacrifice. Besides this, the Christian ascetic acquires the grace of clairvoyance and the gift of penetrating into the souls of other people. Finally, such an ascetic at the highest stage of his perfection becomes the direct conductor of the higher spiritual power; he performs healings and miracles.

Second, in the same example of St Seraphim of Sarov we were convinced that the super-consciousness of an Eastern Christian ascetic is concentrated in his fervent heart. There, *within himself*, he senses the fire of the Divinity, senses Christ. This feeling of inner unity with God comes down upon him naturally and freely, as the direct result of his spiritual growth, as the result of work on himself in the path of humility and repentance. According to the mysticism of the East, all these inspirations of the higher senses appear in a humble person *unexpectedly,* for the ascetic in his humility does not feel that he is worthy even of this.

Third, in the mysticism of the West we see something else. St Francis in his notion of Christ was most of all struck by the earthly life of Christ, His suffering image. This impression came upon Francis from outside, and Francis yearned for visions of the suffering Christ. Thus developed the mysticism of St Francis, proceeding from an external impression, from the image of Christ and His suffering. The result of this was that Francis's mysticism had to incline to the side of the imagination and sensuality, for if Christ was for Francis an object, if Francis proceeded in the notion of Christ from an *external impression*, then one of the means for developing this mysticism was by exciting the imagination to this external impression. And if the imagination had been excited, then sensuality must have been affected as well.

Here, by the way, we should say that this sensuality is a highly characteristic property of all Catholic mysticism in general. It is even reflected in the external side of the Catholic religion: in its icons and in the text of its prayers. The *most* superficial comparison is sufficient to be convinced that original Orthodox iconography is more strict and more spiritual than Catholic iconography. Merely compare, for example, the modern iconographers of the East and West—Viktor Mikhailovich Vasnetsov and William Adolphe Bouguereau. The same contrast can be found in prayers. To illustrate this position, we first cite a sample text of a Catholic prayer, for example, a prayer of St Ignatius Loyola that is recited in the Catholic world to the same degree that the prayer of St Ephraim the Syrian is recited in the Orthodox world. Here is this prayer:

> Soul of Jesus, illuminate me,
> Body of Jesus, save me,
> Blood of Jesus, give me to drink,
> Water from Jesus' rib, cleanse me,
> Passions of Jesus, strengthen me,
> O good Jesus, hear me.[52]

And analogous with this Catholic prayer, here is an Orthodox prayer, taken from the akathist of Communion of the Holy Mysteries, from Eikos 1.

> O Jesus, burn up the thorns of my many sins.
> O Jesus, create in me a clean heart and renew a right spirit within me.

O Jesus, lead my poor soul from the prison of passions.

O Jesus, destroy in me impure thoughts and evil lusts.

O Jesus, guide my weak steps in the path of Thy commandments.

O Jesus, God of my heart, come and join me to Thyself for ever.

In comparing these two prayers, the quality of sensuality inherent in the first prayer stands out in relief.

Fourth and finally, we see that Ignatius Loyola led this mysticism, in which the power of the imagination played a large role, to extreme limits; but the results attained by this mysticism could not be anything but negative. The premeditatedly excited imagination, like everything that is unnatural and exaggerated, can easily evaporate. With the decline in the flashing of the cerebral imagination will also diminish the religious feeling that has been fanned by artificial exaltation. In this mysticism, the impulses it arouses cannot be firm, deep movements of the spirit, cannot be those profound ecstasies that are spoken of by the Christian ascetics of the *Philokalia*.[53] The ecstasies of Catholic spiritual leaders, judging from how the Catholic clergy were ecstatic in the throng of pilgrims at Lourdes, are exaggerated transports, external rushes. It is our deep conviction that if miracles do occur in Lourdes, then they occur not from these external methods of the Catholic clergy, but from the fact that among the thousands of pilgrims suffering from sicknesses, there burst forth (in spite of the artificial Catholic mysticism) real surges of higher spiritual super-consciousness. The gifts of divine grace, that great, super-universal Godly power, are, of course, poured out in Catholicism on people who believe sincerely and deeply, who have a heart undarkened by mentalism.

In conclusion, it remains for us to mention as well that Western mysticism, besides its negative sides—its attraction to the external to the detriment of the internal—besides these aspects that we have indicated, it also had its positive aspects. This mysticism, manifesting it characteristic differences in the typical guidance of Ignatius Loyola on spiritual exercises, did much in another regard, namely, in the external unification of Catholic Christianity. It united the Catholic clergy and monasticism into a powerful organization under the supremacy of the pope. The Catholic clergy, exercising enormous influence over its flock, was able to organize a militant church, possessing political, external cultural power. Thanks to this, even in France with its present atheistic government,[54] in spite of the general decline of religious feeling among the intelligentsia, the Catholic clergy just the same bolsters the significance of the church, bearing on high her banner, as a cultural force.

In contrast to the Catholic clergy, the clergy of the Eastern Church was always weakly organized in the sense of a social, external cultural force. And in this sense it is weak even now. But in return, our Orthodox asceticism, judging by such representatives as, in recent times, St Seraphim of Sarov, stands immeasurably high; and only in Orthodox asceticism, based on the principles of the Eastern Church, do we see the pledge of the rebirth of the earthly man into the spiritual man. Only in the penetrating instructions of the Christian ascetics of the *Philokalia* is the possibility of mankind approaching the great ideal of the kingdom of God made feasible, toward which instinctively strove and do strive our people, a people strong in its spiritual leaven, a people thirsting deeply for the acquisition of the Holy Spirit of God.

CHAPTER 6

⁓

Striking Features from the Lives of the Saints

Pskov fool-for-Christ Nicholas Sallos offered Tsar Ivan the Terrible a piece of meat. "I, a Christian, do not eat meat during Great Lent," answered the Tsar. "But human blood you drink?" asked the fearless saint. And the cruel tyrant, the incarnation of terror, recoiled from the saint in fear.

—From the life of Pskov fool-for-Christ Nicholas Sallos

In the previous chapters, we spoke mainly about the life of Seraphim of Sarov. Now we will pass on to the lives of other Christian ascetics of the Eastern Church, carrying out their spiritual struggles in Christ. If we paused in detail on the life of Seraphim, comparing it with the life of Francis of Assisi, this was because Seraphim represents a typical example for judging the lives of the saints of the Eastern Church. And to this end, information on him was for us most complete. The various episodes from his life imprinted themselves in the memory of the many people who surrounded him, and they were contemporaries of our fathers—these live witnesses of the unusual mysticism of Seraphim, of his Christian activity and lofty spiritual struggles. Yet material on the lives of other Christian ascetics of the Eastern Church, if we examine them in the preserved sources, is not so rich and diverse as with Seraphim. Irrespective of this, Seraphim, as we saw, combined within himself the most diverse manifestations of holiness; this was a type not only contemplative, but active as well.

In this chapter, to avoid repetition we will acquaint our readers only with those characteristic manifestations of the spiritual struggles of the saints that supplement the traits of life we studied in Seraphim. We will also acquaint them with such facts that are interesting in their originality and, finally, with some striking events arising as the result of the special conditions under which these spiritual struggles were accomplished.

We will begin by giving an example of the strong inclination of certain saints to the life of spiritual struggle. Here we will observe what kind of obstacles these saints overcame. As we know, when Seraphim entered the monastery, he did not have to contend with opposing conditions. Seraphim's mother willingly let him go into monasticism. Seraphim's whole life formed favorably for his receiving the monastic spiritual struggle.

We have taken an example of a Christian ascetic struggling with conditions hindering his entering a monastery from the life of the Russian saint Varlaam of Pechersk (eleventh century). We will acquaint our readers with the problems of this struggle using information we found in the *Menologion*.

In Kiev, during the rule of the grand duke Izyarslav Yaroslavich (1054–1068), his closest *boyar,* Ivan, had a son, Varlaam, grandson of Vyshata, great-grandson of Ostromir. In his youth this Varlaam, in his striving for spiritual endeavors, overcame all obstacles hindering his entering a monastery—obstacles that seemed insurmountable.

We will recount the events concerning Varlaam, keeping close to the historical chronicle, preserving it in some places word for word. Here the account in the *Menologion* is interesting in itself as an example of the simple and unaffected language of such chronicles. At the same time, this account communicates the relationship of the chronicler himself to the event taking place: one senses the chronicler's reverence before Varlaam's determination to enter on the path of asceticism; one senses how he relates to this case, as to a lofty heroic deed, as to the act of a man who, for the sake of interests of the life of the spirit, sacrificed the interests of the life of form, riches, ambition, and other worldly goods, sacrificing for this even his right to family happiness.[1]

The young Varlaam often went to the Pechersk monastery, where he was influenced by the instructions and lives of the famous anchorites of that time—Anthony, Theodosius, and Nikon.

In conversations with the Christian ascetics an especially strong impression was made on Varlaam by their explanation of the Gospel saying that it is easier for a camel to go through the eye of a needle than for a rich man to enter the kingdom of God.[2]

Coming one day to Anthony, Varlaam revealed to him his intention to enter the monastery; Anthony approved Varlaam's decision.

The next day after the conversation with the elder, Varlaam, as the chronicle says, left not only his parents, but also his intended bride to whom he was already betrothed. Mounted on his horse and dressed in bright and rich clothing, having with him a multitude of servants on foot leading the caparisoned horse, he triumphantly arrived at the cave. When the holy men came out and bowed to the earth before him, as was then customary to bow to nobility, he himself, having dismounted, bowed down to them. Then he took off his rich clothing and placed it at the feet of St Anthony and put his horses before him, saying, Here, father, are the vain goods of this world: do with them as you wish. I want to live with you in this cave, and I will never return home again. Tonsure me quickly.

Then St Anthony ordered that St Nikon tonsure Varlaam and clothe him with the monastic habit, which was done.

The *boyar* Ivan, when he learned that his favorite son had been tonsured a monk, became enraged at the holy men, and taking with him a multitude of servants, he attacked the monks saving their souls in the cave and drove them all away; and his son he forcibly dragged out and, tearing off his mantia and cuckle,[3] he threw them into a stream. Then he dressed him in bright, rich clothing, appropriate to his lineage, but the saint straightway cast them off, not wanting even to look at them. And this was repeated several times, so that his father ordered his hands tied, again forcibly dressed him, and looking like this he was led home through the town.

When they arrived home, his father ordered him to sit at the table with him: his son was forced against his will to obey, but he ate none of the food served and sat with his head bowed. At the end of the meal, his father let Varlaam go to his room, appointing a servant to guard him so he would not leave.

Then he ordered Varlaam's betrothed to put on her finest adornments to entice him and express her love for him in every possible way. But the Christpleaser Varlaam went into one of the rooms and sat in a corner on the floor. In accordance with the instructions she had been given, his betrothed followed him and begged to sit on his bed. Then he, seeing her foolishness and guessing that his father had sent her to tempt him, lifted up from the depths of his heart a secret prayer to the all-merciful God for salvation from temptation. He sat there three days, not getting up, eating nothing, not dressing, and remaining in just a hair shirt. Meanwhile, St Anthony and those with him in the cave were very saddened by his fate and prayed for him to God.

The servants reported to the *boyar* that already for four days his son did not eat food and did not dress himself. His father took pity on his son and, fearing that he might die from hunger and cold, called him and, kissing him with love, let him go to the cave. "And then something truly amazing happened," said the chronicle.

There was heard in the house weeping and crying as if for a dead man; everyone wept: the father and mother that they had lost their son, the betrothed that she was parted from her intended, the slaves that their kind master had left them, But Varlaam, like a bird escaping from a net, set out quickly for the cave. The monks living there rejoiced wholeheartedly upon seeing Varlaam, and glorified God Who had heard their prayer for him.[4]

In this example, we see how great for some saints was the striving toward asceticism. It overcame all obstacles. The power of spirit in Varlaam triumphed over the interests with which earthly human life beckoned to itself. If the Western Church presents Francis of Assisi as an example of a man's unusually strong propensity toward spiritual struggle, then one could say that the Eastern Church numbered among its saints people like Varlaam. Their attraction to life in the Logos, as we see in the current example, was an elemental force.

———————

The power of attraction to the spiritual life was manifest in all eras. It was deeply rooted in the Russian people. And it is preserved in it even now. It is hidden also in some of the intelligentsia, but unfortunately, the majority of these people are not even aware of it. The germs of spirituality, if they develop now in people of exceptional mystical talent, then most often in incorrect forms, and sometimes completely deformed, because now the vast majority of people have lost the way to higher mysticism—the way shown by Christianity, which alone can direct the *mystical* talent in its real path.

So impulses toward spiritual life always were and will be. And in some eras they became manifest even in whole mass movements of people in the direction of religion. The early Christian era was especially rich in these impulses.

If in our simple people, feeling the need for life in Christ, these impulses reveal themselves in the striving toward monasticism and spiritual exploits (wandering, foolishness, etc.), then in the early Christian era these impulses were manifest first of all in the transition from paganism to Christianity and in unusual cases of conversion of pagans into Christians.

To judge fully the power of the instinctive attraction of some people to spiritual life, we consider not without interest to cite here three examples of the pagan world, when people, moved by the inclinations of their higher reason, not only became Christians, but also straightway became even great Christian ascetics. One such example we will take from the life of a pagan philosopher, another from the life of a pagan courtesan, and the third from the life of an actor.

The first example is the history of the conversion to Christ of the famous saint of the second century, Justin the Philosopher, who later even died a martyr's death, confessing Christianity.

This Justin, before his conversion, was a prominent academician. Having studied the modern schools of philosophy—the Stoics, the Pythagoreans, and others—he stopped at Neoplatonism, as a philosophy that perceived the God-head. But even this philosophy did not satisfy. Then he became interested in Christianity. Those accusations that the pagans cast on Christians, and that at first he believed, proved to be slander, and meanwhile, the Christians so fearlessly died for their faith. And here, at that time when there was born in Justin a sympathy toward persecuted Christianity, he met by chance on the seashore a Christian teacher—an elder—whose conversation made a deep impression on him; this conversation influenced his decision to convert to Christianity. Justin described this conversation in detail in one of his works.[5] The conversation with the elder was of long duration, and its substance was purely philosophical. We will cite from this conversation only the most significant moments that influenced Justin.

Here is how it all happened. One day, Justin, living in a town close to the sea (maybe in Ephesus, says Farrar), being occupied at that time with serious thoughts and questions, went off to walk in a plain not far from the shore, to give himself over to reflection in solitude. He wanted to be alone with his thoughts, but as he was walking back and forth along the seashore he noticed that he was being followed by an unknown old man, very handsome, with a quiet and majestic way of walking. Surprised by this, he turned around and somewhat suspiciously stared at him.

"Do you know me?" the old man suddenly asked Justin.

"No," answered Justin.

"Then why are you staring at me so?"

"I did not expect to meet anyone in this quiet, peaceful place," answered Justin.

But here after these first words a conversation began between them. And this conversation was about philosophical questions.

"Tell me," the old man asked Justin at the height of the conversation, "what is philosophy and in what does it give happiness?"

"Philosophy," answered Justin, "is the understanding of all that exists and the knowledge of the truth; *the happiness rendered by philosophy consists in the possession of this understanding.*"

Let us stop on these words of Justin. Reading them, we involuntarily recall that definition of the purpose of life that we read in the book of P. D. Uspenskii, *Tertium Organum,* which we spoke about in Chapter 2.[6] Namely, Uspenskii maintains that the meaning of life is *in cognition and knowledge.*

After comparing this view with what Justin said to the elder about the happiness offered by philosophy, we see that the pagan Justin the Philosopher is in essence saying the same thing that we now read in the books of our intelligentsia. As we see, nothing has changed in these definitions for all the past eighteen centuries. The inquisitive philosophical mind both then and now finds happiness in knowledge. Yet the Christian heart, as we saw in the *Philokalia* and from the life of Seraphim of Sarov, finds happiness first of all *in the acquisition of the Holy Spirit of God.* And knowledge appears later, as a function derived from the attainment of this main goal.

But let us return to the conversation of Justin with the Christian elder. From philosophy, the conversation switched over to the understanding of the Godhead, and the elder asked Justin, "How can your Hellenic philosophers reason correctly about God and confirm any truth concerning Him, if they have never seen Him, have not heard and, consequently, have not had any knowledge of Him?"

Justin answered, "The power of the Godhead is not seen with bodily eyes.... With the mind alone is one able to perceive God. Thus says Plato whose teaching I follow."

Saying this, Justin became carried away with the interesting theme. He began to develop before the elder how, according to Plato's teaching, the Godhead is perceived. Justin spoke eloquently, but the elder disputed the possibility of such perception. Finally, the elder said very firmly to Justin, "Man's mind, if not directed by the Holy Spirit and not illuminated by faith (i.e., not having acquired the Holy Spirit of God), is totally incapable of knowing and understanding God."

The elder began after this to talk about the Holy Spirit, about the Savior of the world, about the prophets; he concluded his talk thus: "First of all, pray diligently to the true God that He open to you the doors of light, for only he can contemplate and understand divine things whom God Himself has deigned worthy of revelation; and He opens to everyone who seeks Him with prayer and approaches Him with love." Having said this, the elder departed from Justin.

Justin was left alone on the seashore with his thoughts. He never again met the elder, but the words of the elder made a great impression on the philosopher. Justin expresses his feelings at that time in his writings thus:

A kind of fire blazed up within me, igniting my soul with striving toward God, and there increased in me love for the holy prophets and those men who were friends of Christ. Pondering the words of the [elder], I came to realize that the philosophy proclaimed by him was the only truth; I began to read the books of the prophets and apostles and from them became a real philosopher, that is, a true Christian.[7]

But of course Justin was so touched by the words of the Christian teacher only because his heart was already close to sensing God. Justin's higher reason, despite his heathen life, was not completely stifled in him. The instinct of this reason was awakened by the inspired words of the elder.

———————

Let us switch over now to another typical conversion to Christianity—the conversion to Christ of the Antioch courtesan Pelagia.

This event took place in the fifth century, when the breaking up of paganism was at its height. At that time in Antioch, one of the richest cities in Syria, the local archbishop not infrequently had councils with the surrounding bishops for deciding church matters. To one of these councils in Antioch came the Heliopian bishop Nonnus, famous at that time as a preacher. He brought with him to the council the Heliopian deacon James, who was an eyewitness to Pelagia's conversion to Christianity. James the Deacon even left a description of this conversion.

This is how it took place. Arriving in Antioch, Nonnus stayed at the church of St Julian. One day, some bishops came to this church and wanted to hear Nonnus's sermon. They gathered for this on the church porch by the church doors, where they sat to listen to the gifted preacher. Nonnus began his inspired talking. He quickly enthralled the listeners. They listened to him reverently. "At that time," says James the Deacon in his chronicle,

> a certain woman—a heathen, well-known in all of Antioch as a prostitute—was passing by the church doors with great pride, dressed in rich clothing, adorned with gold, precious stones and pearls, surrounded by a multitude of maidens and youths in beautiful clothing, with golden torques. She was so beautiful of face that the worldly youths could not get enough of contemplating her beauty. Passing by us she filled all the air with aromatic fragrance. Seeing her walking so shamelessly, with her head uncovered and shoulders bare, the bishops closed their eyes and, quietly sighing, turned away as from great sin.[8]

With her beauty, the courtesan Pelagia also made an impression on Nonnus. After the bishops had departed and when Nonnus had returned to his cell, he began praying to God with this prayer: "Lord, do not destroy the work of Thy hands: that such beauty may not continue in depravity, in the power of devils, but turn her to Thyself, that Thy Holy Name may be glorified in her; for with Thee all things are possible."[9]

That night Bishop Nonnus had a strange dream. The next morning he spoke of his dream to James the Deacon thus:

"Brother James, listen to the dream I had this night," Nonnus began his account. "It seemed to me that I stood in one of the corners of the altar, and here while the service was being performed, a black dove appeared and it flew around me. And when the deacon pronounced: "All catechumens depart," the dove flew away, and I did not see it until the liturgy had ended. But after the liturgy was finished, when we were leaving the church, I suddenly saw once again this dove in all its squalor, which again flew around me. Stretching out my hand, I caught it and plunged it into the water standing in the porch of the church; in it the dove was cleansed of all its filth, flew out pure and white like snow and, rising on high, became invisible."[10]

On that same day in Antioch, in the main cathedral the solemn archiepiscopal service was to take place, with all the visiting bishops serving. Many people gathered for such a celebration. To see the divine service also came that beautiful courtesan who had made such an impression on Nonnus. Maybe it was not from curiosity alone that she came. After all, she already had had a chance to hear much of what Nonnus said with such inspiration to the bishops seated on the church porch.

At the end of the solemn cathedral service, the bishop of Antioch offered Nonnus to say a word to the people. Nonnus began his sermon. He spoke with power. And Pelagia heard Nonnus's words.

After the sermon, she said to servants, "Wait here and, when that holy man who gave the sermon leaves, follow him, find out where he lives and tell me upon your return."

The servants fulfilled her orders. They informed their mistress that Bishop Nonnus was living by the church of St Julian the Martyr. Then, in her own hand, Pelagia wrote this message to Nonnus: "If, as I hear from Christians, thou art a true slave of Christ, then do not reject me who with thy help wish to come to the Savior of the world and see His most holy face."

Having read Pelagia's message, Nonnus wrote her this answer: "Whatsoever thou art is known unto God and thyself, and what thy purpose is.... If indeed thou hast a desire to believe in my God and dost wish to see me, there are other bishops with me; come, and thou shalt see me in their presence. For thou shouldst not see me alone."[11]

When the bishops had gathered in the church of St Julian, Pelagia came there. She begged Nonnus to make her a Christian. "My lord, I am a sea of sins," she cried, "and an abyss of unlawfulness, cleanse me in baptism."

They baptized her. All her possessions she gave to the orphans, the poor, and the infirm. Pelagia freed her slaves and servants. Fervently she gave herself over to repentance. She yearned for spiritual struggle that would cleanse her soul.

On the eighth day after her baptism, when by custom the newly baptized must remove the white robes received at baptism, Pelagia rose early, removed this robe, and put on a hair shirt. That day she disappeared from Antioch. No one knew where she had gone; only Nonnus knew where she was. Pelagia went to Palestine to the holy places. Dressed in men's clothing, she settled there in solitude under the name of monk Pelagius and secluded herself from everyone. Thus passed three years—three years of spiritual endeavor, full of deprivation and severe asceticism—until death came upon Pelagia. James the Deacon learned of this death, having seen in Palestine the monk Pelagius not long before his death, and only after his death did it become known whom this young monk was.

———

The third example of the turning of a heathen into a Christian we have taken from the life of the pagan actor Porphyrius. The example is striking, but unfortunately, only briefly summarized in the *Menologion.* This is what is said there about Porphyrius:

> One day the people were celebrating the birthday of Emperor Julian. As an actor, Porphyrius was supposed to mock and profane Christians in the theater. At the moment when with this intention he plunged into the water and exclaimed: "Porphyrius is baptized in the name of the Father and the Son and the Holy Spirit," he suddenly believed in the true God, and leaving the water, began openly to confess Christ. For this he was given over to suffering and was beheaded.[12]

This account, as the reader sees, is briefly told, but the fact of conversion speaks for itself. Only in that amazing early Christian era, when the atmosphere was permeated with spiritual power, only then could such a thing have been accomplished.

What in essence really took place here? This actor of antiquity, Porphyrius, possibly a famous mime of that time, like the illustrious Paris (mimic soloist of Emperor Nero), adorning the orgiastic pagan stage; he, who was possibly a great artist, suddenly went out of his mind, his pagan mind, and announcing loudly before everyone that he was a Christian, expressed in this way a protest against the pervading pagan orgy, not only on the stage, but in life as well, and with his fervent act renounced the world. One can imagine what an indignant public outcry arose as a result of this incident, how displeased by Porphyrius's action were the Epicurean philosophers ruling the theater, how malicious was the laughter of the extollers of the pagan theaters—the critics of the ancient world—and what hatred was stirred up against Porphyrius in the heathen crowd, craving only one thing: bread and spectacles! But despite all this, Porphyrius expressed his protest fearlessly. What spiritual power there must have been to dare to take such a step! And one frequently comes across such striking cases in this amazing era.

But from these startling scenes of early Christianity, the scenes of the conversion of the courtesan Pelagia and the actor Porphyrius into followers of Christ, let us switch to the modern era, and let us ask ourselves, can we conceive of anything similar in our time, among us living in the stagnant mire of our lives—in the mire that devours people's striving toward air and light. Can we picture, for example, someone who had devoted himself to the theater, indiscriminant of evil, today just like it was in ancient times; this man, for the sake of some kind of spiritual striving, renouncing his success? Can we conceive that a modern-day courtesan/actress, belonging for example to the ballet world, having attained the adoration of the crowd, could ever voluntarily renounce her precious right to display herself on stage in front of the crowd, shamelessly exposing herself and putting on airs? And finally, let us take another example: Is it conceivable now that an actor of another kind, even some talented court defender, selling his eloquence for money, would renounce his ability to whitewash the guilty in court, would do this for the sake of preserving the purity of his soul, and would begin even to repent that many times he had shamelessly lied in court to make his orations a success?

———————

From the previous descriptions of people who were drawn to the spiritual life, we will switch now to another manifestation of the striving of spirit; we will tell of its manifestations in deeds of philanthropy and unusual benevolence.

Prof. I. V. Popov, in his analysis *St John Chrysostom and His Enemies,* says[13] that only monasticism has made an attempt to carry out in life the Sermon on the Mount, the ideal of self-denying love and nonresistance to violence and offense. In connection with this, Popov cites this example to illustrate the following situation taken from the *Lausiac History* of Palladius, bishop of Helenopolis.[14]

Bishop Vissarion always carried with him a book of the Gospels. In one village, he saw a dead poor man, completely naked, and he covered him with his cloak. Later, he met a live poor man, also without any clothing, and after giving him his shirt, he himself sat naked, covering himself with his hands. When Vissarion was asked who undressed him, he answered, holding out the Gospels, "This undressed me." Finally, to help a poor man he sold his Gospels from which he had never parted, "that very Word," as he recounted later, "which always told me—sell what thou hast and give to the poor."

A case similar to this manifestation of goodness we see in another saint, namely, Anin the Wonderworker, whose life is described in the *Menologion*.

This wonderworker lived in Syria, a short distance from the Euphrates River. His ascetic life made him known throughout the whole area. Many people came to him for advice and help. The local bishop had great respect for Anin.

Learning one day that Anin himself bore water from the Euphrates for quenching the thirst of those who came to him, the bishop sent him a gift of a donkey that could carry water from the river.

It happened that after this gift, there came to the saint a poor man who had nothing with which to pay back his debt to a money lender. This man asked the saint to help him pay the debt. With this, Anin, having nothing else to give, said to the visitor, "My brother, take this donkey, sell it, and with the money received pay thy debt." The man took the donkey and left the saint, and the saint once again began to haul water from the river.

When the bishop learned of this, he sent another donkey to the saint and told him, "I am not giving thee this donkey to keep, but so thou canst use it to carry water; when I will have need of it, I will take it back."

But even this donkey did not serve the saint for long. After a while another poor man came to the saint and also asked him for charity. Having nothing to give except the donkey, the saint gave that to the beggar.

When afterward the bishop came to the saint, says the chronicle, not finding the donkey, he ordered that a large cistern be dug and, using many animals, filled it with water from the river (usually, in waterless and dry areas cisterns were dug and filled with water from rain or melted snow, or brought from a river). Having filled the cistern to the top, the bishop took his animals back; and when the water in the cistern became exhausted, the bishop again sent his donkeys for carrying water to the cistern and later took them back.[15]

Of course, such maximalists in the spiritual struggle of charity as Abba Vissarion and Anin the Wonderworker are conceivable today merely as an ideal of selflessness in aiding one's neighbor. Under present-day circumstances, the actual realization of such exploits is almost impossible.

After these examples of nonacquisitiveness and benevolence, we could not fail to be struck by examples of the extent to which Christian ascetics struggled with worldly glory, how they shunned positions of honor. Biographies of the saints are full-on descriptions of cases when Christian ascetics were practically forced to take higher episcopal posts. We will cite from the lives of the saints two such examples.

At the end of the fourth century, an Antiochean priest John, receiving subsequently the name of Chrysostom, for his holiness of life and eloquence, was chosen archbishop of Constantinople, according to the wish of the Byzantine Emperor Arcadius. John was then already fifty years old. Before his election, he did everything on his part that the cup of this service pass him by, but he was compelled to submit to the force of events. John did not even want to go from Antioch to Constantinople, guessing why he was being called there, but he was brought there by force and subterfuge. A participant in the plot against Chrysostom, the Antiochean noble Asterius, asked the unsuspecting John to visit a chapel with him outside the city walls of Antioch. When John arrived at the appointed place, he was seized and taken by force to Pagri, the first station on the way to Constantinople. There, in spite of his protests, he was seated in the imperial chariot prepared for this purpose, and accompanied by soldiers and envoys they dashed off to the eastern capital.[16]

And here is what we read in the *Menologion* of the life of the famous Christian ascetic of the fourth century, Ephraim the Syrian.

Ephraim the Syrian was full of deep humility, in every way avoiding human honor and temporal glory. One time the people wanted to seize him and forcibly make him a bishop. Learning of this, Ephraim pretended to be foolish and began running around the square, dragging his clothing behind him like a madman, grabbed bread and vegetables being sold and ate them. Seeing this, the people thought he was insane, and he ran from the city and hid until another bishop was appointed to the post which they had wanted to appoint him to.[17]

———

We do not consider it superfluous here to acquaint the reader with the most exceptional circumstances of the life of a certain Christian ascetic, to judge in general the at-times peculiar ways in which the ascetics' activity of doing good to one's neighbor expressed itself. We have taken this example also from the *Menologion,* from the life of a saint named Vitaly the Monk.[18] Here is what the chronicle says about this saint.

When the patriarchal throne in Alexandria was being occupied by Patriarch John the Merciful,[19] there came to Alexandria a monk by the name of Vitaly, from the monastery of St Sirid. This monk, who was sixty years old, chose for himself the kind of life that for people seeing only the outside of a person would seem impure and sinful. The chronicle says that Vitaly "made himself a list of all the prostitutes living in Alexandria and he prayed for every one of them with special fervor to God that He turn them from their sinful life." The elder found employment in the city from morning to evening and for his work took twenty copper coins. With one coin, he would buy himself a bean[20] and before sunset would eat it, because while working all day, he fasted. Then he would set out for the brothel and, arriving there, would give the rest of his money to some prostitute and say to her, "For this money I beg you to keep yourself in purity, committing no sin with anyone."

And having said this, he would lock himself up with her in her room. She slept on her bed, and the elder would stand in the corner and spend the whole night without sleep, quietly reading the Psalms of David and till morning praying for her to God.

So he did for a long time, working all the days in fasting and at night going to the prostitutes, abiding in prayer without sleep. Every night he went to another until having seen them all, he began again with the first.

The *Menologion* says that some of the prostitutes, shamed by Vitaly's virtues, themselves stood up to pray and together with him, on bended knee, they prayed. And many of them left their former sinful life and married lawful husbands. And others, wishing to live in complete purity, entered convents and there in fasting and tears spent their lives. Others lived in the world without husbands, in purity supporting themselves with the work of their hands.[21]

Monk Vitaly's behavior aroused the indignation of many. Not knowing Vitaly's real relationship with the fallen women, people reproached him severely. One day, says the *Menologion*, when at dawn St Vitaly was leaving the brothel, he was met by a young fornicator who was going to the prostitutes. Recognizing Vitaly, the youth struck him hard on the cheek and said, "Cursed and ungodly, how much longer will you not repent and not abandon your impure life so that the name of Christ be not profaned by you?"[22]

But finally the time came when Vitaly's real relationship with the fallen women was made clear to everyone.

When the saint died and when these women whom he saved from sin learned of it, they flocked to his coffin with lighted candles and lamps, weeping and grieving for their father and teacher. Meanwhile they told aloud to all the people the virtues of the elder who came to them to save them.

So only then did the people find out the truth about the monk Vitaly. "And many of those living in Alexandria," says the chronicle, "edified by Vitaly's virtuous life, set a rule for themselves never to judge anyone."

———————

It still remains for us to explain the features of the manifestation of spiritual striving called *foolishness for Christ*. While studying the lives of the saints, one cannot ignore this form of spiritual endeavor; here everyone is struck by the peculiarity of this amazing spiritual struggler.

The saints' foolishness for Christ consisted in Christian ascetics who remained living among people and strove to renounce the customs and conditions of their surroundings, completely disregarding the interests of the life of form, and invisibly to others they devoted themselves to spiritual life. Outwardly, the life of such ascetics seemed strange, incomprehensible, going contrary to everything they had ever met up with. But alongside of this, some actions of the fools involuntarily reduced people around them to reverential compunction; these acts amazed everyone by their profound significance. At the same time, in these fools there sometimes burst forth mysterious and wonderful actions containing in themselves clear allusions to the future, which came true. These were people to whom in many cases was opened a high degree of mystical perception.

The life of fools, as we see from their biographies, represented the most difficult Christian spiritual struggle. Being constantly in the society of people, fools were no less alone than those living in wild deserts. Having completely renounced all possessions, comforts, and earthly blessings, free from attachments to the world, having no definite shelter and subject to all the vagaries of a homeless life, they were like strangers from another world. Food, clothing, and shelter did not constitute for them an essential need. Foolishness for Christ was a voluntary, constant martyrdom, a constant struggle against oneself, against the world and evil, and a most difficult and cruel struggle besides. Not hesitating to tell the truth to a person's face, the fools with their words or unusual actions sometimes sternly reproached and shocked unjust and sinful people, often the powerful and strong of the world, and sometimes they gladdened and comforted devout and God-fearing people. It was not uncommon for fools to associate with the most depraved members of society, with the purpose of reforming and saving them, and many of these outcasts returned to the path of truth and goodness.[23]

The first Christian ascetics of foolishness for Christ appeared early in the Christian era; they appeared in the cradle of monasticism in Egypt, in the second half of the fourth century. In the sixth century in Syria, Symeon the Fool was famous, and his life represents interesting features of which we will speak further on. Besides this, in the same sixth century in Cappadocia (Caesarea), there was a well-known fool, St. Thomas.[24] Finally, in the ninth century in Constantinople, St Andrew the Fool was famous.

With the spreading of Christianity in Russia, the spiritual struggle of foolishness was taken on by our Christian ascetics; the Russian people treated fools with the greatest reverence, as their moral heroes. It is interesting to note what the famous publicist M. O. Menshikov has to say about the honoring of fools by our people. In one of his articles, he writes this about foolishness:

> One should realize that it was not without reason that the people put forth foolishness as one of the striking manifestations of its spirit. Foolishness is one of the national sovereignties, one of the heroisms, one of the heights of attainment. Remember the scene in Pskov: Nicholas Sallos offers Ivan the Terrible a piece of meat. "It is now Lent," answers the Tsar, "I, a Christian, do not eat meat." "But human blood you drink?" asks the fearless saint. And the cruel tyrant, the incarnation of terror, recoils from the saint in fear.[25]

No less highly did the great writer of the world L. N. Tolstoy esteem foolishness. "If I were alone," wrote Tolstoy to Strakhov in 1877, "I would not have been a monk, but rather a fool; that is, I would value nothing in life and do harm to no one."

Here it is interesting to remind the reader of the type of Russian fool so strikingly portrayed by Tolstoy in his *Childhood*. We reproduce the vivid scene from Tolstoy's *Childhood* when Tolstoy, still a child, secretly, along with others his age, observed from a dark closet the fool Grisha when he entered the room drenched in moonlight and began to pray fervently to God.

We were all terrified in the dark [writes Tolstoy]; we pressed close to one another and did not say a word. Almost right after us Grisha came in with quiet steps. In one hand he was holding his staff, in the other a tallow candle in a brass candlestick. We held our breath.

"Lord Jesus Christ! Most Holy Mother of God! to the Father, and the Son, and the Holy Spirit…" breathing in air, he repeated over and over with various intonations and abridgements, peculiar only to those who often repeat these words.

With a prayer he put his staff in the corner and looking the bed over, he began to undress. Ungirthing his old black sash, he slowly took off his tattered nankeen coat, folded it carefully and hung it on the back of the chair. His face now did not express the usual haste and stupidity; on the contrary, he was calm, thoughtful and even dignified. His movements were slow and deliberate.

Remaining in just his underclothes, he quietly sat down on the bed, made the sign of the cross over it from all sides, and obviously with effort (because he winced) he readjusted the chains under his shirt. Having sat for a while carefully examining several torn places in his undergarments, he stood up, with a prayer lifted the candle to the level of the icon case in which there were several icons, crossed himself before them and turned the candle with the flame upside down. It went out with a crackle.

In the windows facing the forest an almost full moon shone. The long white figure of the fool was lit up from one side by the pale silver rays of the moon, and from the other, by black shadow along with the shadows from the frames, falling on the floor and walls and reaching to the ceiling. Outside the watchman knocked on a brass gong.

Crossing his enormous hands on his chest, lowering his head and with constant heavy sighing, Grisha stood silently before the icons, then with difficulty he got down on his knees and began to pray.

At first he quietly said well-known prayers, only emphasizing certain words, then repeated them, but louder and with great animation. He began to use his own words, with a noticeable effort trying to express himself in Slavonic. His words were awkward, but touching. He prayed for all his benefactors (as he called those who took him in), including Mother and us; he prayed for himself, asking God to forgive him his grave sins and saying repeatedly: "God forgive my enemies!" Groaning, he got up and repeating over and over these same words he fell to the ground and again rose up, despite the weight of the chains which gave off a dry, sharp sound, knocking on the floor.

For a long time Grisha remained in this state of religious rapture and improvised prayers. First he would repeat several times in a row: "*Lord have mercy,"* but each time with new power and expression; then he would say: "forgive me, O Lord, teach me what to do ... teach me what do, O Lord!" with such expression, as if he at that moment expected an answer to his prayers; then we could hear only mournful weeping.... He rose to his knees, crossed his hands over his chest, and fell silent.

I [says Tolstoy] quietly stuck my head out the door and held my breath. Grisha did not move; heavy sighs burst from his breast; in the dull pupil of his crooked eye, lit up by the moon, stood a tear.

"May Thy will be done!" he cried out suddenly with inimitable expression, and fell with his face to the ground and began weeping like a child.

Much time has passed since then [writes Tolstoy], many memories of the past have lost for me their *meaning* and have become vague dreams, and even the wanderer Grisha long ago finished his last traveling, but the impression he made on me and the feeling which he aroused will never die in my memory.

O, great Christian Grisha! [exclaimed Tolstoy]. Your faith was so strong that you felt the closeness of God; your love was so great that words poured of themselves from your lips—*you did not believe in them with your reason....*[26] And what high praise you brought to His greatness when, not finding words, you fell with tears to the ground![27]

———————

One must admit that this scene described by Tolstoy is written with genius. It is hard to tear oneself away from it. However, let us continue our theme on fools and study their lives according to historical information. Let us take from the *Menologion* interesting scenes from the life of the Syrian fool Symeon (sixth century).

On the shore of the Dead Sea, not far from Jordan, for about thirty years two anchorites, Symeon and John, were saving their souls in difficult ascetic labor; they led the contemplative life that completely filled them. In this spiritual struggle, Symeon had already reached old age. And here one day he said to John, "We have no need, brother, to remain now in the desert; listen to me, let us go and serve for the salvation of others. Here we are helping only *ourselves.*"[28]

John, however, did not heed Symeon's call; he did not feel himself strong enough for spiritual struggle in the world—he stayed in the desert. But Symeon chose for himself the great spiritual struggle of foolishness. Staying for a while in Jerusalem in the holy places, says the chronicle, "He prayed fervently to God to hide his works before people until he had departed this life, *in order to avoid empty glory and pride.*"[29]

But it was impossible for Symeon not to reveal himself in amazing acts of wonderworking and love, and his works were made known to many. And when the fame of his deeds became widespread, he did all that he could so that people would consider him demon-possessed and not exalt him. The chronicle says that he was able "to hide his wondrous works, accomplished by the Grace of God, by an outward show of foolishness."

From Jerusalem, Symeon went to the city of Emesa and began there his foolishness for Christ. Approaching the city he saw a dead dog in a rubbish heap; taking his belt, he tied the dog to his leg and dragged it into the city, passing quickly through the gates and dragging it around the streets. A crowd of children gathered, who ran after him crying, "Foolish monk, foolish monk!"[30]

Symeon later settled in the city in the following manner. The owner of a tavern took him in to entertain visitors and kept him like a slave. This tavern owner was by nature quite cruel; he rarely fed the elderly Symeon enough, although he received much profit from the fool. With his eccentricities Symeon attracted customers. The townspeople began often to invite one another to the tavern, saying with a laugh, "Let us go drink in the tavern where the fool is."[31]

But here Symeon's miracle working began. One of the townsmen had 500 gold coins stolen, and this man was grieved by the loss of his gold and endeavored to obtain information about it; he was cruel to his slaves and beat them mercilessly. One day Symeon met him on the street with the words "Do you want to find your gold coins?"

"Yes, yes! I do," he answered.

"And what will you pay me if you find the gold right now?" asked the fool.

The other promised ten gold coins.

"I do not need gold, but swear that you will not beat the thief," Symeon demanded, "nor anyone else either."

The townsman swore that he would not. Then the fool revealed to him, "Your baker stole the gold coins, but be careful, do not beat him or anyone else."

The man returned home, says the chronicle, found everything as Symeon had said, took the gold in its entirety from the baker slave, and did not beat him. Later on, when he wanted to beat one of his slaves for some wrongdoing, his arm became painfully stiff, and he could not beat. Remembering his oath, he went to the fool and begged, "Release me from the vow, fool, let my arm act freely." And the other, as if not understanding, played the fool.

And he came to him many times, importuning him to release him from the vow.[32]

However, as soon as people began to consider Symeon holy, he would straightaway do something that would be clear proof not of holiness, but of insanity. Sometimes he walked limping, and sometimes leaping; sometimes he crawled on the ground, knocking up against the legs of passersby; sometimes he would even lie on the ground, kicking his legs. And at the new moon he pretended to be possessed and fell down as one possessed by a devil.[33]

Hearing of Symeon's life, it says in the same chronicle, a certain nobleman living near Emesa thought to himself, "I shall go and have a look at him and find out if he is playing the fool for the sake of Christ, or is indeed mad."

It so happened that just at that time when he was coming into the city, from afar he saw the fool among a group of fallen women. Then the noble thought to himself, "Who is to say that this false monk does not commit sin with these impure women?"

But here something that astonished the noble took place. Symeon from afar felt the judging in the thoughts of this man. He ran up suddenly to the noble, opened his tattered clothing, and showing him his emaciated body, he cried, "Do you think, O wretched one, that lustfulness could arise here?"

The noble was amazed that still from afar the elder knew his thoughts and was convinced that he was a voluntary fool for Christ.[34]

Symeon the fool was friendly with a deacon of Emesa by the name of John, whom he often visited secretly and to whom he explained his words and actions, requesting only that he say nothing about this to anyone until his death.

Two days before his death, Symeon came to John and said that he felt that he was nearing his end.

"I know of nothing within me that would be worthy of heavenly reward," he said with a deep sigh, "for what kind of reward could a mindless fool receive, unless for free my Lord by His benevolence will have mercy on me? But I beg you, brother, do not scorn or reproach any of the poor, especially monks, that your love may know that many of them are cleansed by suffering misfortunes."[35]

———

In conclusion, we will cite here several scenes from the life of an eccentric Russian fool, who, besides foolishness, imposed upon himself a vow of silence as well.

In the seventeenth century near the city of Vyatka, in the city of Khynov there was a famous fool, Prokopius. Besides the spiritual struggle of foolishness, he took upon himself the spiritual struggle of silence. In the *Menologion*, it says that many people in the city, considering him mad, laughed at him; others gave his beatings.[36] But not a word did Prokopius answer to the mockery and derision. In everyone's eyes, he appeared to be mute.

Prokopius did not have a permanent shelter; he spent the night where night found him: on the church porch, on the street, in the dirt. Often he would come to the Church of the Ascension in the city of Khlynov and would pray there. The priest of this church, John Kalachnikov, was Prokopius's confessor. When he came to him for confession, he would then release himself from silence and would converse with his confessor like everyone else and not like a fool.

Here are some scenes from the life of this saint.

Prokopius loved to visit the sick in the city of Khlynov. Being clairvoyant, if he saw that the sick one should get well, then with his own hands he would lift him from his bed and would rejoice and be glad for him. But if he foresaw that the sick one would not be able to regain his health, then he would weep over him, kiss him, cross his own hands over his breast, and with signs show that he should prepare for burial. More than once the blessed one foretold fire threatening the city. Long in advance, he would climb up into the bell tower and ring the bell as if to sound the alarm. Foreseeing the future, Prokopius would foretell it without words, in a visual fashion.

At that time, in Vyatka prison was incarcerated the Moscow *boyar* Michael Tatischev, who had fallen from favor. Prokopius would come to him, sometimes bringing bread, sometimes water. The *boyar* accepted with joy what was brought. During these visits, the blessed one would pull the prisoner through the window or beat the prison lock, knock at the doors. By all this, he was making known the imminent release of the disgraced *boyar*. And the prophecy soon came to pass, says the chronicle. From Moscow came the tsar's *ukase* [decree]: Tatischev was forgiven and was returned once again to Moscow.

One time the blessed one came to the town hall. The governor, Prince Gregory Zhemchuzhnikov, was sitting then in his place. Prokopius took his hat from his head and put it on himself. Then the governor gave him his seat as well. The blessed one sat down at his place like a judge. Later he took the prince by the hand and led him out of the town hall and took him to the prison, locked him up in it, and went away. In a few days, by order of the tsar, the governor was put in prison for a week for some misdeed.

———

We have spoken about the reverence that the Russian people felt toward their hero-fools, like the Pskov blessed one, Nicholas Sallos, or the Khlynov fool, Prokopius. But at the same time, we should also tell about the negative side that this love for fools engendered. Not all fools were holy people; there was much falsification under the name of this kind of holiness. For example, as early as 1636 Patriarch Joasaph I expressed his complaints against fake fools; he wrote that "some go around like anchorites, in black clothing and chains, with disheveled hair, but not for the Lord and not in the Lord." And the Moscow Church Council of 1667 condemned such people

> who imagine themselves to be reverent, but in reality are not, who live among towns and villages like hermits and recluses, hairy, in monastic clothing, some even fettered in irons; also naked and barefooted they go around to the towns and villages of the world, *for vanity's sake,* to receive glory from the people, that they might honor them as saints, thereby deluding the simple and ignorant.[37]

These complaints, of course, are very typical of that time.

But we should mention that the evil of false foolishness did not belong exclusively to the era before Peter the Great. It was manifest later on as well. We cannot remain silent that even at the present time—a time when everyone is being carried away by the mysterious—there are beginning to appear among us various types of fools, and questionable fools at that. For example, even now in Petersburg various blessed ones are appearing. But one must say that these present-day fools, while to all appearances simpletons, in the majority of cases are, as we would say, cunning blades. It seems they carry on their own politics, instigating and undoing intrigues and fashioning their affairs in a way completely out of harmony with their show of holiness. Another, for example, begins with a sermon on religious renewal, and you look again, and he ends with charismaticism; he begins with speeches on nonaquisition, and ends by pocketing a handsome sum. And one must admit that even here, even in a phenomenon such as "foolishness for Christ," there lurks the old familiar evil—the evil of hypocrisy and fakery.

CHAPTER 7

~~~

The Aspiration for Happiness

Religion is one of the ways by which man aspires to happiness and by which he attains it. Religion possesses the miraculous power to transform the most unbearable sufferings of man's soul into the most deep and lasting happiness.

—William James, *The Varieties of Religious Experience*, 164

All of man's life is a search for happiness; the goal of life is to be happy, to feel sensations of joy. The thirst for happiness takes root in man with the first signs of consciousness. But even if everyone agrees on this truth, still many arguments always and everywhere have aroused and will arouse the question of what pleasure consists, what brings happiness and what brings unhappiness, what makes a person happy and what makes him unhappy. In our next work, *The Dark Power*, we tell of evil pleasures and that enchantment that the evil power promises man.

But now we will discuss with the reader the happiness and joys of the Christian ascetics—the joys that gave them invincible energy in their great spiritual struggles. This happiness of the saints consisted in their religious feelings—in prayer, in divine contemplations and ecstasies, and also in the perception of visions, the gift of prophecy, and the gift of performing miracles for the good of one's fellow man. In his study, "The Psychology of Our Righteous Ones," Professor V. F. Chizh says that

esthetic and intellectual feelings can never play such an enormous role in the lives of even the most gifted people, as do those religious feelings which saints experience. For artists esthetic sensations and for scholars intellectual sensations cannot provide such delight that they could be happy in the most unfavorable conditions. In the opinion of Chizh, only religious feelings can make life not only bearable, but even happy for people starving in isolation.[1]

Of those sensations experienced by Christian ascetics, one should place in the forefront those feelings that saints experience during prayer, in divine contemplations and ecstasies. The aforesaid joyful sensations were for them so great that they not only balanced out the physical and other trials to which the ascetics subjected themselves (and these trails, as we have seen, were terribly severe), but they even exceeded them and gave the saints a full abundance of happiness. For example, here is what Macarius the Great says about prayer, how he felt it: "A man enraptured by prayer is encompassed by the infinite depth of that age (of the future life) and he feels such unutterable pleasure that his soaring and transported mind is in total ecstasy and in his thoughts he forgets earthly wisdom, because his thoughts are overfilled, and like captives they are led away into the infinite and incomprehensible."[2]

Here is what St Isaac of Syria says about the same thing:

Look at what bounties are begotten in man by asceticism. Often it happens that a man has bent his knees in prayer and his hands are raised to the heavens, his face is turned to the cross of Christ and all his thoughts he gathers together in prayer to God; and at that time, as the person is praying to God with tears and tender compunction, at that very hour suddenly, unexpectedly in his heart there begins to well up a spring pouring forth delight, his members weaken, his eyes close, he bows his face to the ground and his thoughts change so that he cannot do prostrations from the joy awakened in his whole body.[3]

It is interesting to note that the Christian ascetics themselves recognized perfectly well that the purpose of life was blessedness; and they strived toward this with all the strength of their soul.

As one of the authors included in the collection the *Philokalia*, Theodore of Edessa, says, "The end [purpose] of our life is blessedness, or which is the same thing, the heavenly kingdom or the kingdom of God. And it (blessedness) is ... the reception of the Divine inflow and as it were the receiving of deification (man receives the qualities of the Godhead) and by this inflow receives the completion of what is lacking in us and the perfection of what is imperfect."[4]

Joyful spiritual states that developed in several Christian ascetics in unusually powerful perceptions usually envelop them during prayer, the sensations of which, as we just saw, were spoken of with such enthusiasm by saints such as Macarius the Great and St Isaac of Syria. In our book *Super-Consciousness*, we followed in detail the course of the development of prayerful states of mind in Christian ascetics. We will repeat here briefly the conclusions from this book that are applicable to this case. As can be seen from the material in the collection the *Philokalia*, the transition from the lower degrees of prayer to higher degrees is accomplished in the following way: During ordinary prayer, the Christian ascetic practicing it and reaching its highest degree becomes imbued with a state of special prayer, done only in the heart. As soon as the inspiration of this prayer descends on a person, his own will no longer takes part in the subsequent act of prayer, although the one praying feels this prayer. Such prayer is performed itself within him by the heart. The higher spiritual forces have caught up man's soul; his soul is already in another world; it is enveloped by a wave of spiritual super-consciousness. Great Christian mystics such as the Apostle Paul explain this state by saying that here it is not earthly man that gives it life, but the Lord Himself. Here are the original words of the Apostle Paul defining this state: "The Spirit Himself makes intercession for us with groanings which cannot be uttered."[5]

From the same information in the *Philokalia*, we explained that these spiritual transports in prayer, repeating themselves more and more often, were transformed in some Christian ascetics into higher mystical states—states known as silence and passionlessness, and also into states of higher spiritual ecstasy.

The higher state of silence and passionlessness was attained by St Seraphim of Sarov, whose life we set forth in Chapter 2 of this book, where we also spoke of several cases of ecstasy and spiritual visions of this Christian ascetic. Namely, we spoke there of three characteristic manifestations of St Seraphim's mystical experiences: (1) Seraphim's vision of the Son of Man in glory on the Thursday of Passion week during the liturgy, (2) the descent of the Holy Spirit on Seraphim during his conversation with the landowner Motovilov, and (3) the ecstasy of Seraphim during his conversation with the Sarov monk John, during which Seraphim's face was illuminated by an extraordinary light.

Of these experiences, the first two, although exceptional in their power, are still among those perceptions that left a clear trace in Seraphim's memory and mind's eye. The vision of the Son of Man in glory he could tell to his elders. During the descent of the Holy Spirit on Seraphim and Motovilov, Seraphim was conscious of the sensations of this experience and even shared with Motovilov his impressions of these sensations. But this was not the case in Seraphim's third experience—his spiritual ecstasy in the presence of the monk John, when Seraphim revealed to John that *other worlds* were known to him; he was there, "only I do not know," said St Seraphim, "whether in the body or out of the body ... God knoweth, this is incomprehensible.... And of that joy and sweetness that I tasted there, it is impossible to tell you." And afterward Seraphim said to John, "If you knew what joy awaits a righteous man, then you would resolve to endure all sorrows during this temporary life."

Thus, Seraphim could not communicate the state of this experience to the monk John; for this, he found neither words nor images with which this state could be expressed.

It is precisely these experiences concerning the higher degrees of divine mysticism that we will discuss in detail in this chapter.

———————

Although the ineffability of the delight experienced in divine mysticism is a general feature of higher divine contemplation,[6] nevertheless, in some exceptional Christian ascetics, who, besides mystical talent, possessed the gift of the inspired word and a deep philosophical mind, we encounter more or less successful attempts to communicate in analogies accessible to them these unutterable experiences. Among such attempts we number, for example, the description of the higher mystical state of St Isaac of Syria, which we have taken from the *Philokalia*.

In this chapter of our work, so that we may explain the sensations of such ecstasies, we will use rich material to describe, as far as is humanly possible, the aforementioned ecstasies—material we have drawn from the works of the famous Christian ascetic of the eleventh century, St Symeon the New Theologian.

Like Seraphim of Sarov, this Christian ascetic himself experienced more than once the state of higher spiritual ecstasy. But he strove in his writings to help others feel what kind of experiences these were, and one must say that his vivid language and inspired analogies even overcame, as it were, the "unutterability" in the matter of portraying higher mystical states. In this regard he is significantly higher than other Christian ascetics of the Eastern Church; he is even higher than St Isaac of Syria, whose writings on divine mysticism are recognized as some of the most profound in patristic literature.

But first we will say a few words about the life of Symeon the New Theologian.[7]

The eleventh-century Christian ascetic Symeon the New Theologian (963–1043) was born in Paphlagonia. He was raised in Constantinople by his uncle, who served at that time at the court of the emperor of Constantinople. Upon finishing his studies (what would be called grammar courses), Symeon entered the ranks of courtiers for Emperors Basil and Constantine Porphyrogenitus. But Symeon was little occupied by court life; he was drawn toward introspection and the spiritual life. In Constantinople, he became friends with the then-famous elder of the Studite monastery, Symeon the Reverent, who had an influence on the development of the mystical inclinations of his young disciple. It ended with the young Symeon leaving his secular career and entering the Studite monastery as a monk, where his ascetic life developed under the guidance of that same elder. Later on, Symeon became igumen of the Constantinople monastery of St Mamont. He set this cloister in order and, having turned it over to a new igumen, Arsenius, he devoted himself to anchoritism or "silence," as it says in the biography written by his disciple, Nikita Stifat. But not to the end of his life was he to delight here in the quiet of anchoritism.

A storm arose against him because, not having asked permission from the patriarch, he had instituted a holy day in honor of his reposed elder, Symeon the Reverent, whom Symeon the New Theologian revered as a saint. The intrigues of his enemies cast him out of Constantinople, and Symeon had to settle outside the capital, a certain distance away. He organized there another monastery that soon began to flourish, and Symeon again left monastery administration to devote himself anew to "silence." He died in the first half of the eleventh century. In 1050, his relics appeared; he was numbered among the saints of the Eastern Church.

———

As we see from the writings of Symeon the New Theologian, what stands out in his mysticism are the two accounts of his ecstatic experiences of the Godhead. In these accounts, he strives, as far as it is in his power, to express his "ineffable" experiences. But besides these two mystical descriptions, our attention is drawn to other homilies of Symeon about the process of higher contemplations; here, Symeon indicates the developmental stages of these contemplations and also analyzes mystical feeling itself. First, we will cite two of his accounts of his ecstatic experiences of the Godhead.

It should be noted that both of these experiences were for Symeon *beyond all expectations*; they appeared during states of the deepest *humility*.

This humility is vividly expressed by Symeon in one of the forewords to the account of one such experience, namely, in the ninetieth homily. Symeon, turning to God Who had given him the unutterable joy of contemplations, exclaims,

> How was I to know, Lord, that Thou, Who art invisible and uncontainable, art visible and containable in us?[8] ... And how could I have known that everyone who believeth in Thee is Thy man and shineth with Divinity by Thy Grace! ... All of this I did not know, All-holy King, and never desired and did not seek to receive it from Thee, *but remembering my sins, sought only remission of them* .... For this I think, O King, Lover of men, Thou didst shine Thy holy light in me, sitting in the darkness of this world, in the midst of such evil.[9]

Symeon further explains that long before his spiritual visions of God, his soul had already many times been immersed in the higher sphere, which he sensed as a special ineffable light. This light, as we will see later on, he calls *"the light of the Holy Spirit."*[10] "I often saw light," says Symeon, "and sometimes it appeared within me, when my soul had peace and quiet, and sometimes it appeared from without, at a distance or was even completely hidden." The sensation of this ineffable light brought Symeon inexpressible joy and happiness; therefore, when he says that when the light became hidden, this caused him great sorrow. "Because then," explains Symeon, "I thought that surely it no longer wants to appear. But when I began to weep and shed tears and show all estrangement from everything and *all obedience and humility*, then it appeared again, like the sun when it disperses a thick cloud and little by little shows itself, gladdening, brilliant and round."[11] Symeon writes that when a man, through repetitions of this light, comes close to perfection, then in this higher light he begins to sense God Himself. Of this higher sensation, Symeon says,

> God does not appear in some sort of figure or impression, but appears as simple, formed by light—formless, incomprehensible and ineffable. More than this I can say nothing. However, He shows Himself clearly, is recognized very well, is seen *purely as invisible*,[12] speaks and hears invisibly; God converses by nature with those born of Him *gods by grace*, as friend converses with friend, face to face. He loves His sons like a father, and is loved exceedingly by them and is for them a wonderful vision and fearful sound of which they cannot speak as they ought, but then again, they cannot remain silent.... And they cannot sate themselves of announcing the truth, because they are no longer masters of themselves but are organs of

the Holy Spirit, dwelling in them, Which moves them and is again moved by them.[13]

All the words of Symeon that we have cited here serve merely as a prologue to the following sublime, mystical picture that he portrays in this way. Symeon addresses the Godhead, saying,

> Once, when Thou didst come and bedew and wash me with waters, immersing me repeatedly in them, as it seemed, I saw lightning flashing around me and rays of light emanating from Thy countenance mingling with the waters; and seeing myself washed in these luminous, radiant waters, I fell into ecstasy.... Some time went by, and then I saw another awesome mystery. I saw Thee ascend to heaven and take me up with Thee—though I do not know whether *in the body Thou didst bear me there or out of the body*. Thou alone, the accomplisher of this, knowest. After I had spent there with Thee almost an hour, in wonderment at the greatness of the glory (but whose glory this was and what it was I do not know), I fell into ecstasy from its exceeding loftiness and I began to tremble all over. But again Thou didst leave me alone on the earth where I had stood before. Having come to myself, I found myself weeping and amazed at my sad impoverishment. Then a little while later, as I prostrated myself, Thou didst deign to show me the heights in heaven opened, Thy countenance like the sun, without image and form....
>
> Again Thou didst appear, invisible, intangible, imperceptible ... and Thou didst allow me to see Thy glory even more abundantly. All the while Thou wast growing larger and spreading Thy radiance more and more; and as the darkness[14] disappeared Thou didst seem to come closer and closer, as we experience when observing sensory things. For, when the moon shines and the clouds swiftly drift by in the wind, it seems that the moon itself moves faster, although in reality it keeps its usual pace.
>
> Thus, O Lord, it seemed to me that Thou, being motionless, wast coming towards me; being unchangeable, wast growing larger; and having no image, didst assume an image. Sometimes a blind man who gradually grows accustomed to seeing and taking the whole image of another man, or the entire outline of a human body portrays him little by little within himself the way he is—like, I say, a blind man who does not have and does not transform the image of a man in his eyes, but as the eyes of a blind man becoming more and more purified, they finally see the image of a man as he is—when the likeness of a person's image is being outlined in the eyes

and through them passes into the mind, being imprinted in his memory as on a tablet.[15] So Thou too, having completely purified my mind, didst clearly appear to me in the *Light of the Holy Spirit*; and as my mind perceived Thee more clearly and perfectly, it seemed to me as if Thou wast stepping out of somewhere, brightly radiant, and allowing me to see the features of Thine imageless countenance.... When I asked Thee, saying, "O my Lord, Who art Thou?" then, for the first time Thou didst grant me to hear Thy sweet voice, and Thou didst talk to me with such sweetness and meekness that I fell into ecstasy, trembling in amazement, thinking and speaking to myself: "How glorious and resplendent this is!" Thou didst say to me: "I am God become man, out of My love for thee. I am speaking to thee through the Holy Spirit, Who speaks to thee together with Me. This I have given thee only because of thy desire and thy faith, and I shall give thee even more than this."

Under the impression of this divine contemplation, St Symeon exclaims in rapture, "What else could be more resplendent and exalted than this?" And he hears an answer, that the apprehension of the future life is higher than this happiness. "Thy soul is extremely small," hears St. Symeon, "if thou art satisfied with this happiness, because in comparison with the future bliss it is like a drawing of the sky on paper that someone holds in his hands in comparison with the real skies; *even much more does the future glory surpass the one thou hast witnessed now.*"

"And little by little," Symeon says further, "Thou didst become hidden from my eyes, my most sweet and good Lord. And I do not know if I departed from Thee or if Thou didst leave me. Meanwhile, it appeared to me as if I had come from somewhere and entered my abode and only here did I completely come to myself."[16]

In this striking account by Symeon of the vision of God that he experienced, what first of all attracts attention are the following words of the mystical scene, full of secret meaning: "When Thou didst come and wash me, immersing me repeatedly in the waters, as it seemed, I saw lightning flashing around me and rays of light emanating from Thy countenance and mingling with the waters; seeing myself washed in luminous, radiant waters I fell into ecstasy."

After reading these words, one involuntarily asks, how is one to comprehend these inspired writings of Symeon? How does one understand the hidden meaning of his words about his being bedewed in the waves of some experience unknown to us? And maybe, as he says, these "waters which washed him" were those tears of ecstasy that poured from his eyes and that St Isaac of Syria often mentions as a sign of the inspiration of a deeply religious ecstasy on an ascetic.[17] What did Symeon feel here; what did he experience?

To get at least an approximate understanding of this, let us have recourse to our sole means for comprehending mystical experiences, to analogies accessible to us from the realm of experiences of strong feeling—to analogies drawn from our life, which is poor in bright experiences.

Let us first of all ask our readers, have any of them experienced the feeling of ideal pure love, which in rare cases, like a happy illumination, sometimes descends upon youths when they are imbued with this bright feeling, while they are still virgins and not poisoned by the pleasures of the flesh? Have any of them experienced this feeling at least in the years of childhood, the possibility of which is testified to us by L. N. Tolstoy in his short story "Children and Adolescence"? If our reader has not experienced *this,* then has he not experienced at some time in his life the special unspeakable joy when, after a long separation from a loved one after storms and disturbances, finally the long-awaited meeting arrived and it seemed that unexpectedly, as if by the waving of a magic wand, sorrow disappeared and tears of happiness were shed that the oppressive and tormenting burden of life had passed by? Finally, I will ask the reader again if he ever experienced, for example, the feeling—was he ever at the soul-stirring divine liturgy when during the magnificent Cherubic hymn of Bortniansky, the priest and deacon standing before the altar call to the Lord, exclaiming, *Let us who mystically represent the Cherubim ... put away all worldly care....* Meanwhile, one feels that these ministers of God are truly praying, and their prayerful mood is passed on to others in the church. And for some of those present, tears come to their eyes and maybe they themselves do not understand what mysterious power is compelling them to weep.

Using these analogies from our life that is poor in bright experiences, maybe the mystical feeling of our readers will sense to some extent what Symeon wanted to express when he spoke of the immersion of his feelings in the washing waves of rapture, saying these inspired words, "I saw lightning flashing around me and rays of light emanating from Thy countenance and mingling with the waters; seeing myself washed in luminous, radiant waters I fell into ecstasy."

From this mystical scene, let us pass on to an account of another inspired ecstasy of St Symeon the New Theologian.

Defending himself from the attack of those who saw in his precepts pride and the undeserved attributing to himself of spiritual power, Symeon said first of all,

> I did not write anything in order to display myself[18] ... but I cannot bear to be silent about the wonderful gifts of God.[19] The love of God moves me to reveal before you, my brothers, the unutterable mercy and love which God has for you....[20] And do not rebuke me who speaks to you with the word of Grace ... for saying this, I am a slave and speak to you the words of God, I am revealing the gift of the teaching given to me and am opening to you the hidden mysteries of God.[21]

After this introduction, Symeon surrenders himself to his inspiration and, as it were, in ecstasy in the following manner tells of what he heard from Christ Himself. He begins this place thus: "Be instructed," he says,

> that not only in the future life, but even now is the present there lies before your eyes and before your hands and feet an ineffable treasure which is higher than any principality or power, about which I say to you: it is the light of the world. *And I do not say this from myself, but this treasure itself, that is to say, Christ, says*: I am the resurrection and the life.... As I am visible now in the present life to those who sought and found Me, so in the future life I will shine in them and above them all, as I now shine in them, being hidden, higher than all the heavens. I, being uncontainable by nature, am contained in you in the present life by Grace. I, being invisible, am visible, I appear not as I am, although I remain all visible, but as much as can contain the nature and strength of those who see Me.... In My paradise I set to live those who believe in Me and are reborn by the Grace of the Holy Spirit—who can sin no more; and the prince of this world—the devil—has no authority or power over them, for I am in them and they in Me and they conquer the world, because they are outside of the world and they have Me, the Most-Powerful of all, with them.[22]

Symeon's reasonings are interesting, based as they are on his experience, from which he makes his conclusions concerning manifestations of spiritual super-consciousness. Here he first endeavors to analyze mystical feeling; second, he points out the various stages of development of divine contemplations, speaking also of their beneficial effect on man; and, third, he discourses at length on the main and most essential experience of man during this contemplation—the experience of mystical light or, as he calls it, "mental light."

Let us begin with the first; let us explain how Symeon analyzes the mystical feeling of man.

But before this we should say a few words on what exactly is meant by mystical feeling or, as we called it earlier, "spiritual vision."

Earlier in the introduction, while discussing the higher reason, we said among other things that in connection with the features of the higher reason to sense and perceive God, some highly gifted people, progressing toward perfection by way of lofty ascetic endeavors [spiritual struggles], may develop a special aptitude of that higher reason—the aptitude of "spiritual vision" to penetrate into the higher spiritual world, the aptitude leading to divine contemplations and what we call spiritual ecstasies.[23]

Here we should explain that spiritual vision is not the seeing (observation) of visions, as many are inclined to understand it, derived from the sensation of physical vision. This is a completely special sense, a sensing of special spiritual sensations, only analogous to our vision, representing a totally special, extremely intense intuition.

Symeon the New Theologian speaks of this mystical feeling of man in his writings. He explains that this sense, being one, as it were, contains in itself all five of our bodily senses. By this, Symeon wants to express how powerful is this sense in its perception. Here are his very words: "It [this one sense] has within itself all five senses *or to be more precise, more, inasmuch as they are all one*."[24] Further Symeon says that when "God *appears* through a revelation to a single reasoning soul, then to this soul is revealed all goodness and *at the same time is contemplated* (perceived) *by all the senses together.*[25] Therefore, according to St Symeon's explanation, it is difficult even to convey in human language the sensing of this experience. During this experience, Symeon says further, "We cannot portray or explain with many words all that in one moment we perceive and comprehend, hearing with our sight and seeing with our hearing, learning through contemplation, listening through revelation."[26]

One cannot help but recognize the unusual depth in the aforesaid thoughts of St Symeon. To understand these ideas fully, we can draw an analogy from our physical life. As the uniting of rays in the focus of a magnifying glass multiply to infinity the power of the heat of the light of these rays, likewise in uniting all man's senses into one sense, into one mystical feeling, these senses are transformed into one single unusual power of perception—a power incomparable to any of our physical senses and representing something totally separate from our ordinary senses of vision, hearing, smell, and so forth.

And the divine light contemplated by this one sense is not the same as the light that is perceived by our corporeal eyes. This is a special light, a mystical light. St Dionysius Areopagite gives it a totally special name: he calls this light *divine darkness*, indicating by this the inapproachability of its rays to our physical sight. Dionysius speaks of this light thus: "Divine darkness is the unapproachable light in which the living God is confessed."[27] Regarding the mystical sense that perceives the light of the Godhead, inaccessible to physical vision and its powers, another ascetic, St Macarius the Great, writes the following: "There are eyes," he says, "which are more internal than these [physical] eyes and there is hearing which is more internal than this [physical] hearing."[28] St Macarius the Great obviously felt and understood this internal mystical sense, but we do not find that his analysis of this sense is similar to the one St Symeon the New Theologian gives us in his writings.

We will now discuss Symeon's explanations of the various stages of divine contemplation. As the reader will recall, in the mystical illustration of experiencing the Godhead, which we cited before,[29] Symeon says that God appeared to him *in the light of the Holy Spirit*. In other places in his works, Symeon also calls this light *mental light*, that is, light comprehended by the mystical sense of the higher reason, about which we were just now talking. Speaking here essentially about the mystical perceptions of the *mental light (light of the Holy Spirit)*, Symeon also explains through which stages a Christian ascetic passes in his divine contemplations.

To best assimilate the process and course of the development of the aforesaid mystical perception, Symeon first of all advises representing the ordinary world of our soul as a prison of passions and feelings—a prison in which faintly shines man's instinct toward the Godhead, according to Symeon's words, a man enlightened by only "some small vision from divine scripture."

Then we should imagine that suddenly in the roof of the prison in which is incarcerated the man who has not yet seen real daylight, "somehow by chance a small crack opens up and he suddenly sees, in as much as the size of the crack allows, the light of the heavens which until this time he had never seen nor imagined."[30] Then, says Symeon, the man "suddenly falls into ecstasy and as if existing outside himself, for hours gazes with wide eyes on high and wonders at the spectacle which has suddenly been opened to him."

Such, according to Symeon the New Theologian, is the first stage of mystical perception. After this, from the words of St Symeon, if the imprisoned man often looks at the opening, then he will become used to this light and at the same time "his first great ecstasy will lessen. And the soul of such a man," Symeon says further, "becoming used to the *mental light,* is not struck so strongly any more by the mental light, as it was the first time, because it concludes from the small light seen by it that there is still a more perfect light."[31]

Such, according to Symeon the New Theologian, is the second stage of a Christian ascetic's mystical development.

Finally, St Symeon speaks of the onset of the following higher state. About this, he expresses himself thus: "When a man abides in such a state of light, not turning back to the world, then heaven is opened to him," that is, the whole light of this heaven is opened up before him and "this light enters within his soul." Of this process, which is difficult to transmit in human language, Symeon tries to give an understanding with the following two illustrations. In saying the phrase "Then heaven is opened to him," Symeon explains that one can understand this opening not as the actual opening of heaven or the illumination of man by mental light, but rather as the opening, as the illumination of man's *eye of the heart*, receiving finally the ability to see clearly this light. This *eye of the heart* of man Symeon also calls here the *mind*.[32] Here are Symeon's own words concerning this state: "Then whether heaven is opened to him, or the eye of his heart, that is, the mind, he cannot say definitely: I repeat, whether the mind opens more (the higher reason) or heaven and this light enters into his soul, a light most luminous and wonderful and while he is no longer in ecstasy, but sees both himself and what is around him, that is, he sees the state that others are in."[33]

Here it should be noted that these last quotations that we took from Symeon concerning the description of the higher degrees of contemplation have much in common with what St Isaac of Syria says on the same subject. St Isaac says that a man "in becoming accustomed to the mysteries of the spirit and to the revelation of knowledge *rises from knowledge to knowledge, from contemplation to contemplation, and from comprehension to comprehension.*"[34]

Assertions such as those of St Symeon and St Isaac have great meaning for us because they are based on their personal experience. At the same time, these assertions convince us that man's feelings of the joys in the sphere of the Holy Spirit are exceedingly rich in the diversity of these ineffable perceptions.

In conclusion, we will cite here the following interesting words of Symeon concerning these contemplations and ecstasies. "This sweetness, given in drink," says Symeon,

> and this gladdening brilliance coming from the sun banish from the soul all sorrow and make a man rejoice always; and no one can harm him, no one can prevent him from drinking his fill from the fountain of salvation. The ruler of this world, dominating this world with his evil, the sovereign of earthly things, the lord of darkness, the deceitful devil, ruling all the waters of the sea and playing with the world as with a small bird held in the hands, will not dare with all his hosts and with all his power to approach him and even touch the heel of his foot, much less look at him boldly. For the brilliance of wine and the rays of the Sun light up the face of him who drinks it, they enter within him and are transmitted to the arms and legs and to all his members and make all of him a powerful fire in all his parts, so as to burn the enemies who approach him. And he becomes the favorite of the Light, friend of the Sun and His beloved son, by virtue of the pure and bright wine which is poured out on him like rays of sun and light.[35]

The comparison of mystical perceptions to sensations of light is encountered quite often in the writings of Symeon the New Theologian. Besides the expressions—*light of the Holy Spirit* or *mental light,* we also find in Symeon the following analogies. In his nineteenth homily, in discussing that same light of the Holy Spirit or mental light, St Symeon calls this light "a *reflection of that first Eternal Light,*"[36] that is, the reflection of God Himself that fully agrees with the Orthodox symbol of faith in which the Holy Spirit proceeds from the Father. Besides this, Symeon even says that man's mind (the higher reason), capable of seeing God through contemplation, itself becomes all illuminated and becomes like light, although it cannot comprehend or express what it sees.[37]

Finally, more than once in his writings Symeon compares to light not only God the Father and God the Holy Spirit, but also the whole Divine Hypostasis of the Holy Trinity. In his fifty-first homily, we read, "Light the Father, Light the Son, Light the Holy Spirit: these three are one light, timeless, indivisible, undissolved, eternal, uncreated, inexhaustible, immeasurable, *invisible* inasmuch as it is above all, which no man could ever see before being purified and could not receive before gaining sight."[38] And in Homily

79, Symeon says, "God is light and all those deemed worthy to look upon Him see Him as light and those who have perceived Him, have perceived Him as light. For the light of His glory goes before His countenance and without light He cannot manifest Himself."[39]

As regards this last statement, we should share with the readers the thoughts that it evokes.

In his analysis *The Mystical Justification of Asceticism,* Prof. I. V. Popov, quoting this same statement of Symeon, expresses the thought that the light that St Symeon talks about here is not a metaphorical expression of a particular, mystical mental light, but rather by this is meant an actual sensation of light. Popov says also that the aforesaid statement, as well as similar statements of St Macarius, *should be understood literally,* that Symeon is talking here about a real light and in this light he sees the manifestation of the divine nature itself.[40]

Comparing this saying of Symeon the New Theologian with his other sayings, in particular with those that we have cited from his writings, we cannot fully agree with Popov's explanation. In our opinion, if Symeon talks here about light, then it is *first of all* about that light that is apprehended not by physical vision, but by that mystical sense of which we have spoken and which Symeon calls in his writings the *single sense* or the *eye of the heart.*

St Symeon's treatise on the stages of development of the contemplation of *mental light* supports our opinion. And our opinion about this is supported also by the undoubted metaphoricalness of the expression in the statement under examination, for Symeon is speaking here about "the Light of His Glory" and that "the Light of His Glory goes before His countenance."

––––––––––

But if in the given case we so understand Symeon the New Theologian, this does not exclude our general acknowledgment of cases of divine visions when the visions manifest themselves not on the spiritual plane of man, but in his physical substance. The Light of the Godhead can be sensed not only by spiritual vision: there are also exceptional cases when the sensing of the Godhead can penetrate into man's normal consciousness, can break through into his brain, like the sensation of bodily light, which appears then like a reflection of the Godhead on man's physical plane. Historical examples prove this. Let us recall the vision of the holy Apostle Paul before Damascus, when in the beginning of the vision Paul sensed an unusually bright light from which he even lost his physical sight for a time. Gospel history tells us that during the Transfiguration of the Lord on Tabor, the apostles with their

bodily eyes saw the light illuminating Christ. The descent of the Holy Spirit
on the apostles was expressed in a vision of fiery tongues coming down upon
them. And finally, in the previously mentioned events from the life of St Seraphim of Sarov, we can see the same thing. It is sufficient merely to point to
the inspired conversation of Seraphim with the landowner Motovilov when
the latter saw how the face of Seraphim began to shine with an extraordinary light.[41] According to the testimony of the famous Christian ascetic and
mystic of the fourteenth century, Gregory Palamas, "Saints, seeing by Divine
power the brightness of God and being filled with this unutterable brightness can themselves appear brilliant."[42] St Macarius the Great says the same
thing, namely, according to his words, the very body of a Christian ascetic can
appear brilliant. He writes, "[T]here appeared to [Christian ascetics] a kind
of bright raiment the like of which does not exist on earth in this age and
which human hands could not fashion."[43]

The aforesaid divine light, leaving its mark in man's physical vision, has
received its own name in patristic literature—it is called the *light of Tabor.*
Visions of this light of Tabor are noted in the lives of the saints.

As an example of such a vision, we will cite here the very characteristic
writing about this same kind of light by the personal secretary of the famous
Ambrose of Mediolan (fourth century), Paulinus the deacon—a description
of how he saw the light of Tabor (light of the Holy Spirit) descending upon
Ambrose. Paulinus's account is similar to what Motovilov wrote upon seeing
the descent of the Holy Spirit on Seraphim. Paulinus writes that one day
Ambrose (not long before his death) was working with him, dictating to him his
interpretation of one of the psalms of David: "When suddenly," says Paulinus,

> looking at him I saw fire like a shield around his head; gradually this fire
> coiled up and entered his mouth. Then Ambrose's face became white just
> like snow. This vision plunged me into such horror that from fear I could
> not write, but then Ambrose's face again took on its usual appearance. I
> told about this to the honorable deacon Katul, and the latter, himself filled
> with the Grace of God, explained to me that I had seen the Holy Spirit,
> descending in the form of fire on our bishop, as in the time He descended
> upon the holy Apostles.[44]

In the writings of Symeon the New Theologian, we have not found a
specific indication of this light of Tabor. In his *Homilies* he speaks most of
all about *mental light,* comprehended, according to his expression, by the
"eye of the heart," that is, a special mystical sense. Only in one place of his

works did we find that he, as it were, refers to light visible to the bodily eyes appearing to him, namely, in the ninetieth homily, excerpts of which we cited previously.[45]

"I often saw light," says St Symeon in this discourse, "and sometimes it appeared from without, at a distance or was even completely hidden." But one can also understand these words of St Symeon as referring to mystical light, for in the same homily he speaks of God, Who "is often seen as *invisible*,"[46] that is, invisible to the bodily eyes, but sensed by spiritual vision.

———

Concerning all these references to the light of Tabor, it is interesting to note that something similar to the light of Tabor was experienced even by pagan mystics, for example, the Neoplatonist Plotinus, but there this light was *purely material*. With Christians, if the light of Tabor does leave an impression of light in the organs of vision, then this is invariably combined with deep mystical feeling, by which the Christian clearly recognizes that this light *proceeds from the Logos itself*.

In these instances, the Christian was first of all totally absorbed by his fervent feeling for the Logos. The impression of light appeared in him as the result of this absorption; it was the product of that mental light that illuminated the soul of the Christian.

But the source of the light in pagan mystics was completely different, which is why it bore a completely different character. In the following analogy of Plotinus, we will see how material was this impression in him of pagan light. He says that "that light was similar in this case to an eye, which having been pressed on by the hand, sees light within itself." Plotinus gives his own particular origin for this light; he identifies it with the unveiling of the qualities of the Godhead, *existing, in his opinion, in man himself*. According to Plotinus, God always exists in the soul anyway, but it does not always see Him.[47]

Whereupon, according to Plotinus, in order that the soul feel its divinity, it should "remove from itself all evil, *even all good*." To attain the ecstasy of sensing in oneself the divine Light, Plotinus advises strict asceticism with such denial of everything that, as he says, "a true wiseman would preserve imperturbable calm even if his native city were destroyed or when his fellow townspeople perished."

Thus, according to Plotinus, by such stoic asceticism is attained the sensation of God within oneself—the sensation of divine ecstasy (light); it is attained by the asceticism of "stony insensibility," against which Christians have always fought. Here we should note that this stoniness of feeling is in essence the same thing that yogis do to attain Samadhi (see *Super-Consciousness,* chs. 10–12). From these quotes of Plotinus, one can already conclude what must be the enormous difference between cold pagan ecstasy and flaming Christian ecstasy, the foundation of which is the sublime emotional movement of love for one's fellow man and for God. And therefore the sensation of light in Christian ecstasy should be totally unlike that of the ecstasy of pagan Neoplatonists, or of yogis, although both ecstasies can leave the impression of light in man's bodily eyes.[48]

The gifts of grace, as we saw in the life of Seraphim, were felt by him not only in the perception of joyful spiritual ecstasies and visions, but also in what we call *clairvoyance.* From information on Seraphim's life, one can explain the psychology of his clairvoyance by observing the clairvoyance that he showed to those who came to him for spiritual healing. As the reader will recall, we concluded from the words of Seraphim himself that his clairvoyance appeared as the result of complete renunciation of his conscious (cerebral) will. In the moments of clairvoyance, Seraphim's entire soul no longer belonged to him, but to the First Principle—Logos, creating in man the light of true understanding. "As iron to the forger, so I give myself and my will to the Lord God,"[49] said St Seraphim in explaining his clairvoyance.

Here we will cite some striking examples of clairvoyance, as well as spiritual visions, of several other ascetics of the Eastern Church. Experiences of these perceptions are also part of the mystical joys of saints, concerning which certain of the ascetics themselves testified to people around them. Thus, St Anthony the Great, as can be seen from his biography composed by Athanasius the Great, told of his visions to his disciples "for their benefit," so they would know "that asceticism has good fruit and visions are frequently a comfort in labors."[50]

First we will cite interesting examples of the clairvoyance of several saints, a different kind of clairvoyance than the one about which we spoke when examining the life of Seraphim of Sarov. Namely, we will show two cases of *spiritual second-sight,* one occurring with Sergius of Radonezh (fourteenth century) and the other with the ascetics Theodore and Pammon in Egypt (fourth century).

In memory of the first occurrence concerning the life of Sergius of Radonezh, there exists up to this time in the Trinity–Sergius *lavra* in the refectory during the brethren's dinner a certain custom that usually startles laypeople who happen to be taking part in the common monastery meal for the first time.

Before the final course, at the sound of a bell, all the monks stand up, and the priest whose turn it is pronounces, "By the prayers of our holy fathers, Lord Jesus Christ, have mercy on us," after which everyone sits down to finish their meal.

This custom was established in the Trinity monastery long ago, after the following incident from the lives of Sts Sergius of Radonezh and Stephan of Perm. A contemporary of Sergius of Radonezh, Stephan of Perm had a deep love for St Sergius, but he rarely had the opportunity of seeing the famous elder because Perm was far from Moscow. One day, Stephan was summoned from Perm to Moscow on urgent diocesan business. Stephan hastened to the city but did not have time to stop at the Sergius monastery, even though the road he was traveling passed close by the monastery, only seven versts away. Upon arriving at the turnoff for the monastery, instead of going on to the monastery, Stephan limited himself to ordering the people to stop in view of the monastery. He himself got out of the carriage and recited, "It is meet and right...." and completing the usual prayer, he bowed with these words directed to Sergius: "Peace to thee, spiritual brother!" After which, he sat in the carriage and continued on his way to Moscow.

Meanwhile, the chronicle says, it happened that at that moment Sergius, together with the brethren, was eating in the refectory. Understanding in spirit the salutation of the bishop, Sergius rose immediately, stood for a little while, recited the prayer, and in his turn bowed to the bishop and said, "And thou rejoice, pastor of Christ's flock, and may the blessing of the Lord be with thee."

Everyone was amazed at the saint's unusual behavior; and some of them understood, says the chronicle, that "the saint had been deemed worthy of a vision." After the meal the monks began asking Sergius about what had happened, and he told them, "At that moment Bishop Stephan stopped opposite our monastery on his way to Moscow, bowed down to the Most-Holy Trinity and blessed us sinners."

Some of Sergius's disciples hastened to the indicated place, caught up with the holy bishop, and confirmed that all had happened exactly as Sergius said.[51]

The case of spiritual second sight from the life of two Egyptian ascetics, the igumens of monasteries, Theodore and Pammon, was written down by a witness to the occurrence, St Athanasius the Great. This event relates to the period of Athanasius's life when he was undergoing persecution by the Emperor Julian the Apostate. Athanasius then hid from Julian's agents in Egypt with the Thebaid anchorites. Once during these persecutions, he had to secretly escape pursuit by sailing on the Nile in Abba Theodore's boat, accompanied by Abba Pammon. "The wind was unfavorable," writes St Athanasius,

> Being heavy of heart, I prayed; Theodore's monks got out of the boat and drew it along. Abba Pammon was comforting me and I answered: "Believe my words that my heart is filled with firm faith not so much during the time of peace as during persecution. For I am certain without a doubt that suffering for Christ and strengthened by His mercy, if I am killed, then all the more will I obtain mercy from Him." Before I had even finished saying this, Theodore, looking intently at Abba Pammon, smiled. Because Abba Pammon almost began laughing, I said to them: "Why do you laugh when I say this? Could it be that you judge me to be afraid?" But Theodore said to Abba Pammon: "Tell him why we were smiling." And as Abba Pammon answered, "You should say it," Theodore continued: "At this very hour Julian has been killed in Persia.... Therefore you need not trouble yourself to go into the Thebaid, but it would be better secretly to join Julian's retinue, because when you meet it on the way and are sincerely received by it, you will return to the church. And Julian will soon be taken by God." And so it happened.[52]

And this was indeed so, says the researcher of St Athanasius's life, Farrar. At that time, Julian (in 363), not yet having reached the age of thirty-two, was killed by a stray arrow in his ill-fated expedition into Persia.

Finally, we consider it interesting to tell also of the following two spiritual visions from the life of St Sergius of Radonezh. Here is the first vision.

One day Sergius was serving liturgy with his brother Stephan and his nephew Theodore. In church at that time, among others, there was a Christian ascetic called Isaac the Silent. When with the previously mentioned persons Sergius was serving the mystery in the altar, according to the words of the chronicle, Isaac then suddenly "saw a fourth man in the altar, in brilliant robes and shining with an extraordinary light." During the small entrance with the Gospel, this server followed the saint, his face shone like snow so that it was impossible to look at him. The wonderful appearance startled Isaac, says the chronicle, and he opened his mouth and asked the monk Macarius standing next to him, "What is this wonderful appearance? Who is this extraordinary man?"

Macarius had also been deemed worthy of seeing the vision, says the chronicle. Astonished and amazed, he answered, "I do not know, brother; I myself am terrified looking at such a wonderful appearance; did not some clergyman come with Prince Vladimir?"

Prince Vladimir Andrievich Serpukhovsky, on whose ancestral estate the Trinity *lavra* was located, was at that time in church. The elders asked someone in his entourage whether a priest had come with the prince; he answered that there was no priest with them. The monks understood, says the chronicle, that an angel of God was serving with St Sergius, and they asked him about it. At first, the Christian ascetic did not want to reveal the mystery to them. "What sort of extraordinary apparition did you see, children? Serving the liturgy were Stephan, Theodore and myself, a sinner; there was no one else."

But his disciples continued asking him; then the saint answered them, "Children, if the Lord God Himself revealed this to you, then can I keep it hidden? The one you saw was an angel of the Lord; not only now, but always when it happens that I, unworthy one, serve the liturgy, he by the will of God serves with me. But do not tell anyone what you have seen while I am alive."[53]

And here is another vision from Sergius's life, accompanied by the light of Tabor.

Sergius was serving liturgy. During this service, one of his disciples, Simon, suddenly saw that fire was floating around the communion table, illuminating the altar and surrounding Sergius, who was serving, so that the saint was enveloped in flame from head to foot. And when Sergius approached the communion of Christ's mysteries, the fire arose, coiled up "like some marvelous winding sheet," and immersed itself in the chalice from which St Sergius was taking communion. The amazed Simon stood there speechless. After partaking of communion, having left the communion table and understanding that Simon had seen a vision and was under its strong impression, he called him to himself and asked, "Child, why is thy soul so afraid?"

"Father, I saw a wonderful vision," answered Simon, "I saw the Grace of the Holy Spirit acting with thee."

"Tell no one what thou hast seen, not until the Lord calls me to Himself," said Sergius.

And they both began to give fervent thanks to the Creator Who had shown them such mercy, adds the chronicle.[54]

All of these visions are of the same type as the one we cited in the life description of Seraphim of Sarov, when serving in church he saw the Son of Man in glory. These visions left profound, joyful impressions on the Christian ascetics. These visions influenced them by strengthening them in future spiritual struggles.

CHAPTER 8

On a Good Death

The supernatural gifts of communion with God, received by the soul here, serve as a pledge of heavenly blessings. Already in the present life such a man experiences blessedness and delight, similar to the eternal joy in the age to come.

—Saying of St Macarius the Great

In order to be free from the delusions of faith in the miraculous, a man should acknowledge as true only that which is natural, that is, which agrees with his reason, and acknowledge as falsehood all that which is unnatural, that is, which contradicts reason.

—*The Christian Teaching of L. N. Tolstoy*, sec. 231

When in the previous chapters, the examples of the lives of the Christian ascetics unfolded before us in vivid images, when in these examples we sensed the "Light Invisible" illuminating their lives, then along with these majestic pictures we were relentlessly haunted by the thought of our miserable reality. We were haunted by comparisons of the manifestations of "light" that we have described with the darkness of our real life, and these comparisons involuntarily forced their way into our account. But here before us is a chapter on how the saints died living in the Logos, acquiring for themselves the Spirit of God, regenerating their faith in the firm awareness of receiving eternal life, the beginning of which they sensed while still in the earthly encasement. Information on how these saints died is of great interest for our investigation. After all, when one comes down to it, it must be admitted that a man's predeath state and the very moment of his death are for him the most important experiences of all that he has ever lived through in his earthly life. In a way, death is man's most important examen and first of all an examen of his religion, an examen of to what extent his worldview (philosophical knowledge) comprehended the fact of death itself and not only made this fact comprehendible, but, as we will see from the example of the saints, made it even easy, and not only easy, but even joyful, as joyful as when a man is liberated from difficulties that disrupt his happiness.

And involuntarily, when we will read about how the saints died, we will also, as earlier in our work, be persistently haunted by the thought of how we are passing this terrible examen of death, how we, the Russian intelligentsia, this salt of the earth, are passing this examen—we, supposedly a people strong in spirit, ruling the minds of the nation, holding in our hands the strings to its prosperity, and possibly (if we are on the wrong path) to an increase of its sufferings. Therefore, parallel with the investigation of the death of holy Christian ascetics, we feel a desire to give ourselves at least an approximate accounting of how we will endure this great test. Here we hasten to express the reservation that if we are confronted with such a question, then to resolve it we do not intend to discuss how total unbelievers die: materialists, positivists, and others. We will not enlarge on how these people die, for what kind of death can a person have in whom is instilled the consciousness that by death he is completely destroyed— the death of a man whose chief desire is to die suddenly or, similarly, to avoid death through an unconscious death? Concerning the death of such people, one answer can be given, a short answer. Such a death is either a feeling of horror or a feeling of dull despair, hidden under a mask of apathetic indifference. In any case, such a death is the result of a senseless life. Of such a death, there is nothing to be said. The question of interest to us, how the Russian intelligentsia dies, relates to its better people, who recognize in life a certain meaning, who in their earthly path strive to find a definite rational goal and more or less attain it.

To resolve such a question, we would of course have to do a great deal of research. But we will attempt to adopt for our purposes a shorter way, capable (despite its abridgment) of leading to interesting comparisons and conclusions. This way is to select for investigation the most typical case of death of a prominent intellectual and, comparing this death with how people died who had acquired the Holy Spirit of God, come to a certain definite conclusion. Therefore, we are choosing this much shorter way for our investigation.

Now if we have chosen this path and intend to search out an appropriate example, then life itself is not tardy in suggesting one to us. And it suggests it to us in an event that startled us not long ago. We are speaking now of a great loss felt by all; we are speaking about the death of a brilliant representative of Russian educated society, Count Leo Nikolayevich Tolstoy. Here we should note generally that Tolstoy was always amazingly typical of our Russian intelligentsia. In his life, as a focal point, are expressed all the chief vicissitudes of this intellectual life: from the middle of the last century to the present time, from the time of the heroic period of the Sevastopol war, the liberation of the serfs, and the interests consuming our society during the second half of the nineteenth century. And we must say that the Russian intelligentsia deified its idol—this great writer of the Russian land—for it recognized that he raised it to the heights to which it strove; and it felt that its idol, Tolstoy, had the ability to express its impulses brilliantly, that he was its most typical representative. We will speak in detail of Tolstoy's death in the current chapter. But before we speak about the death of this great Russian writer, we will first begin with our main theme, namely, how the holy Christian ascetics died.

Let us recall first of all the circumstances of the death of Seraphim of Sarov, as it appeared to the monks of the Sarov monastery, when they found Seraphim dead in his cell on his knees before the analogion with his hands crossed over his chest. This end speaks for itself and gives us to feel in what a prayerful disposition Seraphim of Sarov met the great moment of death. Unfortunately, this saint's experiences right before death have remained for us a mystery. No one was a witness to how Seraphim prayed in these minutes, no one knows precisely what were the last movements of his soul. Meanwhile, firsthand information on the predeath state of such a great clairvoyant, as everyone knew Seraphim to be, could have been very instructive for those around him, and through them for us, thirsting for a knowledge of the truth.

So we do not have information on Seraphim's last moments. Therefore, for us to picture the passage of a Christian ascetic into the next world, we will present information on the deaths of other righteous ones. From the numerous descriptions found in the *Menologion*, we have selected just a few typical examples: from the lives of Sts Basil the Great, Joasaph Kamensky, and Nikon of Radonezh. Here are these examples. The renowned Christian doer and ascetic, archbishop of Caesarea, St Basil the Great, performed before his death an extraordinary spiritual struggle bearing testimony to the power of his spirit.

This spiritual struggle was directed toward the salvation of the soul of his fellow man, in this case, a Jewish man whom he turned to Christ. We will describe what the chronicle says. In the archepiscopal residence in the city of Caesarea, where Basil was destined to die, there lived a Jewish man by the name of Joseph, famous in the city as a physician who was unusually skilled in his profession. St Basil knew this physician and loved him. Earlier, he often had talks with him on subjects of faith, desiring to convert Joseph to Christianity.

At the end of Basil's life, when he took seriously ill, Joseph the physician was sent for so that he would examine the sick one and give his advice. "What have you to say about me?" asked St. Basil when the other had examined him. "Prepare everything for burial," declared Joseph to the people of Basil's household. "Death can be expected at any minute." Hearing this, Basil said, "You know not what you say." Joseph answered, "Believe me—your death will come upon you before sunset." Then Basil said to Joseph, "And if I should stay alive till morning, to the sixth hour, what will you do?" "Then may I die," answered Joseph. "Yes," Basil said to this, "die, but die to sin, in order to live for God."

"I know what you are talking of," answered Joseph, "and now I swear to you that if you remain alive till morning, I will fulfill your wish." Then Basil, as the chronicle relates, began to pray that his life be prolonged until morning for the salvation of Joseph's soul. Basil's wish was fulfilled. Joseph did not guess Basil's hour. The next morning Basil was still alive. In the morning, the archbishop again sent for the physician, but the latter did not believe even the servant who told him that Basil had not yet died.

However, Joseph went to see him (as he thought) already dead. When he came to the archbishop and saw Basil alive and fully conscious, he was so astounded by the prolongation of Basil's life that under the impression of this occurrence and his previous conversations with Basil about faith, he announced to the archbishop that he intended to be baptized. Upon hearing this, Basil, in spite of the fact he was dying, said to Joseph that he would baptize him himself. Then Joseph, approaching the saint, touched his right hand and said, "Your powers, master, have weakened and you whole body is finally exhausted; you cannot not baptize me yourself."

But despite all this, Basil rose. The chronicle relates that he went into the church and before everyone baptized Joseph and his whole family and then served liturgy.

Right after this, having given everyone the last kiss, he died fully conscious. His last words were "Into Thy hands I commend my spirit,"[1] In such a way, St Basil's power of spirit was manifested in its greatness in his dying hours, the power of calmness before the face of death, confident in the future life, power directed moreover toward the salvation of one's neighbor, toward bringing him to Christ.

Striking in its touching simplicity is the description of the repose of the Russian saint Joseph Kamensky, wonderworker of Vologod.

It was the 10th of September, 1457—the day of the saint's repose. When the brethren had gathered around Joseph, he ordered that the reading of the rule[2] begin, and when this was finished, he rose from his bed, took the censor with incense, and told the igumen to cense the holy icons and all the brethren. Then he said a prayer to the Lord and to the Mother of God, pouring out in it his petitions not only for himself but also for the whole monastery in which he strove with selfless labor for its spiritual flowering. At the end of the prayer, the saint again "lay down on his bed and prayed about his departure, not grieving in the least, but rather rejoicing in the hope of future blessedness, and with prayer on his lips he quietly passed away. His face was bright, as if he had not died, but had fallen asleep."[3] In conclusion, we will cite here a description of the death of Nikon of Radonezh, disciple of St Sergius of Radonezh, who inherited after him the abbacy in Trinity *lavra*. Sensing the closeness of his death, Nikon ordered that the brethren be summoned to him. When they came, he turned to them with a final word of edification. Upon finishing his instructions, Nikon fell silent. "And here in a vision," relates the chronicle, "still before the separation of the soul from the body, he was shown the place of his future repose (in the higher spiritual world) with St Sergius." In his humility not revealing this clearly to the brethren, Nikon in his dying exhaustion said unexpectedly, "Carry me into that bright chamber which has been prepared for me by the prayers of my father [Sergius of Radonezh]; I do not want to remain here any longer."

Having said this, Nikon partook of the Holy Mysteries. After this, to warn the brethren of the approach of his death, he pronounced, "Here, my brothers, I am released from bodily union and depart to Christ."

Giving his last blessing with the words directed to himself, "Depart, my soul, for the place prepared for thee to abide, go with joy: Christ is calling thee!" and having made the sign of the Cross, with prayer Nikon gave over his soul to the Lord. This was the 17th of November, 1428.[4]

There are many similar descriptions in the *Menologion*, but we have recounted enough to judge how Christian ascetics of the Eastern Church died. One cannot fail to be struck here by the fact that the Christian ascetics not only calmly but even joyfully experienced the approach of death—that very death which for us is so horrifying. And involuntarily, when reading these touching descriptions, one asks oneself, whence did these people have such an unwavering certainly in the blessedness of eternal life, whence did this power of faith spring up in them, bringing them to a direct sensing of the blessings of the future life while still here on earth?

This power of faith, this sensing of the future life, this calm and even joyful death with full reconciliation with life was given to our Christian ascetics by the religion of Christ—transforming, as we have seen, ordinary people into people of life, full of real spiritual struggles, full of real self-denial. All this was given to them by religion, which they knew by experience, through their spiritual struggle. What essentially is the Christian religion? It is faith in a personal God, faith in Christ as God–man, faith in the grace of the Holy Spirit, giving people spiritual strength to fight with evil passions, giving them personal joyful immortality. This religion was born in an expanded conscious-ness (super-consciousness); it appeared as a revelation coming from the Logos, incarnate as man, as a revelation received not by people's intellect, but by the instinct of their higher reason. The purpose of life according to this religion is acquisition of the Holy Spirit of God,[5] giving a foretaste of the blessedness of the future life. This is faith that gives meaning to and makes acceptable the fact of death—a fact that is frightening and seemingly senseless to the major-ity of people who do not have this faith in their heart. "When a man is living in negligence [that is, not in the life in Christ]," says St Isaac of Syria, "he fears the hour of death; but when he comes closer to God ... then this fear is swal-lowed up."[6] "Acquire purity in your works so that your soul may be illumined in prayer," teaches this same Christian ascetic, "so that by the remembrance of death joy will be kindled in your mind."[7] "He who lives in love reaps life from God, while still in this life, sensing here that breeze of the resurrection."[8] And here is what St Macarius the Great says on the same subject:

People who are approaching perfection, while still in this world, already become sharers in the Mysteries of the Heavenly King, have boldness before the Almighty, enter His chamber where the angels and the spir-its of the saints are. For although they have still not received the perfect inheritance prepared for them in the future age, with this pledge which they received now, they have secured themselves as already wedded and ruling, and with this abundance and boldness of Spirit they do not find it surprising that they will rule with Christ, because while still in the flesh they already had within themselves that feeling of sweetness, that action of power. Super-natural gifts of communion with God, received by the soul here, serve as a pledge of heavenly blessings. Already in the present life such a man experiences blessedness and delight, similar to the eternal joys in the age to come.[9]

Judging by the words of St Isaac of Syria and Macarius the Great, such is the psychology of those righteous ones whose lives we have described. The sublimity of their passage from the earthly world to the spiritual world is explained precisely by the state of their soul, which had acquired the Holy Spirit of God.

———————

The righteous ones of the Russian Orthodox Church, as we have already explained in the book *Super-Consciousness*, were the only teachers of the Russian people in the doing of the Christian moral life.[10] They taught the simple Russian people to understand the meaning of life, taught them not to fear death, but to accept one's end with calm greatness of spirit. And one must admit that this calmness before the face of death in our people is truly remarkable. L. N. Tolstoy in *A Confession* says, "As a calm death, without terror and despair, is the rarest exception in our [intellectual] circle—in contrast to this, a troubled death, defiant and joyless, is the rarest exception among the simple people.... And I saw," he writes further, speaking of the simple people, "not two, not three, not ten, but rather hundreds, thousands, millions of people who understood the meaning of life. And all of them, endlessly diverse by nature, mind, education, position, they all identically and in complete contrast to my ignorance[11] knew the meaning of life and death, quietly labored, endured privations and sufferings, lived and died, seeing in this not vanity, but good."[12]

In his story "Childhood," Tolstoy portrayed for us an example of how simply and calmly Russians from among the common people know how to die. We read in this story the touching description of the death of Tolstoy's nanny, Natalia Savishna. The description of this death is so interesting that we will cite it here right now. At the same time the reader, upon hearing this description, will see much in common in the death of Natalia Savishna with the deaths of those Christian ascetics of whom we have spoken, although Natalia Savishna was not a Christian ascetic devoting herself entirely to the spiritual life alone, and although she did not possess the mystical gift of insight. Natalia Savishna was an ordinary Christian, one of those whom Tolstoy had met in his time, as he said, one of those thousands of Russian people. Here is Tolstoy's description of the death of Natalia Savishna: For two months, Natalia Savishna suffered from her illness and endured her suffering with true Christian patience, not murmuring, not complaining, but only, as was her habit, ceaselessly calling upon God. An hour before her death with quiet joy she confessed, received communion, and was anointed with holy unction. She asked everyone in the household for forgiveness for the offenses she might have caused them and asked her confessor, Fr Vassili, to tell us all that she did not know how to thank us for our kindness and asked us to forgive her if in her foolishness she had ever grieved anyone; "but I was never a thief and I can say that I never stole even a piece of thread from the master." This was one quality she valued in herself. Having put on the readied morning dress and cap and leaning on pillows, she did not stop talking with the priest till the very end. She remembered that she had not left anything to the poor; she got ten rubles and asked him to distribute them in the parish. Then she crossed herself, lay down, and for the last time sighed and with a joyful smile pronounced the name of God.[13]

Struck by the beauty of Natalia Savishna's death, Tolstoy exclaimed impetuously, "Great God! Send me ... such superstition, such delusions, and such a death!"[14]

But Tolstoy exclaimed thus long ago, during his youth. Later on, Tolstoy created his own particular faith, and in the eighty-second year of his life he himself was obliged to stand with this faith before the face of death. And what is very difficult for all of us—when he stood before the face of death, he had to die tragically and cruelly. Tragically and cruelly, mainly because the religion that he had created was not sound, was a fantasy religion. This religion was merely a temporary form of solace for him. Even before death, he was still searching for God, not satisfied in the depths of his soul with his own religion. But death caught him unawares, when he had still not found the true faith. And Tolstoy's fantasy religion dispersed like smoke before the horrible face of death. To understand the tragedy of Tolstoy's death, one must first of all study the essence of his religion. Therefore, before we speak of his death, we will explain to the readers Tolstoy's religion, in which he died.

———

In citing the exclamation of Tolstoy concerning the death of Natalia Savishna—"Great God! Send me such a death!"—we said that Tolstoy thus exclaimed long ago, during the time of his youth. After this earlier period, Tolstoy's emotional impulses and his relationship to life underwent significant and diverse changes. He went through being carried away by his passions and satisfying his egotism with human glory and also the despair of ever finding happiness in life. At times, he was totally absorbed in family life, which satisfied him; and at other times, he experienced painful feelings, feelings of anguish and the aimlessness (as it seemed to him) of his life. Once when he was almost fifty years old, he even thought seriously of suicide. He became an atheist when he was still young. His faith in God began to waver when he was eighteen years old.[15]

But here with the onset of old age, Tolstoy began to be overtaken by a new break, serious and important—a break from atheism again to religion. When Tolstoy was already fifty years old, at that time his higher reason, still unextinguished in him, manifested its thirst for true life. This higher reason, through irrational means, not through the brain but from the heart, revealed its attraction to the Godhead, asserted its need to search for God.[16] In his confession, Tolstoy says that since he began searching for God, only then did he begin truly to live; he says that he truly lived only when he was searching for God and that he died when he lost faith in the existence of God—"God is life!" flashed the great thought overshadowing Tolstoy. Live, searching out God, he said to himself, and then there will be no life without God.[17]

And as soon as Tolstoy found for himself this main task of his life—the task of searching for God, then, according to his words, his life received great meaning. "And more strongly than ever before, everything lit up within me and around me and this light no longer left me."

And so Tolstoy began his great task—the search for God. We will not describe here how Tolstoy found his faith, we will not set forth his religion in detail; this would extend far beyond the framework of the present work. We will tell here only the following main theses of Tolstoy's religion, namely, (1) what kind of God Tolstoy found and (2) how he represented to himself the future life.

———

And so let us first talk of what kind of God Tolstoy found. In his religion, Tolstoy created his own God, an impersonal God. His understanding of God dissolved into abstraction. In his diary on the 1st of November, 1910 (six days before his death), Tolstoy wrote, "God is that unlimited all, of which man is conscious of himself as a limited part. Only God truly exists. Man is His manifestation in matter, time, and space." In this way, according to Tolstoy, man contains within himself elements consubstantial with the Godhead.[18] This universal abstract God, according to Tolstoy's teaching, is splintered as it were into separate human entities. "Why did the Single Spiritual being become divided in itself?" asks Tolstoy, and gives this answer: "the purposes of which are inaccessible to man."[19] So according to Tolstoy, God in man—this is a desire for good to all that exists, which Tolstoy identifies with what we understand by the word "love."[20]

Here it is interesting to note to what extent this view of Tolstoy does not agree with Christian teaching. According to Christian teaching, God remains

God and man, man. Only the one God–man, Jesus Christ, is consubstantial with God the Father, Light from His Light, God uncreated, but Himself that very God. According to Christian teaching, man, no matter how lofty his life, cannot turn into God, he can only be like God by the grace of the Holy Spirit given him by God.

In allowing this identification of desire for good with love, Tolstoy fails to notice that he is confusing two concepts. The desire for good to all that exists can be the perception by man's reason of a moral law; it can be a purely rational perception, man's rational submission to this law. This is the foundation which the pagan-Stoics Marcus Aurelius and others[21] placed as the cornerstone of their worldview. Now love, as we understand it and as Christian ascetics understand it, is not a rational, cerebral movement, but rather the very deepest emotion. "God is a fire that warms and kindles the heart and inward parts," says Seraphim of Sarov. "If we feel in our hearts coldness," he continues, "then let us call on the Lord, and He will come and warm our hearts with perfect love not only for Him, but for our neighbor as well." According to Christian teaching, Christian love is something completely special and altogether incommensurable with what we understand by the words "a desire for good to all that exists," which desire the pagans had who recognized an abstract God (as did Marcus Aurelius, for example) for good to all that exists (secs. 24 and 25). And the desire for good to all that exists is love (sec. 32) is God (secs. 28 and 32).

Between the abstract God of Tolstoy—a God of rational desire for good to all that exists, and between the personal God of Christians, a God of fervent, sublime love (according to the words of Seraphim of Sarov, "that warms and kindles the heart and inward parts") there is such a difference as between polar and tropical climates. Such is the difference, by its force, between these two movements: between the mental movement toward a certain good and the profound movement toward that fervent heart. Christian ascetics made a sharp distinction between these emotions. Hence, Bishop Theophan the Recluse says that with mental impulses, life is not real. The heart is absent here, and it is left with the possibility of being attuned in its own way, independent of mental reasonings. It moves slightly under the impression of mental representations, but superficially, similar to how the surface of water ripples from a light breath of air. As movements of this kind do not pass into the depths of the heart, so its formation and attunement go their own way, and maybe, totally out of correspondence with the mental construction.[22]

Having created in this way his own understanding of an impersonal God, Tolstoy rejects Christ as God, as a Person of the Holy Trinity, and rejects divine revelation.[23] According to Tolstoy, every man knows God within him-self from the moment there is born in him the desire for good to all that exists.[24] For such a man revelation from above is not needed. He can be his own revelation. According to Tolstoy, man's religion is his subjective revela-tion, the product of his spirit. According to Christian doctrine, the Chris-tian religion takes as its first cause revelation proceeding not from people, but from the personal single Godhead. This religion has its source in Jesus Christ, in this exalted most-perfect Being. Tolstoy's religion denies the whole mystical essence of Christianity—it is created by rationality; this religion came into being as the result of the egocentric consciousness that fettered Tolstoy's spirit.

Christian religion, on the contrary, was born in the expanded conscious-ness (super-consciousness); it appeared as revelation proceeding from the Logos, incarnate of man, as revelation perceived not by people's rationality but by the instinct of their higher reason—"He who has ears, hear," said the Great Teacher, and these thousands of people received the revelation expressed in the following divine words of the Teacher: "I am the way, the truth, and the life,"[25] and "As the branch cannot bear fruit of itself, unless it abides in the vine, neither can you, unless you abide in Me."[26] Thus, in Tolstoy's religion the center of gravity is in man. For Christians, the center is in the Godhead—in Jesus Christ.[27]

––––––––

Now let us switch over to how Tolstoy represented to himself the future life. Contrary to the Christian religion, based on faith in the grace of God, giving man personal joyful immortality, Tolstoy teaches that belief in a future personal life is a very low and crude representation.[28] Tolstoy says that for a man's rational consciousness, there can be no representation of a future life.[29] "It will be well with me,"[30] declares Tolstoy, speaking of his own impersonal future life, but by this life he understands something abstract, unrepresented by man, something diffused in the idea of God, as the desire for good to all that exists, in an idea that is eternal. And man's individuality, as understood by Tolstoy, being in itself limited, perishes with man's physical death.[31] Hence, according to Tolstoy, there is no personal future life; belief in a personal future life is, as he says, a very low and crude representation. If Tolstoy called the Christian representation of a personal future life crude and low, then this was because Tolstoy was in general poorly informed in our patristic literature. We will further cite facts that prove that he was poorly informed in this regard.

Already from the material that we cited in this book, in speaking of the lives of the saints, one could judge for a certainty what a lofty poetic aspect this future life represented to Christian ascetics, not crude and low. For example, in the previous chapter where we cited the description of the mystical revelations of Symeon the New Theologian, we see references to this future life, full of exalted happiness. We remind the reader that to the question of Symeon, ablaze with the ecstasy of contemplating the Divinity, "What else could be more resplendent and exalted than this?" Symeon heard this answer: "Thy soul is extremely small if thou art satisfied with this happiness, because in comparison with the future bliss it is like a drawing of the sky on paper that someone holds in his hands in comparison with the real skies; even much more does the future glory surpass the one thou hast witnessed now."[32]

One cannot help but acknowledge the lofty poetry in these illustrations of St Symeon's vision, portraying his understanding of the future life. In the aforementioned illustrations, we see one side of the saint's representation of this life, namely, as a life of the greatest blessedness in the contemplation of God.

And here is the other side of the saint's representation of that very same personal future life. This concerns his relationships in this life, with those who still remained on earth. We will remind the reader of the following words of Seraphim of Sarov:[33] "When I am no more," Seraphim said to his spiritual children, "come to me at my grave . . . fall to the ground as to a living person, tell me everything, and I will hear you. All your sorrow will fly off and pass away. As you always spoke with a living person, it is the same here. For you I am alive and will be forever."

We could cite still more material to prove that Tolstoy's opinion of the crudeness of the Christian representation of a personal future life is erroneous, but this would divert us far from our main theme. And these words of Symeon the New Theologian and Seraphim of Sarov are sufficient to see the error of Tolstoy's view.

As a result, we have before us the following main propositions of Tolstoy: (1) Tolstoy rejected a personal God, rejected divine revelation, rejected the action of grace, and rejected the personal future life; and (2) besides all this, Tolstoy acknowledged God in every man entering on the path of desiring good to all that exists, acknowledged a collective, abstract God of all people, uniting them in this desire, acknowledged the future life as an impersonal life.

With this his religion, Tolstoy was obliged at the end of his days to stand before the face of death. And it turned out to be weak and unstable, this religion of Tolstoy's. It did not support him in the difficult moment of trial. We will see from the description of Tolstoy's last days that he died in darkness, with a restless soul.

Moreover, what is tragic is that Tolstoy himself felt the instability and weakness of his faith, and he was aware of this long before his death, not knowing how to extricate himself from his doubts, not knowing where and how to find the true faith.

––––––––––

We said before that Tolstoy was unlearned in our spiritual literature. Yes, he simply did not want to know it. He ignored the writings of Christian ascetics—these teachers of the Russian people. When we spoke of this, we promised to cite factual information that proved Tolstoy's lack of knowledge in this regard. Now we will tell how we personally come to be convinced of this during our short acquaintance with Tolstoy. In the life of every person, there are strange occurrences to which at first he does not ascribe proper significance and only begins to value them later on when life itself underscores their importance. Such a chance occurrence happened to us in our relationship with the great writer of the Russian land. Not long before Tolstoy's death, we had the opportunity to become acquainted with him and have a conversation with him, to which at that time we did not ascribe the significance it deserved. But later, after Tolstoy's great drama, this conversation acquired for us profound meaning and clarified much for us concerning Tolstoy. It happened that I, the author of this book, became acquainted with Tolstoy three months before his death, and besides this, was a personal witness of how Tolstoy, while apparently still living peacefully in his family circle, showed that he was unsettled in his religious searching, showed also that he had very little knowledge of our religious literature. On the other hand, I had the opportunity to experience personally how eccentric this man was, strange in the sometimes inexplicable prejudice of his views.

How Tolstoy's strangeness expressed itself and also what Tolstoy's moods were shortly before his death (three months)—all this the reader can discern from the following account. It was the last days of July 1910. I came to Tolstoy with my wife and another one of our acquaintances, S. V. Chirkin, director then of the Russian consulate in Bombay, on leave at that time in Russia. We arrived in Yasnaya Polyana at the agreed-upon time[34] of seven o'clock in the evening. At that time in Yasnaya Polyana, besides Sophia Andrievna Tolstoy, there were also Tolstoy's two sons, Lev Lvovich and Andrei Lvovich with his wife, also Count Biriukov with his wife and children (it seems that Biriukov at that time acted as Tolstoy's secretary and librarian), the pianist Goldenwieser, and Tolstoy's ever-inseparable Dr Makovitsky. At exactly seven o'clock, Lev Nikolayevich (Tolstoy) came out to us from his study; he was dressed as always in his traditional outfit, a smock shirt; his gait was fast and he carried himself straight.

Tolstoy's face was tired; his expression was very serious. "How is your health, Lev Nikolayevich?" I asked him after the usual greetings. (Not long before our meeting, Tolstoy had been ill.)

"What of health!" he answered, "One has to prepare for death." When we had all arranged ourselves in a circle around the table in a corner of the room, he turned to me and asked, "I've heard that you're writing something?" "I'm interested in everything concerning the life of our Christian ascetics and saints," I answered. "I am now working hard on researching this life."[35] Tolstoy looked at me rather severely and attentively.

"And this does not interest me in the least," he said. Having said this, he turned to one of the others present. "How can it be that Christian ascetics don't interest you?!" I burst out. "Those Christian ascetics don't interest you who created the Akim type in 'The Powers of Darkness'?" Tolstoy turned to me and said, "What of Akim? Akim was just a good man." "That's not all," I objected. "He's not only a good man, he is a Christian ascetic, a light.... He gives off light. Why, Akim is bone of the bones of our Orthodox Christian ascetics!"

"Akim is no more than a very good man," Tolstoy continued. "Well then, that means we have a disagreement in words," I persisted. "We're using different terminology. You say that Akim is a very good man, and I say that too, adding only that in his constant striving for good, he manifested himself in this sense as a Christian ascetic. Agree after all, Lev Nikolayevvich, that Akim is a type of Christian ascetic, he is an ascetic among the peasants." "And what's so special about your spiritual striving which you are studying?" asked Tolstoy. "There is a great deal that is special. Permit me to cite as an example the philosophical saying of a Christian ascetic of the sixth century. It concerns the interrelationship in man's soul of love for God and love for people. Does this interest you?" "Speak on," said Tolstoy, "the subject is interesting."

"The Christian ascetic expressed this interrelationship thus: 'Picture to yourself a circle,' he said, 'and in its center is God. From the circumference people are striving toward God. The paths of their lives are the radii from the circumference to the center. Insofar as they, traveling these paths, come closer to God, in like measure they come closer to one another in their love, and insofar as they love one another, in like measure they come closer to

God.' Don't you agree that's a good one?" "Yes ... that's a good one," said Lev Nikolayevich. He was silent for a moment. "That's even amazing," he added. "What is the name of this Christian ascetic who gave this scheme?"

"Abba Dorotheus—a sixth-century Christian ascetic." "I'll show you right now," Tolstoy interrupted the silence. He drew from his pocket a notebook and began leafing through it. "Now here I have ... Not long ago I wrote to a friend ... Look here," he continued, having found the page in the book on which a circle was drawn. "I wrote him that we must love one another more. Here in the center I have God, and my friend and I are on the circumference and relate to one another along the circumference. So instead of circling and so we will come closer together, we make a chord. Along the chord we will come closer together and will be closer to God.... Why my idea is the same as your ascetic's." "No, Abba Dorotheus's is better; there it is more clear, more vivid."

"Yes, it's better," Tolstoy agreed. "This is very, very interesting. Where did you read it?" "In the *Philokalia,*" I answered. "And what is the *Philokalia?*" asked Lev Nikolayevich. "It is a very large collection of writings edited by Bishop Theophan. In it is contained excerpts from the works of thirty-eight Christian ascetics of the Orthodox Church. And Abba Dorotheus is there. And that is where I found this." "Why is it we know nothing about the *Philokalia?*" Tolstoy turned to Biriukov, who was present with everyone else during our conversation. "What do you mean know nothing!" answered Biriukov. "I've told you so many times.... You forgot." "This is very, very interesting," Tolstoy continued animatedly. "We must by all means obtain this collection." "You will find many more things there," I said. "You will come across such pearls as will amaze you." "By all means we must obtain the *Philokalia,*" said Tolstoy. "Abba Dorotheus expressed this very well." "We have all this," Biriukov said as if to himself in a dissatisfied tone. At this point, the conversation on the *Philokalia* broke off.

After this, Tolstoy began asking me about the trip around the world I had just completed. We spoke a great deal about India, about Japan; Tolstoy asked Chirkin many things about India, after which he talked about the Hindu ascetic Vivekananda whom he was then studying and whom I knew from his treatise on Raja yoga.[36] I will not recount this conversation because it does not relate to the matter in question concerning Tolstoy's spiritual state before the onset of his drama.

The conversation lasted for more than an hour at the round table. Sophia Andreyevna asked everyone to come to the big table where tea was being served. The whole group moved to the long table. There my conversation with Tolstoy resumed, and by chance we got on the subject of occult powers.

I stated that I fully acknowledged these powers and began to assert fervently that they exist. "That's all nonsense," said Tolstoy, "I don't believe it. We also have women here in the country who say all sorts of nonsense. And I advise you not to believe whoever says this." "How can I not believe it, when I have reliable information?" I objected. "Here, ask my wife; she's sitting right here. She will tell you how in my presence in Algiers the hypnotist Pikman put her to sleep against her will; she didn't want it, but he put her to sleep just the same." "And I'm not about to ask," said Lev Nikolayevich. "All this is trivial. In this world that surrounds us there are no special mysterious powers. There are no such perceptions." "How can there be no such perceptions?" I continued. "What about music?" "What about music! What has music got to do with it?" said Tolstoy.

"In that it exerts influence on my soul … that I cannot explain this using any of our physical powers. Isn't this a special power?" "There's nothing special here," Lev Nikolayevich persisted. "It's just pleasant to the ear, it titillates the ear. And you delight in music." "But no, that's not all," I continued unabated. "Music does not titillate, it uncorks."

At these words, Tolstoy burst out laughing; evidently he liked my comparison. "But look, we have our own corkscrew sitting here," said Tolstoy's son, Andrei Lvovich, pointing out to me the pianist Goldenweisser, who at that moment was earnestly writing something in his notebook.

So ended our conversation on the subject of occult powers. But in any case, it was confirmed to me then what I already knew from Tolstoy's writings, namely, that he did not believe in any mysterious powers. All these acknowledgments of special powers were, in his opinion, nonsense and trifles. Meanwhile, at the table we talked about culture and civilization, and about the harm they produce. We talked on various other subjects, we talked a great deal. The time passed quickly. The clock already showed ten o'clock in the evening; it was time to get up. When bidding goodbye to Tolstoy, at my wife's saying that our conversation might have tired him, Lev Nikolayevich said that, on the contrary, he had enjoyed it and that he was grateful that we had come and would himself soon visit us at our estate.

Four days passed. Tolstoy and Dr Makovitsky came on horseback to us in Basovo.[37]

"I've come to visit for a few minutes," said Tolstoy, entering the house. "I came to see you and to look at the *Philokalia* Let's go in and you show me the *Philokalia*" We went into my study; I took from the bookcase all five volumes. Tolstoy began looking them over and leafing through them. Then he took out a notebook and began, apparently, to enter there the title of the edition and make some other notations. At that time, I explained to Tolstoy that the *Philokalia* was not the only one of its kind of interest, that the *Philokalia* contained only excerpts, that for example, the original complete collections of the writings of the ascetics St Isaac of Syria, Symeon the New Theologian, and others contain wonderful pages.

In my study, Tolstoy happened to notice a large album with Japanese landscapes that I had collected during my trip around the world. He became interested in the album; we began looking through it; I gave explanations.

Finally, Tolstoy remembered the time. He quickly rose, said goodbye, and went out with Makovitsky to the horses. Going up to his horse, he began patting it, with one hand grabbed hold of the saddle and, before I knew it, with the ease and agility of a young man, he sprang into the saddle. From the way he jumped on the horse, it was apparent how vigorous he was, and I never thought then that I was seeing him for the last time,[38] that his end was so near.

The short acquaintance with Tolstoy as described gave me quite interesting material for judging this amazingly eccentric man. Indeed, isn't this astonishing? From Tolstoy's writings, I knew that for thirty years Tolstoy had worked on creating his own religious worldview, had studied Confucius, Socrates, Lao-Tse, Zoroaster, Marcus Aurelius, and others. And here it seems for all this, to the end of his days he stubbornly ignored a whole group of great religious thinkers, the teachers of the Russian people—that very people before whose strength of spirit he bowed down. Tolstoy did not know our patristic literature, had no idea, for example, what sort of book the *Philokalia* was, or who were the philosophers St Isaac of Syria, St Ephraim the Syrian, St Abba Dorotheus, and others who created our Russian saints. To such an extent did he not want to know all this, that in prejudice he would turn away without further converse from anyone who was seriously interested in Orthodox spiritual endeavor. So when in conversation I had occasion to inform him that I was doing research on their lives, he, without even thinking, with a touch of total contempt, said, "And this does not interest me in the least," and immediately turned the conversation to another subject. And only then, when I practically forced into Tolstoy's ears the brilliant words of St Abba Dorotheus, did he feel their power, and no sooner had he felt this, than there awoke in him an interest in Christian ascetics and the *Philokalia*.

Here we cannot overlook a certain characteristic trait of Tolstoy's surroundings that we noticed at that time. We saw clearly the impression that Tolstoy's sudden interest in the *Philokalia* made on the Tolstoyan Biriukov who was present at our conversation. We saw how Mr Biriukov seemed to want to lead Tolstoy away from this book, giving us to feel that all this, as they say, is common knowledge and old.

But Tolstoy was not the sort of man to easily leave off the studying of ideas once he had become interested in them, even though these ideas did not agree with the stereotype pattern of his Tolstoyans. And here, not having found the *Philokalia* collection in his own library, and probably not having found the willingness in his secretary Biriukov to order this collection, Tolstoy rode ten versts on horseback for these books, and one of his first words upon entering were "Show me the *Philokalia*." And so we see that Tolstoy needed some sort of special occasion, a special impulse to jolt him out of the false course into which his philosophical–religious searchings often fell. It should be said that, in general, Tolstoy's philosophical thought did not possess clear vision; it was often darkened by the bonds of his prejudiced opinions, opinions nurtured by the Misters Tolstoyan who in a tight circle surrounded the great writer, infecting him with their extreme views.

And here, as a result of all this, what amazing contradictions we see. On one hand, before us is Tolstoy's artistic genius—he creates the striking type of peasant Akim from "Powers of Darkness," creates the type of true ascetic in whom one senses spiritual power. And on the other hand, before us is Tolstoy the religious seeker, studying with great interest the Hindu yogi Vivekananda, but knowing very little, for example, about the great ascetic, Seraphim of Sarov, immeasurably more powerful and interesting than Vivekananda, and besides more closely related to the peasant Akim, to that very Akim who was created by the artistic genius of that very same Lev Nikolayevich Tolstoy. In addition to these thoughts which involuntarily came to mind after my short acquaintance with Tolstoy, there also remains with me a strong impression from the first words he said in answer to my question about his health. Tolstoy then answered outright, "One must prepare for death," and his face was sad, the expression of his eyes very serious. Undoubtedly Tolstoy at that time was thinking persistently about death, and he did not feel solid ground beneath him before his oncoming death. The precariousness of his religious worldview was the most characteristic feature of his rationalistic philosophy. So, for example, two days before his departure from Yasnaya Polyana, that is, October 26, 1910, in his letter to Chertkov expressing his views on the present and future life, Tolstoy added, "Sometimes this seems to me to be true, and sometimes it seems like nonsense." In general, Tolstoy's whole religion was very unstable. This is apparent, by the way, from one event that took place in 1904, about which we will inform the reader. His teaching, in which he calls faith in the mysteries "false teaching" (sec. 386 of Tolstoy's book *Christian Teaching*), Tolstoy decided to make public in 1897, and he published this book (as can be seen from his letter of September 2, 1887, to Chertkov), with the purpose of giving "something useful to people." Meanwhile, after this publication, in 1904, when Tolstoy' s brother, Count Sergei Nikolayevich, was dying,[39] L. N. Tolstoy, totally unexpectedly for everyone, expressed complete sympathy with his brother's decision to act in accordance with what he earlier called "false teaching," that is, to partake of the Holy Mysteries.[40]

But now come days full of anxiety, fateful days for Tolstoy. Approaching Tolstoy is a cruel drama. Clouds begin to obscure the sky. Of these days— sorrowful for all of us to whom Tolstoy was so dear—we have detailed information only from the moment of his departure from Yasnaya Polyana. On October 28, 1910, something happened that none of us expected. Tolstoy runs away from home, and runs not to the Tolstoyans, but to his monastic sister, with the purpose of living close by her.[41] Tolstoy flees unbeknownst to everyone; the only one to know about it is a certain Dr Makovitsky whom Tolstoy takes with him. Tolstoy is thirsting for the possibility of retreat from everyone; he thirsts for a peaceful life close by his monastic sister, he wants to get away even from his Tolstoyans. And this is not all—we learn further of another unexpected action by Tolstoy. Having left his home to go to his sister in the Shamordino Convent, he does not go there directly, but rather decides to stop by Optina Pustyn'. Why does he go to Optina Pustyn'? We ask this question and have a definite answer to it, supported by factual information. Tolstoy goes to Optina with the purpose of seeing the Optina elders.

This fact, more than any other, strengthens the conviction we came away with upon meeting Tolstoy, that Tolstoy was not satisfied with his religion. Of late the thought of death did not leave him, and this death was not far off.

Tolstoy, sensing the instability of his own religious worldview, rushes to the Optina elders. He rushes to find support from them. Maybe he will hear there powerful words, similar to the words of Abba Dorotheus—words to enlighten the truth; maybe the doubts that have seized his soul will be cleared up. The Optina elder will appear before him in the full armor of his faith, in the full armor of his inspiration. But here something cruel for Tolstoy takes place. Tolstoy is prevented from seeing the elder by a more powerful force acting contrary to this impulse. This force is Tolstoy's own pride. Tolstoy goes to the hermitage, goes up to the outer doors of the elder's cell, stands for a few moments before the doors, but unable to make up his mind to enter, turns back. "But why didn't you go in to see the elder?" he was asked later. "I couldn't make up my mind. After all, I'm excommunicated." "And will you go again?" he was asked further. "If he were to invite me!" answered Tolstoy.[42]

So here is Tolstoy's will. This will is bound by his pride. His decision—to visit or not to visit the elder—depends first of all on whether the elder invites him to come in. The elder had to guess that Tolstoy was waiting to be invited. Tolstoy's pride told him that it was already more than sufficient that he—excommunicated from the church—had decided to come to Optina Pustyn'; it was enough that he, Tolstoy, openly announced his intention to see the elders, announced this to the innkeeper, Fr Michael.

From Optina Pustyn', Tolstoy and Makovitsky came to Shamordino on October 29. Tolstoy went to his sister and announced to her his intention to live nearby her in Shamordino. But here an obstacle arose; a new circumstance came up that overturned Tolstoy's final intention.

On October 30, there arrived in Shamordino two vehement Tolstoyans—Lev Nikolayevich's daughter, Alexandra Lvovna, and her friend, V. N. Feoktistova. They brought alarming news—news that Tolstoy's wife, Sophia Andreyevna, had found out where her husband had gone. "Mama will most certainly come here," Alexandra Lvovna told her father. This was sufficient to frighten Tolstoy away from Shamordino.[43]

Although toward evening of that day Tolstoy was already feeling ill, yet that did not hinder a new decision; it did not prevent Tolstoy's daughter, Alexandra Lvovna, the young Miss Feoktistova, and Dr Makovitsky from taking the ailing eighty-year-old Tolstoy from Shamordino early the next morning in very bad weather.[44] It seems they all decided to travel to Rostov-on-the-Don, where there was a colony of Tolstoyans. Obviously, such forced travel for a seriously ill old man could not pass without incident, could not go on for long. During this trip—a trip totally without comfort, in terrible weather—Tolstoy's illness could not but get worse, and as we know, this is what happened, quickly and mercilessly. Soon Tolstoy had no strength to continue traveling; he was forced to leave the train at the station in Astapovo. In Astapovo, Tolstoy's illness progressed quickly, and already on the morning of November 4 (three days before his death) Tolstoy began to realize that he was dying.[45]

Up to this time, Tolstoy still hoped there was a possibility that he would get well. But from November 4 this hope began to leave the sick man. From this day began the serious test of the powers of his soul, the test of his religion. Thus commenced the trial of a man before the terrifying passage into another world—into that world from which there is no return.

———————

To judge Tolstoy's last days, we have two documents: (1) the doctors' record from November 9, 1910, of the sickness and death of Tolstoy, written in Yasnaya Polyana, and signed by D. P. Makovitsky, D. N. Nikitin, and G. M. Berstein (the newspaper *New Time* of November 12, 1910, No. 12454); and (2) the article by V. Chertkov on the last days of L. N. Tolstoy, printed in all the Russian newspapers in January 1911.

Of these two documents, the first represents a detailed account of the progress of Tolstoy's illness; only in one place in the record is there any mention of the words that Tolstoy spoke, characterizing his emotional state. As regards the second document, it gives more information on the moral sufferings of the great writer as he was dying. Concerning the doctors' report, one could say that it was written fairly objectively; but this could not be said of the second document. In it there is much of a personal nature, relating specifically to Chertkov, much that obscures the description of the kind of emotional drama Tolstoy was experiencing in these last days of his life.

In the article, Chertkov talks much about himself, and talks of Tolstoy's feeling of love for him (Chertkov describes scenes illustrating this love); he tells how he—Chertkov—loved Tolstoy; and he tells how Tolstoy did well to leave his home and wife, and that all good people approved of Tolstoy's action.

Expatiating on all this, Chertkov does give some information on Tolstoy's actual emotional state during these difficult days. All the while, Chertkov, in this same article, unfortunately obscures this information with his commentaries. But because at the present time, after the publishing of reliable material on Tolstoy, it has become possible to verify to what extent these commentaries correspond to actual events, so we have grounds on which to discard those judgments of Chertkov that prove incorrect.

To give the readers an understanding of how Chertkov generally errs in his commentaries, we cite the following example. So, in explaining why Tolstoy did not want to die (i.e., in other words, he was dying with a feeling of sorrow), Chertkov writes that this occurred because Tolstoy, before his final illness, "had managed to extricate himself from his hopeless situation. He intended to begin life anew, independently, in an environment which had for a long time attracted him, amongst simple workers" (i.e., Tolstoyans). Therefore, so Chertkov thinks, Tolstoy did not want to die mainly because death frustrated these plans of his. But such an explanation contradicts Tolstoy's actions. Tolstoy, as we know now, fled from Yasnaya Polyana not to the Tolstoyans but to Shamordino, to his sister, Maria Nikolayovna, close by whom he wanted to live in retreat, and it was these very Tolstoyans who frightened him away from Shamordino with the news of his wife's apparently imminent arrival.

We will not recount Mr Chertkov's description relating to him personally. Nor will we enlarge on how Tolstoy, judging by Mr Chertkov's information, showed himself to the end of his days to be a writer faithful to his calling; how, during this time, he related to his family, to his close ones, and in general to people.[46] We will pass directly over to the material of most interest to us, namely, to Tolstoy's highly significant words, which in the last days burst forth from the depths of his soul, while he was fully conscious—to the words revealing how Tolstoy's soul reacted to the onset of death.

Meanwhile, we should mention that during these difficult days Tolstoy was conscious for the most part. The doctors' report says that on November 4 and 6 his mental state was "absolutely clear," and on November 5 it was "clear," although at times Tolstoy was unconscious and delirious.

The death agony, when Tolstoy was no longer able to speak, began after midnight on the 7th of November, although according to the doctors' report even then he still remained conscious. Tolstoy reacted to flashes of light. Only at five o'clock in the morning of November 7 did his breathing become shallow, and at 6:05 A.M. Tolstoy passed away.

———————

Tolstoy's death was dark and tormented. The readers themselves will be convinced of this when they delve into the desolate meaning of the dying man's words, if they take these words without Chertkov's commentaries that strove to ascribe to this death a calm and bright character, if they take these words such as they were spoken. We will now cite Tolstoy's very significant exclamations: "I don't understand what I am to do.... But the peasants, how the peasants die!... Apparently, I will have to die in sins.... This is the end and nothing more." Let us closely analyze these words of Tolstoy. "I don't understand what I am to do." We have two versions of this exclamation: (1) Chertkov, in his article on the last days of Tolstoy, says the following: "On the eve of his death, when Tolstoy was in great distress, he, apparently wanting to fulfill his obligation, said to me—I don't understand what I am to do"; and (2) according to the words of Tolstoy's sister, Maria Nikolayevna Tolstoy, "During the last days we heard from Tolstoy the words: 'What am I to do, O my God, what am I to do.' His hands were folded as in prayer."

The first explanation of Tolstoy's words by Chertkov we cannot understand at all: What sort of obligation for Tolstoy is Mr Chertkov talking about here, and what does he mean by "apparently"? Even without Maria Nikolayevna Tolstoy's version, if we were to understand even Chertkov's version, only freeing this version from his commentaries, then the meaning of Tolstoy's exclamation—"I don't understand what I am to do"—undoubtedly indicates the lightless state Tolstoy was in, seeing no way out for his emotional consolation, not knowing what he was to do in these hours before death. And we understand these words of Tolstoy, "I don't understand what I am to do," in just this sense. In any case, whichever version of these words one takes—either Chertkov's version, "I don't understand what I am to do" or Maria Nikolayevna Tolstoy's version, "What am I to do, O my God, what am I to do"—one must in any case conclude that Tolstoy's religion, placed before the face of death, gave him no solace. Tolstoy's last days were the days of a man tossed about, not knowing what he should do.

"But the peasants, how the peasants die!" As can be seen in Chertkov's article on Tolstoy's last days, this exclamation of Tolstoy's is understood by Mr Chertkov to mean that Tolstoy was expressing the pangs of conscious of a well-to-do man before peasants, deprived of material means, dying in need and deprivation. But Mr Chertkov in this sentimentality completely forgets that Tolstoy always admired how the peasants died peacefully and joyfully. In accordance with this, Tolstoy's exclamation "But the peasants, how the peasants die!" must be understood in a completely different sense than Mr Chertkov understood it. This exclamation expresses Tolstoy's grief that he is incapable of dying as the peasants do. And in this very same sense we should understand Tolstoy's next exclamation, "Apparently, I will have to die in sins…. This is the end, and nothing more."

This exclamation Mr Chertkov likewise explains in his own way, striving to lessen its significance. He juxtaposes it with an exclamation of a completely different character, half-jokingly said by the sick man while delirious; namely, with Tolstoy's words, "Now, Mother, don't be offended." But by making such a comparison, Mr Chertkov belittles totally how Tolstoy pronounced the outcry, "This is the end and nothing more." He pronounced these words, as the doctors' report testifies, in the following manner. We take the original words of the report: "On November 6th at approximately 2:00 p.m.—unexpected agitation: he sat up in bed and in a loud voice said clearly to those around him, 'This is the end and nothing more.'"

After reading these words of the report, involuntarily one asks oneself why Tolstoy said the word "nothing" in such extreme agitation. What kind of agitation was this? And perfectly naturally it comes to mind, was not this agitation the result of the very awareness contained in this word "nothing," in the word directly behind which already stood the icy death of his personal life. Now if one were to juxtapose Tolstoy's outcry with another of his light-less outcries, "I don't understand what I am to do!" then this last cry of Tol-stoy's soul, "This is the end and nothing more," takes on a meaning totally unlike what Mr Chertkov tries to ascribe to it. And as a result, we cannot but come to the conclusion that, regardless of how Mr Chertkov deceived himself and others, striving instinctively in his defense of Tolstoy's delusion to extinguish the true meaning of all these words of Tolstoy, Tolstoy's death with these outcries all the same causes every impartial person to feel that the state of the dying man's soul was turbulent.

This was the slow, fully conscious death of a philosopher who had not found solace in his own philosophy, and what is all the more tormenting, a philosopher under the watchful eye of his disciples, blind in their slavelike devotion to his delusion. Under the impression of Tolstoy's outcries we invol-untarily think back to one place in *A Confession*, written thirty years before, when Tolstoy says, "I was like a man lost in the woods, struck with horror that he is lost and thrashing about wanting to get out on the road—knowing that his every step entangles him even more—and cannot stop thrashing about."[47]

But back then when Tolstoy wrote these lines, he had hope of getting out of the woods. Back then, Tolstoy felt in his heart that there is a God, and he felt relieved, for he had decided to search for God. But unfortunately, it was not with his heart that he instinctively strove toward God, but rather he began searching for Him with his reason (the lower reason), which Tol-stoy blindly believed in.[48] He spent the first stage of the way in these search-ings. He got as far as the pagan God and, in getting this far, thought he had found the truth. He took the abstract God for the real God, that has power to save him. But what Tolstoy had found proved to be a mirage when fac-ing this terrible trial. The mirage dispersed like smoke in the face of death. And here in the last minutes Tolstoy found himself again in the dark woods. Death caught him unawares, and no one was nearby him who would show him the road. Around him were people who were as yet much more dark-ened than he was, and so his cries of despair were natural and even outright unavoidable: "I don't understand what I am to do.... But the peasants, how the peasants die!"

Yes, we can say that the peasants do not die like this, nor do their instructors—the great Orthodox Christian ascetics—die like this. These died peacefully and majestically, for they knew for a certainty where they were going. "Depart, my soul, to the place that is prepared for thee," said St Nikon of Radonezh in ecstasy before death. "Go with joy. Christ is calling thee." Whence was this, their awesome and immense confidence in Christ?—Confidence equal to visible proof.

It is attained not by the brain in which Tolstoy had such faith, but by the heart, with that heart that overturned the whole history of the world from the time of the coming of Christ—Christ Who gave to the world "the Light of men"—Light Invisible to our eyes. This light dawned on and saved man and gave him immortality of a personal joyful life. And poor Tolstoy in his conceit imagined himself to be a light! But this weak human light went out instantly, just as soon as icy death touched him and darkness embraced him, and "nothing," as Tolstoy himself felt in despair.

———

In concluding this chapter, we cannot but express the bitter truth that with no more consolation than Tolstoy does our intelligentsia die, who in the overwhelming majority are even far away from searching for God. The majority of this intelligentsia are completely unconcerned with thoughts of the unavoidable reckoning with life, of how this reckoning will go. It dreams only of one thing—postponing for as long as possible payment of the bill that, nevertheless, no matter how much one postpones, must still be paid. When after all these postponements, the unavoidable moment of liquidation comes, it appears as something unexpected, usually catching the person unawares, and here he begins to thrash about and suffer morally.

Nevertheless, for our consolation we can point to cases of majestic and peaceful dying among people of the Russian intelligentsia. But these people were true Christians; they did not strive to create for themselves a God dispersed in abstraction; rather, they strived to know with their heart the personal God, the living God—that Logos that John the Divine proclaimed to the world. As an example we cite one such death. May the picture of this death smooth over for us the painful impression we were left with from the death of Count Lev Nikolayevich Tolstoy. We will tell how A. S. Khomyakov died.

The famous writer on religious matters, Alexei Stepanovich Khomyakov, died September 25, 1860, from cholera, far from his family on his estate in Ryazan. An account of Khomyakov's last days was left by the neighboring landowner, Leonid Matveyevich Muromtsev. Here is an excerpt from this account. When Murometsev went in to Khomyakov and asked what the matter was, Khomyakov answered, "Oh nothing in particular, it's time to die. This is very bad. Such a strange thing! How many people have I healed but myself I am unable to heal." According to the words of Murometsev, in his voice there was not a shadow of regret or fear, but rather a deep conviction that there was no way out. "About one o'clock in the afternoon, seeing that the sick man's strength was giving out, I," says Murometsev, "asked if he wanted to receive the Last Rites. He accepted my offer with a joyful smile, saying, 'I would be very, very glad.' During the whole time the Sacrament was being performed, he held in his hands a candle, in a whisper continued in prayer and made the sign of the cross." After a while it seemed to Murometsev that Khomyakov was better, which he intended to tell his wife: "I am sending the good news that, thank God, you are better." "*Faites vous responsable de cette bonne nouvelle; je n'en prend pas la responsibilité,*"[49] said Khomyakov to Murometsev, almost jokingly. "Of course you are better, look how you have become warmer and your eyes have brightened up," observed Murometsev. "And tomorrow how bright they will be!" answered Khomyakov. "These were his last words," says Murometsev. "He saw more clearly than we did that all these signs of an apparent recovery were merely his last exertions of life. A few seconds before his end he firmly and in full consciousness signed himself with the cross. Alexei Stepanovich Khomyakov died well."[50] He died so well because his heart sensed the live touch of divine power toward which he strove—the touch of power that conquers death, giving to people the assurance of a joyful, personal future life. "I give them eternal life, and they shall never perish," said the Savior of the world.[51]

CHAPTER 9

Manifesting the Light Invisible

Placed in the arena of the circus, Martyr Ignatius the Godbearer said in a loud voice: "Men of Rome, looking upon my present struggle! You know that not for some kind of unlawfulness am I condemned to die, but for the sake of my one God, by love for Whom I am encompassed and to Whom I earnestly strive. I am His wheat and will be ground by the teeth of the beasts so that for Him I will be pure bread."

—*Menologion*, Book 4, 560

Before beginning the main subject matter of this chapter, we consider it necessary to make the following introduction. When studying modern philosophers, we often come up against differences in their understanding of terminology. If for Christian ascetics these differences occurred as a result of inadequate contact in their era among the writing brethren, then the reason for these same phenomena at the present time is hidden elsewhere.

These days, when the movement of philosophical thought is splitting up into many schools, when philosophy has begun to be elaborated in its complex details, among these schools there have arisen endless disputes concerning both subject matter and also philosophical language—disputes that make it difficult for the disputers to agree with one another in exact and uniform terminology. There is a dispute going on even concerning terms that have already entered into general use, and therefore it would seem that they could not provoke any doubts as to their meaning. We are dwelling now on this phenomenon because it concerns us personally in regard to a term that is of utmost importance to us. Namely, we are talking about the term "Logos" and what we should understand by this word, and also by the words "religion of the Logos" and the expression "strugglers for the Logos"—the expression we have chosen to define the subject of this chapter.

In my opinion, to the word "Logos" should be ascribed the same meaning that St John the Divine gave it; therefore, by the words "philosophy of the Logos" and "religion of the Logos" should be understood Christian religion and philosophy. Now strugglers for the Logos are those people who in their lives and words devoted themselves to the work of defending Christian beliefs and ideas, thereby upholding and strengthening them in the public consciousness. What serves as the basis for our understanding is first of all the main rule of rational terminology—to use a term in that sense that everyone is accustomed to understand it, as the term has already been adopted by the overwhelming majority of people.

All of us who belong to the Christian world know that the Gospel of St John has inspired the whole Christian world with the understanding of the Logos in the sense of divine power creating the universe, in the sense of power creating the light of men, and finally, in the sense that the Logos is the incarnation on earth of the Son of God, Jesus Christ. The Gospel of St John has been read by the whole Christian world and it is accustomed to the word "Logos" precisely in the same sense that divine revelation has spoken of it to mankind. With its content, Christianity gave life to the ancient idea of the Logos, and the great word "Logos," having received after the Gospel of St John a holy meaning for Christians, became the lasting inheritance of the whole Christian world. This is why when using the expressions "life in the Logos "and" strugglers for the Logos," we apply in these expressions the word "Logos" in precisely the Christian sense.

———————

And so let us talk about the strugglers for the Logos in the sense that Christians understand this term, that is, let us talk about people who in their lives and words devoted themselves to the work of defending Christian beliefs and ideas and in this way upheld and strengthened them in the public consciousness. We already saw in the examples cited in the last chapter what miracles of spiritual power people manifested in the last minutes before death—people who felt with their hearts a personal living God. From this sensing of a personal living God, from this sensing of the God–man close to mankind, conquering death, an ever-living God, there was born in them another great state of consciousness—consciousness of personal joyous immortality given by the living God to every man who strives toward God. And man, when earthly death approached, passed over into the other world with triumphant peace, passed over to Him Who first conquered death—to the God–man Jesus

Christ. This life that triumphs over death, given by the personal living God-head, accomplished among Christians miracles of extraordinary power, in all ages and under all conditions. But it manifested its power in particular brilliance during the early Christian era. The "Light Invisible," shining forth then from its great spiritual Sun, accomplished in this era miracles of superhuman power. Inflamed by the fire of this light, people burned brightly in the struggle for its propagation. The power of this light was something special; it issued forth from a mysterious fountain and it surpassed immeasurably any human energy that could come from a man's small "I." "The origin of Christianity," says S. N. Bulgakov,

> is bound up with the mysterious, miraculous birth into the world of a new faith and new life. On the day of Pentecost, tongues of fire coming down on earth kindled a religious flame, blazing up into an all-world, historic fire; the light and warmth of this fire are enlightening and warming us to this day. Faith in the risen Savior with invincible power blazing up in the world, the feeling of His actual presence, streams of Divine love and forgiveness wrested from souls religious songs of prayer, joy, reconciliation, rapture and love, which hitherto had never resounded in the world. Early Christianity is represented in the history of Christianity as those forty days after the resurrection, when the Lord, though invisible, is close and appears to His waiting disciples, answering the call of a burning heart. He appears to them during their daily work of catching fish and blesses their work by His taking part in it; on the way to Emmaus He is met as an unknown traveller and reveals Himself to them "in the breaking of bread"; He is indulgent of their doubting and gives tangible proof of His realness, and at the same time is triumphantly revealed as having all power in heaven and on earth. The early Christian atmosphere is imbued with a feeling of the continual working of the miracle of an incipient worldwide transfiguration.[1]

Here is what we experience as a reflection of this burning of spirit in early Christian times: Now has begun the second millennium since these first flaming impulses; but the light emanating from there gives forth its warmth even to us, people of this age of reason; it makes itself felt in those who with attentiveness pause in their study of the spiritual struggles (*podvigs*) accomplished in the early centuries. This light warms our hearts in spite of our all being enclosed in cold universal rationalism—a rationalism striving to create its own cold religion without the living God.

To convince the reader of the extent back then of the power of this mystical light penetrating the hearts of men, we present several scenes from early Christian life. We took these scenes from the *Menologion* and from material collected by Christian historians.

The framework of our endeavor has not permitted us to pause on the numerous examples of the manifestation of this power, but these few cases with which the reader will become acquainted are sufficient to judge concerning the bearers of Light, the great strugglers for the Logos in the first centuries.

The first strugglers for the Logos were martyrs of Christianity. Martyrdom is a heroic period of Christian history. Exercising world dominion at that time, the Roman Empire had many reasons to persecute Christians. In the eyes of the Roman authorities, Christianity represented a rejection of the pagan order of things; it represented a rejection of the religion, way of life, mores, and social life of the empire. The rulers and pagan priests considered Christians to be conspirators and mutineers, shaking the foundations of government and society. And the people, the uneducated heathen masses, took their lead from the powers above. The masses, attached to their pagan cult and their festivals, at first sincerely hated the representatives of the Christian movement; they considered them to be godless and eagerly assisted in executing the punishments of the pagan law upon them.

In our time, it is doubtful that we can draw an exact picture of this malicious hatred toward Christians, says F. W. Farrar. It already had manifested itself as early as the reign of Nero. This monster in human form, of course, could not have transferred from himself to the Christians the terrible suspicion of setting fire to his own capital had he not known that they were the object of the people's hatred. To deflect public rumor harmful to himself, Nero (says Tacitus) publicly imputed guilt to people hated for their disgraceful practices, people whom the common folk called Christians. Recalling the condemnation of Christ by Pontius Pilate, Tacitus adds that "this terrible superstition, having been suppressed for a time, appeared once again, not only among the Jews, where this evil had arisen, but even all over the city which is a public sewer and capital of all that is either repugnant or shameful."

Among writers of that time, it was the custom to describe Christianity in just the way Tacitus did. Pliny, in his letter to Troyan, calls Christianity "a repulsive and monstrous superstition, aggravated still more by a stubbornness and unbending obstinacy." Svetony calls it "a new and pernicious superstition." "Christians are public enemies" was the general verdict of the Romans; "People of a disgraceful, unlawful and desparate faction."[2] This hatred was aggravated by the fact that people of various free professions that actively served paganism (and there were many such people) understood perfectly well that with the spread of Christianity there appeared the threat of losing the work dear to them, and therefore they all stirred up the crowd against the Christians as much as they could. As Farrar says,

> All those who worked in preparing idols, selling flowers, obtaining sacrifices, architects of temples, sculptors, artists, decorators, oracles, soothsayers, augurs, astrologers, gladiators, wrestlers, athletes, actors, mimics, singers, dancers, tavern keepers—this whole mass of dissolute people who received their livelihood from furnishing criminal pleasures— all of them rose together against the Christians whose triumph threatened to be their downfall.[3]

And here the cries "Down with the godless ones!" and "Throw the Christians to the lions!" at the beginning of the Christian movement were the most common cries not only in Rome, but also in other cities in the amphitheaters of Greece and the Roman colonies.

> But despite all this, despite fire and pillory, the swords of thirty legions and the burden of constant persecution, Christians, both old and young, rich and poor, gloriously stood their ground and remained exaltedly steadfast. They looked joyfully upon the plundering of their possessions, knowing that they were destined for a far better possession and abode. They went bravely to death, because for them death was life. And as a consequence they conquered the world, and through the darkness and disturbance of the ages passed on to us the blazing torch of revelation and truth.[4]

In the matter of the spreading and strengthening of Christianity, martyrdom was of primary significance. Carefully writing down the dates of the martyrs' deaths, Christians gathered together on these days to celebrate their memory. In the Christian Church, there were special scribes who wrote down everything that happened to Christians in prisons and tribunals. During the time of the first persecutions of Christians, Pope Clement placed these scribes in various districts of Rome. Despite the fact that the pagan government threatened these scribes with the death penalty, the notations continued uninterrupted for the whole time of the persecutions. These records, in which one can sometimes find detailed information concerning the questions of the judge–torturers and the martyrs' answers to them, are known as *The Acts of the Martyrs*. Among these acts, one comes across whole court proceedings composed during the very time of the judgment of the martyrs. This is a copy of the official court records that Christians obtained from the pagans for a high price.[5]

Our *Menologion* is filled with accounts of the martyrdom of saints. Included among these accounts are many that are a direct retelling of what was written in *The Acts of the Martyrs*. To give the reader an exact understanding of the kind of terrible trials the martyrs had to endure before their death, we cite here first, as an example, what was written down about the sufferings experienced by three Antiochean martyrs for their steadfast confession of faith in Jesus Christ. The names of these martyrs were Trophimus, Sabbatius, and Dorymodontus. This was in the third century during the reign of the Roman Emperor Probus.

Back then, to the tribunal of the ruler of Antioch, Heliodorus, were brought among others two people, Trophimus and Sabbatius, openly confessing Christ. Heliodorus ordered them to be separated from one another and had Trophimus brought to him first, whom he began to question concerning his name, life, and faith.

The Christian answered, "My name is Trophimus and I was born of free and noble parents; but having fallen under the power of sin, at first I lived godlessly, until through holy baptism I received true freedom and nobility."

Then the tribune asked, "What is your faith?" Trophimus answered, "I already told you, but listen—I will tell you more clearly: I am a Christian, a slave of Christ and I wish to be a sacrifice to Christ." The tribune asked, "Are you a foreigner or a Roman citizen?" Trophimus answered that he was a traveler. At this, the judge asked, "Have you read the imperial decrees concerning Christians?" "I read them," answered Trophimus. "But what are they to us? Between godliness and demonic delusion there is such a difference as between day and night." The words drove Heliodorus into a rage; he ordered Trophimus to be stripped and, with arms and legs stretched out, to be beaten mercilessly. The martyr was beaten for so long that the earth became crimson with blood. Later, the judge ordered them to stop beating him and said, "Offer sacrifice to the gods, Trophimus, otherwise I will send you to Phrygia, to Dionysius." (Dionysius was famous for his cruelty and inhumanity, explains the chronicle.) Trophimus answered, "It is not important to me whether I am to be killed by you or by someone else, whether you torture me or Dionysius; either way, there will be only one death, because the both of you have one intention: to kill those who serve the true God." The tribune became even more enraged; he ordered the saint to be hung on a tree and his body to be tortured. Straightaway he was surrounded by executioners with sharp instruments with which they tortured the martyr, slicing his body to the bone and even to his very innards. The martyr said softly, "O Lord, help Thy slave!" After these torments Trophimus was thrown in prison. Next, the other Christian, Sabbatius, was brought to the judgment seat and the tribune asked him, "I am not asking you if you are a Christian, but first you tell me: What is your calling?" Sabbatius answered, "My calling, dignity and fatherland, glory and riches, are Christ the Son of God, ever present; His providence establishes and rules the universe."

The judge, taking this answer as an insult to himself, became enraged and, striking him on the cheek, said, "Answer the question you are being asked, and before I destroy you by means of tortures; approach the gods and offer them sacrifices." When Sabbatius refused to do this, at Heliodorus's command he was hung up and torn by iron claws until his bones were laid bare. Because whole pieces of flesh had already fallen from his bones and his insides were all torn, there was nothing left for the torturers to lacerate. Therefore they unbound him from the tree, and Sabbatius at that moment gave up his soul into the hands of his Lord.[6]

After this, Heliodorus, despairing of turning Trophimus from Christianity to paganism, sent him from prison to the ruler of the Phrygian city of Sinad, Dionysius, with a letter informing him of his inability to prevail over this unyielding Christian. When Trophimus was brought to Dionysius, the latter said to him, "You remain unsubmissive and call upon the ineffectual and useless Christ, who was guilty in the death of many people.... Give up the hope which you had in Him, offer sacrifice to the gods so you will be delivered from cruel torments and death." Trophimus did not yield; he endured all the torments and firmly expressed his readiness to die for Christ. Dionysius ordered Trophimus to be scourged with a heavy whip and meanwhile said to him, "Just promise to offer sacrifice to the gods and straightway you will be delivered from torments."

Trophimus was silent. At his command, Dionysius's men took vinegar and, mixing it with mustard, poured it into Trophimus's nostrils. After this, they hung him on a tree, cut into his sides, inflicting deep, oblong wounds, and from his ribs issued streams of blood. Seeing Trophimus's tenacity, Dionysius said, "Your hope is in vain, Trophimus, and your thoughts are futile; for who will come to you from heaven and deliver you from your present suffering?" Trophimus answered, "I will never renounce my true and living

God."[7] Then Dionysius in a rage said to the servants, "Torture him more." And they began to torture him with extreme cruelty, burning his ribs with lit candles. After this, they again threw Trophimus into the prison.

In the city where these tortures were taking place, there lived a senator by the name of Dorymedontus. He was a Christian, but hid the fact for fear of Dionysius. Learning of all that Trophimus endured, on his part he did everything he could to lighten his sufferings. He often came secretly to Trophimus, managing to see him in prison, washed away his blood, wiped his scabs with clean towels, bound his wounds, and cared for him in every way. Word of this reached Dionysius. Designating soon after an official worship of the gods on the pagan festival to Dioscuri,[8] Dionysius ordered Dorymedontus to be present at the worship service. Dorymedontus refused. Then Dionysius commanded that Dorymedontus be brought to him. Being satisfied from the words of Dorymedontus that he was a Christian, he ordered him to be arrested. A short while later, Dionysius sent his confidantes to Dorymedontus to persuade him to repent, but this proved unsuccessful. The next day Dionysius went to the tribunal and ordered Dorymedontus to be brought in. "You deluded man!" he said to Dorymedontus. "What happened to you yesterday that you forsook the gods and refused to obey the command of the Caesar? Can it be that you are not pleased that you are respected by all and that you occupy among us a position of no mean rank?"

Dorymedontus answered to this, "He who loves God sets no value upon worldly honor and glory." Dionysius, at first with kindness and later with threats, tried to persuade Dorymedontus, but getting nowhere, finally ordered him to be stripped and to commence the torturing; he commanded that Dorymedontus be hung up and his ribs burned with red-hot iron stakes. "Let me see if Christ comes to help you," said Dionysius meanwhile. Despite the tortures, Dorymedontus remained a Christian and cursed the pagan gods. Then Dionysius turned his anger on the servants who were torturing Dorymedontus and reproached them for not being able to enforce silence on a man who was cursing their gods. Becoming enraged, the servants tore the saint's face with iron claws and knocked out his teeth.[9]

Later, they lit a fire under the martyr and put him on the hot coals. It was to no avail. Finally, they threw Dorymedontus into prison. Dionysius began to take council with those close to him concerning what kind of death they should sentence Trophimus and Dorymedontus to. They decided to feed the martyrs to the beasts in the circus.

Whence did Christians draw this terrible strength to oppose paganism? A clear and precise answer to this question is given by one of the confessors of the Christian faith, Cyprian of Carthage, who himself died a martyr's death in 258. In one of his treatises, Cyprian writes, "Christ Himself was present at the struggle of those battling and striving for His name. He Himself encouraged, strengthened, inspired. And He, Who once conquered death, always conquers in us.... He not only looks upon His slaves, but He Himself contends in our person; He Himself battles along side of us. He crowns those who strive and is Himself crowned."[10]

From these words of the struggler for the Logos, Cyprian, we clearly see the kind of power of faith in the personal living God that was in the martyrs—the power of faith in the God-man Jesus Christ. And what could the pagan god do against this living power? For example, what could the abstract god do here, such as the god of the Roman Emperor Marcus Aurelius, persecutor of Christians, a god born of the cold speculation of the Stoics? This god must undoubtedly be conquered by the Christian God—by the living and true God, as He was called by the martyr Trophimus.

In the *Menologion,* we have hundreds of similar martyrdoms of Christians, taken from *The Acts of the Martyrs.* These descriptions vary according to the circumstances of each martyrdom, but generally they are similar in character, and what we just saw in the above-cited examples typifies perfectly the general rise of the spiritual power of Christians in their heroic struggle with paganism.

The steadfastness and immovability of the sufferers who bravely went to death worked powerfully on the hearts of the pagans. Under the impression of the titanic power of martyrdom, the pagans themselves began more and more to turn to Christianity. In this way, the blood of Christian martyrs, as expressed by the Christian writer of the second century, Tertullian, was the seed for new Christians.

We cite here another account of martyrdom that gives a vivid picture of that heroic era. From this account, one can see how powerfully martyrdom back then influenced the hearts of people not totally ruined in a moral sense by paganism. This event is described in the fourth book of the *Menologion,* on the 19th day of December. It is called "The Suffering of the Holy Martyr Boniface."

We cite this event from the chronicle in abbreviated form. During the reign of the Emperor Diocletian (in the time of the four rulers), there lived in Rome a woman by the name of Aglaida; her father had at one time been a ruler of the city. She was young and beautiful, owned rich estates inherited from her parents, and lived a free life without a lawful husband. She had a faithful slave who managed her household and estates; he was young and handsome. His name was Boniface, and Aglaida lived with him, satisfying her fleshly desires. At that time, there was severe persecution of Christians. As the chronicle says, a thick, idolatrous cloud covered all of the East, and many of the faithful were tortured and killed for Christ. To Boniface's mistress, Aglaida, came the thought and unconquerable desire to have in her home relics of the martyrs. She instructed Boniface to obtain without fail such relics. Aglaida gave Boniface much gold because it was impossible to obtain the bodies of martyrs without gifts and gold. The torturers, seeing the Christians' strong love and zeal for the relics, did not give them away for free, but rather sold them for a high price and in such a way made big profits for themselves. Boniface took from his mistress much gold, also prepared many perfumes, linens, and all that was needed for wrapping up the bodies of the martyrs. Taking with him numerous slaves, helpers, and horses, he made ready to depart.

As he was leaving the house, he said laughingly to his mistress, "And what will you do, my lady, if I find not the body of a martyr, and my body, tortured for Christ, is brought to you instead—will you accept it then with honor?" Laughing, Aglaida called him a drunkard and sinner.

Boniface reached Asia Minor and the famous Cilician city of Tarsus; in this city at the time, a cruel persecution was raised up against Christians, and the faithful were subjected to severe tortures. Leaving the slaves at the inn, Boniface told them to rest and he, not stopping to rest, went straightway to see the sufferings of the martyrs of whom he had heard earlier. Coming to the place of torture, Boniface saw a multitude of people gathered to watch the Christians as they were brought to torture. The tortures laid upon them were various and sundry: One was hung upside down while on the ground under him was lit a fire; another was tied in the form of a cross to four poles; another lay sawn asunder; another was lacerated with sharp instruments; another's eyes were gouged out; another was dismembered; another was put on a stake that was lifted up and secured in the ground so that it pierced his body up to the neck; many had their bones broken; and another's arms and legs were cut off so that he rolled on the ground like a spool.[11]

At the sight of these terrible sufferings, at the sight of the steadfastness with which the Christians endured the tortures, Boniface shuddered in his heart. As related in the chronicle, he was filled with divine fervor and, standing in the middle of the place where this was happening, he began to embrace all those who had shown themselves to be martyrs, of whom there were already twenty people, and cried out in a loud voice, "Great is the Christian God! He is great because He helps His slaves and strengthens them in such great torments!"

Having pronounced this, he once again began kissing the martyrs. By doing this, he drew to himself the attention of all those present at the torturings. When the tribune who was overseeing the tortures saw this foreigner Boniface displaying such strange behavior, he ordered him to be apprehended and brought to him. "Who are you?" he asked Boniface. "A Christian," answered Boniface. "I came here from Rome; but if you want to know the name given me by my parents, then I am called Boniface."

"And so, Boniface," said the tribune, "approach the gods and offer them sacrifice, or else I will rend your body and bones." But Boniface proved himself a steadfast Christian. He did not submit to the tribunal's demands. Then he also, like the other martyrs, was subjected to tortures, and having endured the torments, passed away while confessing himself to be a Christian.

In the meantime, Aglaida's slaves who had come with Boniface to search out relics, knowing nothing of what had transpired, sat at the inn and waited for Boniface. Seeing that he had not returned by evening, they were surprised; then not seeing him all night and the next morning as well, they began to judge him and speak disparagingly of him (as they recounted later on), assuming that he had gotten drunk somewhere and was spending his time with prostitutes.

They said, laughing, "This is how our Boniface has come to look for relics!" But as he did not return the next night and the following day, they became perplexed and began to search for him, walking throughout the whole city asking for him. By chance they met a man who was the brother of the head of the prison and asked him whether he had seen a certain foreigner who had arrived there. He answered that the day before a certain stranger, having suffered for Christ at the place of torments, had been sentenced to death and was beheaded with a sword. "I do not know," he said, "if this is the one you are searching for. Tell me, what did he look like?"

They described Boniface's outward appearance, that he was not tall, had red hair; they also described other facial features. Then this man told them, "Surely this is the very one you are seeking!" But they did not believe it, saying, "You do not know the man we are looking for." And conversing among themselves, they remembered Boniface's former character and reviled him, saying, "Would a drunkard and profligate suffer for Christ?!" But the brother of the prison warden insisted that he was right.

"From your description of his outward appearance, this man was indeed tortured at the tribunal yesterday and the day before," he said. "Besides, what is keeping you? Go yourselves and look at his body lying on the place where he was beheaded." They set out after this man and came to the place of torture where a military guard stood so that the bodies of the martyrs would not be stolen by the Christians. Going on ahead, the man pointed out to them the beheaded martyr lying there and said, "Is this not the one you are looking for?" When they saw the martyr's body, they at once began to recognize their friend, and when his head, which had been lying separately, was joined to the trunk, they were completely convinced that this was Boniface and were greatly amazed; and at the same time they began to feel shame because they had thought and spoken badly of him.

Then they gave the torturers 500 gold coins and took Boniface's body and head. Anointing them with aromatic ointments, they wrapped them in clean shrouds and, putting them in a reliquary, left for home, taking the martyr's body to their mistress.[12]

Learning of this, Aglaida was horrified, and she remembered Boniface's words that he had said upon leaving. On her estate, which was situated fifty stadia from Rome, Aglaida built a wonderful church in the name of the Holy Martyr Boniface, says the chronicle, and placed his holy relics in it.

After this, Aglaida herself, having distributed all her possessions to the poor and needy, renounced the world and, living another eighteen years in great repentance, died in peace and was joined to the Holy Martyr Boniface, being placed alongside his sepulchre.[13]

Thus ends this brilliantly artistic account of the chronicle of the martyrdom of Boniface.

In explaining the circumstances that are spoken of in this chronicle, we should say here that one of the distinctive features of Diocletian's persecution (when Boniface was martyred) was the extraordinary cruelty of the tortures, reaching the highest degree of brutality. According to the French historian of early Christianity, Allard, this is testified to not only by the hagiographic writings, but also by eyewitness accounts, such as the historian Eusebius. Another feature of this persecution was the great number of martyrs slain at a time; in some places, says Allard, there were put to death ten, twenty, thirty, up to sixty and even a hundred in a single day.[14]

One should mention here that up until the time of Diocletian's persecution (303–305), Christianity had spread in the eastern part of the empire to such a great extent that believers already made up the majority of the population.[15] That Christianity at that time was very widespread can be seen from what we have just read in the chronicle about Boniface, namely, how Aglaida's slaves regarded Boniface, saying of him, "Would a drunkard and profligate suffer for Christ?" Already from these words we can see that in the eyes of the slaves accompanying Boniface Christianity stood very high, that in essence they themselves were already secret Christians.

Diocletian's persecution was one of paganism's last efforts to wipe out Christianity. After this unsuccessful attack, paganism, of course, was obliged to surrender. Soon after this, in 311, Galerius, Licinius, and Constantine issued a general decree of religious tolerance. And not for long did the Christian church have to wait for its complete triumph.

These few pages on martyrdom are sufficient to judge the nature of the heroic struggle of Christianity for the Logos. We will say no more concerning other similar cases of martyrdom. Neither will we recount the martyric deaths of such famous saints as Ignatius the Godbearer, suffering under the Emperor Troyan, or Polycarp of Smyrna, suffering under Marcus Aurelius. The martyrdoms of these saints are well known even from textbooks. Now we will turn to another type of defender of the faith, after the church had become established in the world, which had become, for the most part, Christian. We will turn to outstanding pastors of the church, protecting Christianity from within from any influence that that might weaken the spirit of the true faith.

We have a whole series of examples of the apologetic and homiletic works of the defenders of the religion. The labors and lives of the ascetic strugglers, Athanasius the Great, Basil the Great, Irenaeus of Lyons, Tertullian the Cyprian of Carthage, Clement and Origen of Alexandria, Martin of Tours, Gregory the Theologian, John Chrysostom, and Ambrose of Milan are examples of spiritual energy, interesting for studying the era when Christianity was growing, developing, and, finally, came together into its definitive forms; when the many councils, ecumenical and local, came together to decide church and dogmatic questions.[16] That was the time when Christianity lived an ebullient inner life, when interest in questions of the spirit caught up everyone, beginning with the lower levels of the population and ending with the highest. At that time, there arose various currents in Christianity; they arose in the direction of extreme asceticism (montanism) and in the direction of materialism (chiliasm). Back then, Christians were drawn toward other religions: to Judaism (the Ebionites), the religion of Zoroaster (the Manicheans), and so forth. Then in Christianity there appeared various interpretations of Jesus Christ's Divinity; there appeared what we call heresies: Arianism, Apolinarianism, Nestorianism, Eutychianism, and so forth. This internal life of Christianity itself, this conflict of differing opinions, required a tremendous effort on the part of the leaders of the Christian movement to understand all of these currents and not deviate from the main channel along which the fundamental ideas of the religion should develop.

From all these differing opinions, shaking the essence of the Christian faith, opinions captivating contemporary minds, by far the most interesting movement of the time is the movement created by Arius. It is interesting for us because in this movement one can sense a similarity with what is now going on in the present age within our intelligentsia, calling themselves Christian. As we will see further on, the Arian heresy strove, as much as was possible under the circumstances of that time, to rationalize the Christian religion. Arianism, in its subtle and outwardly acceptable form of interpreting the Christian God (its particular understanding of the relationships of the Hypostases in the Holy Trinity), led the adepts of this interpretation to renounce the Godhead in Jesus Christ. Arius strove, in essence, to lower Christ to man and in this way to diminish His significance as the Godhead. The Christianity of Arius was the creation of the human spirit, and not divine revelation.

In Chapter 8, we saw in the example of Tolstoy's religion what also appears in the present era as the striving to rationalize the Christian religion—only this is carried out in a different way. What is created under the pretext of "Christian teaching" is a religion without a live, personal God and, moreover, deifies man himself. We, just like Jesus Christ, are consubstantial with God, imagine to themselves the Tolstoyans, Theosophists, and many others. In this way, with them Jesus is also put on a level with men, only this is done in a different way. This is done by deifying man. This is done through faith that every person can himself win for himself divinity, can unveil God within himself,[17] with his own personal powers, with his own personal spiritual struggle. Naturally, with such views the teaching about divine revelation and grace given by Christ, as adopted by Christians, loses its meaning and significance with Tolstoyans, Theosophists, and others. According to their understanding, in the matter of religion every man can be his own revelation. In the fourth century Arius, considering himself a Christian, could not bring himself to go so far in his rationalism as Tolstoy has done now. Back then, he did not dare even think of affirming that man was consubstantial with God. In those times, human pride did not venture to flatter man so temptingly and boldly. The Christian religion was always a religion of humility, and not pride.[18]

But let us return to our subject. To give the readers an understanding of the nature of the apologistic strugglers for the Logos of that era, we will now inform them concerning two of the very greatest activists of that time fighting against the Arian movement, namely, Athanasius the Great and Basil the

Great, fervently standing in defense of faith in the living personal God Jesus Christ, for it is precisely in this faith that the main essence of the Christian religion consists.

Athanasius the Great was born in Alexandria in 297, fifteen years before the famous edict of Constantine halting the persecution of Christians and allowing the subjects of the empire to freely receive the Christian faith. The childhood of Athanasius coincided with a period of persecution of Christians under Diocletian. The time when Athanasius entered the arena of public service (when he was about twenty years old) coincided with the beginning of the triumphant flourishing of Christianity.

As we already said earlier, that era was remarkable in that all of Christendom lived a deeply religious life. The extent to which interest in everything religious seized people at that time is apparent from the following event described by the historian Rufus, an event concerning the early youth of Athanasius. It seems that at the time even children were attracted to the Christian religion, were attracted by its cult. Here is the interesting case. At that time in the city of Alexandria where Athanasius was raised, the Christian metropolitan was Alexander, taking over the cathedra of Archbishop Peter, who had been martyred by the pagans.

One day Alexander, as the historian Rufus recounts, was celebrating the anniversary of the death of his martyred predecessor, Peter, and awaited several of his clergy at the feast in his home. His windows opened out to the sea, and as he stood looking in the direction of the harbor, he saw a group of boys on the shore. They were playing at religious ceremonies. Assuming that the children had gone too far in their play, the metropolitan told some of the clergy to look into these games and then ordered them to bring the boys to him. After some pressuring the boys admitted that in their game they had made their comrade, Athanasius, bishop, and that he baptized those of them who were catechumens by submerging them in the sea with all the established forms.

Metropolitan Alexander, finding that the questions at baptism were asked in the proper way and the answers given were correct, decided to acknowledge this baptism as valid, but completed it with chrismation. He summoned the parents of the boys who acted as priests and advised them to raise them to enter the clergy. Athanasius he allowed to finish his education and then had him come to live in his own house.[19]

The young Athanasius soon became secretary to Metropolitan Alexander. When still a very young man, Athanasius attracted to himself universal attention with his treatise "On the Incarnation." This work revealed Athanasius's burning conviction in the truth that all of Christianity is concentrated in the Divine Person of the Savior.[20] Athanasius quickly became the metropolitan's right hand; he was the chief activist who inspired Alexander in the latter's incipient struggle with Arius.

Arius was a priest in one of the most ancient churches in Alexandria. Not many years of Alexander's bishopric had passed before he began paying serious attention to the teaching of his priest, which was beginning to become widespread. When Athanasius was made archdeacon of Alexandria, at which time his influence on Alexander became considerably stronger, Alexander understood the danger which Arius's teaching represented to the Christian Church. To resolve the arguments that had arisen with Arius, at first Alexander felt it necessary to summon a council of his clergy in Alexandria.

This council was convened in 321. At this council by far the strongest opponent of Arianism was Athanasius. His steadfast conviction that Christ is God incarnate gave Athanasius's words unusual power. At this council Arius's teaching was condemned by the Alexandrian Church. It is interesting to note that the dispute with Arianism at the time caught up all Christians in the Alexandrian Church. To spread his teaching, Arius resorted to the most widespread publicity. He put his teaching to rhythms, accompanying them with songs. Arius's songs resounded on the lips of fishermen and peddlers; meanwhile, his views were the subject of disputes among the clergy.

But Arius, as we already said, thanks to the persistence of Athanasius, was condemned by the local Alexandrian Council; he himself and his followers were excommunicated from the church. However, Arius did not consider himself defeated by this. He withdrew himself to Palestine and turned to the local bishops with complaints about his unjust excommunication and succeeded in having another local council convened in Nicomedia by Bishop Eusebius, which acknowledged Arius's teaching to be correct. In such a way, the matter began to catch fire; it reached as far as Constantine the Great, and to resolve the question concerning Arianism, it became necessary to convene an Ecumenical Council, which was opened by the emperor personally in Nicaea on July 5, 325.

———————

The main task of the Nicene Council was to compose a definition of the faith (symbol). The council diligently studied the question of Arius's teaching. The majority of the council sessions were devoted to this matter. More than once, Arius was invited to the sessions to defend his teaching. He displayed all the power of his eloquence, but he found for himself a powerful adversary in the young Deacon Athanasius, whom Metropolitan Alexander put forward at the council as a talented apologist for the true faith.

And here there began a great dispute at the Ecumenical Council. Arius, speaking of Jesus Christ, expressed propositions from which it follows that the Son of God is created; he maintained that between the Father and the Son there could be no consubstantiality, but only likeness in nature. In this way, by denying in the Savior His perfect Divinity, Arians were in reality atheists within Christianity.[21] They strove to diminish the significance of Christ.

On the contrary, Athanasius, firmly convinced that Christ is God incarnate, insisted that He is consubstantial with the Father. "Arians call themselves Christians," exclaimed Athanasius, "and at the same time have changed the glory of God into the likeness of corporeal man."[22]

Arius considered Christianity to be a subjective revelation, a product mainly of the human spirit. Athanasius accepted Christianity as the divine revelation of eternal, objective facts.[23]

The power of truth in Athanasius's words acted irresistibly. To no avail, Bishop Eusebius of Nicomedia, who sympathized with Arius, offered to the fathers of the council for their acceptance the Arian creed; it was rejected with obvious disapproval. The council acknowledged the Son of God "uncreated" and "consubstantial with the Father." The Greek word *"homoousia"* (consubstantiality) became the main bulwark of the Orthodox faith, says Farrar.[24]

When the symbol of faith[25] accepted at the Nicene Council was read, Emperor Constantine offered everyone to sign it. The Orthodox signed it; many of the Arian bishops signed it, even Eusebius of Nicodemia. Only Arius and two of his faithful adherents, Theon and Secundus, rejected the Nicene Creed. Then all three were excommunicated from the church and were divested of their cathedras. The emperor exiled them to Illyria.

––––––

And so Athanasius's undertaking appeared to be finished in the sense of the triumph of the true faith. But it just seemed that way at first. In essence, despite the decision of the Nicene Council, this matter was far from being over. Persecution of Athanasius and trials for the church from Arianism were still ahead; they were about to begin with great force.

The Arian bishops signed the Nicene Creed insincerely. After the council, they began plotting and intriguing against the defenders of this creed. Soon they managed to take control of important cathedras in the empire (Antioch, Caesarea). Eusebius of Nicomedia, who more than anyone supported Arius at the Nicene Council, was able to gain the trust of the Emperor Constantine. He succeeded in dispelling Constantine's prejudice against Arius. Arius was returned from exile. The Arians concentrated all their energy against their chief enemy—Athanasius—who during this time had been made patriarch of Alexandria after the death of Alexander in 326. Eusebius of Nicomedia prevailed upon Emperor Constantine to require Athanasius to receive Arius into communion with the Alexandrian Church. Of course, Athanasius could not give in to Constantine's demand to return Arius to Alexandria. This refusal enraged Constantine, making him receptive to all sorts of lies and slander against Athanasius.[26]

These slanders did not take long to appear—there arose accusations against Athanasius, accusations that were totally unbelievable. For instance, one accusation was no less than murder and sorcery. This accusation charged that Athanasius had apparently murdered Arsenius, bishop of Ipsus, had cut off his hand and used it for sorcery.

With all these accusations, the Western bishops, of whom the great majority belonged to the Arian party, met in 335 in Tyre with the emperor's permission to judge Athanasius. Although Athanasius did not find it difficult defeating all these charges and defending himself (he defended himself against the charge of murdering Arsenius by presenting Arsenius himself at court alive and with both hands), nevertheless, this did not disarm Athanasius's enemies. They set new traps. The emperor, seeing their determination in persecuting Athanasius and fearing major disturbances within the church, considered it best to remove Athanasius from Alexandria for a time. In 336 he sent him to Gaul. But in this very same year Arius died, and in 337, the Emperor Constantine the Great also passed away.

The new ruler of the East—Emperor Constantius—at first returned Athanasius from exile. But Athanasius was not to stay long in Alexandria; again snares were set for the defender of the Nicene Creed. Circumstances turned out unfavorably for Athanasius. Constantius became a rabid Arian, and he too began to persecute Athanasius. We will not recount here all the misfortunes that Athanasius had to undergo during the reign of Constantius for his steadfast confession of the faith. We will say only that more than once he was forced into exile. This took place not only under Constantius, but also during the reign of Julian the Apostate and the Emperor Valens.

Valens, just as Constantius, was a confirmed Arian and fervently supported the Arian creed. But neither exiles, nor threats, nor diverse deprivations to which Athanasius was subjected (many times the life of this great struggler was in danger)—nothing could shake his confession of the faith. He continued, as much as he was able, to fight against Arianism. He influenced his flock; while in exile, Athanasius was in constant contact with bishops faithful to the Nicene Council, and every time when conditions became favorable for Athanasius and he was able to return to his flock (during this time, the emperors changed often and under the reign of a new one, Athanasius would be called back), he did everything to return the church to harmony and he accomplished this.[27] And here, after the reign of Julian the Apostate, Arianism finally began to weaken.

We must note that the simple people, in the majority, did not like the Arian teaching. It had difficulty taking root in the simple-hearted belief of the people. Besides this, it met with stubborn opposition in monasticism and asceticism of that time, which greatly influenced the masses. So the great defender of the Logos, Athanasius, lived almost his whole life in distress, exile, and constant struggle for faith in Jesus Christ. He was bishop of Alexandria for forty-six years, about twenty of which he spent in exile (five exiles in all). He died on the 2nd of May, 373, at the age of seventy-six, in full control of his bishopric.[28] As bishop after him, he placed a loyal friend, the presbyter Peter. Farrar, in his analyses, says that Athanasius the Great represents in Christian history an example of such a pure and noble man as the church saw only at the time when the Apostle Paul accepted a martyr's death in Rome. Athanasius, in his faith, was firm as a rock; at the same time, this was a man who attracted everyone to himself with his extraordinary meekness and greathearted patience.[29]

———

The struggle for the Logos in the era when the Orthodox world was shaken by the Arian heresy revealed many examples of how people of spiritual endeavors, while appearing weak in all externals, firmly confronted imperial despotism and vanquished it with their spiritual power.

Besides Athanasius, we see further another such example in the person of Basil the Great; this was the continuator of the defense of the Nicene Creed after Athanasius's death. In this matter, Basil had to withstand a serious ordeal from the Arian Emperor Valens, and in the end Valens was obliged to retreat before Basil. The latter was able to unite Christian forces and direct them toward the victory of the universal recognition that Christ is true God. This victory of the Nicene Creed came into effect two years after Basil's death, in 381, at the Second Ecumenical Council (of Constantinople). Basil's spiritual trial began soon after he assumed the cathedra of Caesarea, while Athanasius was still alive. Right after his election, Basil was obliged to endure a fierce attack by the Emperor Valens, who, under the influence of the Arian bishops, was striving to raise up the Arian standard over the East and spared no means to accomplish his purpose.

Valens, in his fight with Orthodoxy in Caesarea of Cappodocia, used the services of one of his courtiers; for this he chose the praetorian prefect Modest, well known for his cruelty. Modest was inquisitor during the reign of Constantius, offered sacrifices to idols under Julian the Apostate, and changed to a baptized Arian under Valens.[30]

In 372 Valens sent this Modest to Caesarea with the intent to break Basil's power. Modest arrived in Caesarea accompanied by the Arian bishops. Basil's friends advised him to flee, but he remained and bravely awaited the storm.

We will cite in detail the scene of Modest's discussion with Basil. This discussion is very characteristic.

Modest called Basil to himself. "Basil," began Modest, "what do you want to accomplish with your obstinacy and impertinent opposition to the great imperial power?" "What do you mean?" answered Basil, "What obstinacy?" "All the bishops," said the prefect, "gave in and humbled themselves; you are the only one that refuses to accept the religion of the emperor (the Arian Creed). What do you think of us? You really think we are nothing?" "You, prefect," said Basil, "are one of the most brilliant of men, but you must not be honored more than God." "How is that, you mean you are not afraid of my power?" "Why should I be afraid of it?" answered Basil. "What can they do to me?" "What can they do? Everything that is in my power," proudly answered Modest. "For example?" asked Basil. "Confiscation, banishment, torture, death," answered the prefect. "And that is all," said Basil.

None of this frightens me. He who has nothing cannot be subjected to confiscation, unless you wish to take away these worn out and ragged clothes and the few books which constitute all my possessions. Banishment? I have not the slightest understanding of it. I am not bound to any place. This earth on which I now live is not mine, and any country to which I could be exiled is all mine, or more truly, is all God's, in which I am only a stranger and sojourner. Torture? I do not have the kind of body that could withstand torture: one blow would be sufficient, and it is this one blow alone that you have in your power. And concerning death—death is a benefactress, for she will all the more quickly bring me to God, for Whom I live and Whom I serve.

"No one has ever answered Modest so boldly," exclaimed the astonished prefect. "No one has ever spoken with such fearless confidence!" Answered Basil,

Apparently you have never met a bishop before—otherwise, he most certainly would have talked in this way, carrying on the dispute in similar fashion.... Where there is a question about God, we look only upon Him; and in this case, fire, sword, wild beasts and iron nails which tear the flesh, are sooner for us luxury than fear. Therefore, insult me, threaten, do all you want, delight in your power. And let the emperor hear about this as well. You, in any case, will not convince me to enter into union with dishonor, even if you threaten me with worse things.

Basil's words disconcerted the prefect; he could not bring himself to use force against the bishop. Returning with all haste to the emperor, he said, "Emperor, we are vanquished by the bishop of the Church. He stands above threats, is too firm for arguments, too strong for convincing. We must try with someone higher up. Why this man will never submit, will never give in to threats, will yield to no one, except possibly overt force."[31]

After the death of Athanasius, Basil the Great remained the most influential defender of the Nicene Creed in the East. Finally in 378, there was a cessation to persecutions of Christians who acknowledged Christ as God Incarnate, of one essence with the Father. In that year their last persecutor, Emperor Valens, perished.

The new emperor of the West, Gratian, summoned from imprisonment all the bishops exiled by Valens; and his Eastern co-ruler Theodosius I, at the Council of Constantinople, gave final victory to the supporters of the Nicene Creed. Basil the Great, having worked to prepare this victory, did not live to see it by two years; he died in 379. We portrayed his death in the previous chapter to show an example of how the holy ascetics died with such greatness of spirit.[32]

———

Nothing communicates the spirit of this era so vividly as examples of actual people and descriptions of the stirrings of their soul. No kinds of reasoning of logical deductions from historical facts, no matter how well founded, can give those real-life pictures that are involuntarily drawn in the eyes of the reader when he becomes acquainted with an account from a primary source, if that primary source is composed by a gifted hand. Therefore, in our accounts about people of Christian spiritual struggle, we have striven, wherever possible, to keep to those vivid examples and portrayals that we found in several of the chronicles, taking these accounts almost in their entirety, except for a few abbreviations. It is in these stories from the lives of individual people, that we now, in this chapter, acquaint ourselves with the era of struggles for the Logos, the struggles of the martyrs and apologists in the first centuries of Christianity. In these fragments that we have taken, we feel their internal overall bond, we feel the nerve of this whole movement. This nerve, giving life-strength to this movement, consists in people's fervent faith in a living, personal God. This faith in the Divinity of Jesus Christ, attaining the power of visible certainty, showed to the world the victory of the Christian religion. But likewise, as before in earlier parts of our work, after scenes of this heroic movement in defense of the Logos, we now cannot but be transported in our thoughts from the Light of the phenomena described to the darkness of our present life, to our present era that, in contrast to the early Christian era, could easily be called the age of the weakening of the life of the spirit in men's hearts.

The coming generations will have to live through terrible trials, and these trials have their profound meaning. So that the work of the God–man may triumph, there must be dangers and upheavals; they are sent to people so that they come to their senses. "How else can those who are caught in the bonds of the carelessness of external happiness be sobered up, except by sorrows and misfortune," say Christian ascetic strugglers.[33] And here, when these misfortunes are released, when these dangers are released, when finally everything is in turmoil, then the words of the fervent Christian ascetics, the words of the fervent strugglers for the Logos, powerful in the higher reason—the words of the people who carry in their hearts the Light Invisible—will finally be heard and felt. Then people will see anew the great spiritual strivers in all their greatness, in which they appeared to the world in the first centuries of Christianity.

AFTERWORD

In the examples of the lives of the saintly people cited in this book, we see the reflection of that Light that illumined the souls of righteous people, kindled their hearts with flaming love, inciting them to heroic deeds that were humanly impossible. Great is the power of this Light. If the power of the visible sun seems enormous, giving physical life to the whole earthly world, then unutterably more immense and infinitely greater must be the power of the invisible Sun that illumines the spiritual life of people, binding into one their hearts and conquering, as we saw, the power of physical life.

The law of physical life, drawing its energy from the energy of the physical sun—this is the law of the life of forms—of forms struggling each for its own sustenance, and struggling with one another—this is the law of the struggle for existence. The law of the life of the spirit,[1] drawing its energy from the Light Invisible, poured out by the Logos—this is a law whose theses are directly opposite to the law of the struggling physical world. It is the commandments of Christ: "Love your neighbor as yourself,"[2] and "Love your enemies; do good to those who hate you."[3] The energy of the physical sun is transformed on our earth into a diversified life of forms, into the physical life of the earthly world with its laws. The energy of the immeasurably higher invisible Sun gives life to the spiritual world, gives life to the hearts of men. But it pours out the power of its Light (Grace) only on those who themselves strive toward it, sensing in advance that it is their unobscured source.

In the struggle for existence, the victor of all struggling forces on earth is man. He may deserve to be called king of the earth.

Man has conquered everything on earth; but he has not conquered one thing, the most important thing. He has not conquered with his own efforts the evil within his own being. This evil consists in man's egotism—the source of his passions, which nothing can satisfy, full of bitterness, and causing him to suffer.[4] And this evil is inherent in man because he joined himself

193

together with egotism when he waged war with nature and with those who interfered with his life; and this is what he wanted. Egotism not only nestles in man's passions, but also lives steadfastly in the instrument of his thought, in his intellect, which is devoted to egotism and pride.[5] And here we see the power of egotism ruling everyone on earth. This is the general phenomenon of our life.[6]

For man to conquer the evil of egotism, he needs another power, a power higher than man, a power that once and for all uproots evil. For man to rise above himself, he needs another support, higher than his egotistical nature. And man thirsts for this higher power and support; he thirsts to rise above himself, because into his very nature is placed a deep striving to another life—to a truly joyous life, full of love, unpoisoned by feelings of envy, pride, or malice. And here, the Great Source of this love, the Logos Himself, sends down upon people the power they thirst for. This is the Light Invisible, this is the reflection of the universal divinity, the energy of the invisible Sun, able to give to man not only true happiness but also eternal life.

And man, if only the life of his heart has not been completely extinguished, if there is even a faint glimmer of this life in him, he himself senses that Light—the Light of a higher power. And it exists, this power—the power of the invisible Sun—because it kindles man's sensing of the Godhead into a great flame, kindles it in those who strive toward the spiritual Sun, to the true living God. "He who stands in the sun is warmed in his body," says one of the Christian ascetics. "And so he who thinks only of God and divine things is warmed in the spirit. The longer this is done, the more it increases. Finally, the spirit takes fire. This is the kind of fire which the Lord came to enkindle on earth," concludes this same ascetic.[7]

This fire, lit by the Savior of the world, lit by the spiritual Sun, is not an imagined power, as many people think. This is a real power, leading to real results. Even now we sense the Light Invisible from this fire in the examples we have cited from the lives of the saints; we sense it in the works of the ascetics whom we have quoted in brief.

Great is the power of this divine fire. It will not be extinguished by the darkness of human delusions born of egotistical passions—men's pride and self-exultation—and "the darkness comprehended it not," said to us more than 1,800 years ago by the Evangelist John the Divine, announcing the "Light of men."

Terminology of the Christian Ascetics Relating to the Understanding of the *Higher Reason* and *Lower Reason*

Although in the writings of the Christian ascetics of the *Philokalia* we did not come across the expressions *higher reason* and *lower reason*, yet judging by many facts, it seems that undoubtedly the concepts contained in these words were known to them long ago.

We cited in the introduction of this book the words of St Anthony the Great, from which it is obvious that he discerned these concepts, although he gave them a different terminology, calling, for example, the higher reason simply the *mind* or the *good mind*.[1]

We will cite a few more definitions of the authors of the *Philokalia* relating to this current subject. We found a treatise on the question of two human reasons by an ascetic of the *Philokalia*, Theodorus of Edessa. This saint cites in his "Contemplative Word" this parallel. He says,[2]

We call natural knowledge that which the soul can receive through research and investigation, using natural aptitudes and powers, concerning creation and the Author of creation—of course—to the extent this is accessible to the soul which is bound with matter, for the energy of the mind becomes weak from its contact and intermingling with the body, and therefore it cannot be in immediate contact with mental things, but must think of them in the imagination, the nature of which is to create spatial and full bodied images[3] [material in three dimensions]. And so the mind, insomuch as it is in the flesh (that is, according to our terminology, the lower reason), has need of corresponding images of things in order to think of them and understand them. Now the kind of knowledge which the mind, as it is, receives by these natural means, this we call natural. But supernatural knowledge is that . . . in which what is known relatively, surpasses the mind bound with the flesh, so that such knowledge is obviously peculiar to the bodiless mind.

Further on in the teaching of Theodorus of Edessa, one sees that this bodiless mind (cleansed of all material passion) is permeated with divine love and overshadowed by divine grace and that these conditions lead it to "supernatural knowledge." It is obvious that by this bodiless mind Theodorus of Edessa understands what we understand by the expression *higher mind.*

Something similar to this view is also expressed by St Isaac of Syria. He says that a man of holy life can attain to a special knowledge—spiritual knowledge—which is the sensing of something mysterious. This aforementioned knowledge St Isaac contrasts with natural knowledge (or, as he calls it, the first stage of knowledge). According to the meaning of St Isaac's sayings, his terms *spiritual knowledge* and *natural knowledge* have the very same meaning, according to our understanding, as the *higher mind* and the *lower mind.*[4]

The eleventh-century ascetic St Symeon the New Theologian very definitely distinguishes the higher reason from the lower reason. He calls the higher reason the mind of Christ, divine knowledge, and secret wisdom as distinguished from human knowledge (the lower reason), which he calls *external knowledge.* We cite here his exact words concerning this. He says, "Those who are in the darkness of passions, whose mind is darkened by ignorance of spiritual things . . . consider to be irrational he who has the mind of Christ; but he who does not have the mind of Christ, i.e., divine knowledge and secret wisdom, they consider him to be rational because he possesses human knowledge and external wisdom."[5]

Finally, distinguishing the difference between the higher and lower reasons was assimilated also by the Russian Christian ascetics, educated on the writings of the authors of the *Philokalia.* Hence the ascetic St Seraphim of Sarov in his treatise "On the Keeping of Recognized Truths" says, "With a worldly man one should speak of human matters; but with a man who possesses spiritual reason one should speak of heavenly matters." It is obvious that by spiritual reason St Seraphim understands here what we understand by the words *higher reason.*[6]

In general, one must say that in almost every spiritual writer of the *Philokalia* one sees a similar difference in terminology, and this difference can be discerned not only in regard to the terms *higher* and *lower reason*, but also in regard to other extremely important definitions concerning the subject of spiritual super-consciousness. Thus in our book *Super-Consciousness* we pointed out that the higher contemplative state in prayer, which all the Christian ascetics understand identically, in their writings, bear different names. By some it is called spiritual prayer, by others mental prayer, by yet others prayer of the perfect, and also prayer of the heart.[7] This diversity in terminology makes the investigation of the works of the Christian ascetics considerably more difficult, and in order to understand them clearly, it gets to the point where one must first of all familiarize oneself with the expressions of each ascetic. The diversity in the philosophical terminology of the Christian ascetics is explained by the fact that in the era when their main work was created, communication between people was very difficult, and each of the ascetics himself searched for his expressions for defining his thoughts. This diversity is also explained by the fact that as yet book printing did not even exist.

A Short Biography of M.V. Lodyzhenskii

Mitrofan Vasil'evich Lodyzhenskii (1852–1917) was born on February 15, 1852, to Vasilii Vasil'evich and Ol'ga Alekseevna Lodyzhenskii. Both of his parents, as well as three of his four sisters, went on to become monastics. He graduated from the Agricultural Institute in St Petersburg in 1873, after which he worked as a senior forester in the Vologda province. He then served as sheriff in the Tula province, Chern county. From 1884 to 1886, he was chief of the Forestry Department. From May 2, 1896, to August 8, 1898, he was the vice-governor of Semipalatinsk, and later held the same position in Vitebsk (from August 8, 1898, to May 18, 1902), Stavropol, and Mogilev. He was awarded the Orders of St Vladimir (third and fourth degrees), of St Stanislav (second and third degree), and of St Anna (third degree), all of these being civil decorations awarded by the Russian Empire. He was included in the sixth part of the books of noble lineage in the Tula province in 1898.

After retirement, Lodyzhenskii turned his attention to literary work, focusing on the relationship of esoteric philosophy with Christianity. In the summer of 1910, he and his wife Ol'ga Aleksandrovna lived in the village of Basovo, near Yasnaya Polyana, home of Tolstoy, with whom he maintained contact. When that summer Lodyzhenskii visited Tolstoy, their conversation touched on Hindu philosophy, yoga, Theosophy, hypnotism, and science. Accompanying Lodyzhenskii and his wife was S. V. Chirkin, former manager of the Russian consulate in Bombay, who told Tolstoy about India. In late July 1910, Tolstoy visited Lodyzhenskii specifically in order to become acquainted with the *Philokalia*, and later expressed his regret at not having been previously familiar with it. On August 4, 1910, Tolstoy, accompanied by D. P. Makovitskii, visited Lodyzhenskii in Basovo, where they talked about Christian ascetics.

Before his return to traditional Orthodox Christianity, Lodyzhenskii was a friend of both A. L. Volynskii and the occultist P. D. Uspenskii, as well as a member of the Russian Theosophical Society. He spent time in both India and Japan. At a meeting of the Religious-Philosophical Society dedicated to the question of Theosophy on November 24, 1909, Lodyzhenskii declared: "It is possible to be both a true Christian and a true Theosophist." Subsequently, however, he became convinced that this was not the case and renounced Theosophy.

Light Invisible, which was published in 1912, is the second of a series entitled The Mystical Trilogy, the first volume of which is titled *Super-Consciousness and Paths to Its Acquisition* (1906) and the third called *The Dark Force* (1914).

In his 1914 review of *Light Invisible*, Sergei Sergeevich Glagolev, Professor of Apologetics at the Moscow Theological Academy, remarked: "In his book, Lodyzhenskii simply, clearly, and convincingly establishes the apologetical significance of mystical phenomena from an Orthodox perspective."

Lodyzhenskii reposed on May 18, 1917.

NOTES

All references to the *Philokalia* are to the classic Russian language edition of St Theophan the Recluse, organized in five volumes, which will not correspond to the four volumes currently available in English.—Ed.

Introduction

1. John 1:1,3–4.

2. M. V. Lodyzhenskii, *Super-Consciousness and Paths to Its Acquisition* (2nd ed.; St Petersburg, 1912).

3. St Isaac of Syria, "Homily 30," in *Works*, 133.

4. *Philokalia*, 2:617.

5. Regarding spiritual love that unites men in God, we have another, no less profound saying of the ascetic of the *Philokalia*, St Isaac of Syria: "There is love," he says, "like a small lamp, which as the oil becomes used up burns out, or like a downpour of rain which ceases when the rain water becomes depleted. But there is love like a fountain of water gushing up from the earth, which never becomes depleted. The first is human love, and the second is Godly (spiritual), having God as its author" (*Philokalia* 2:661).

6. Lodyzhenskii, *Super-Consciousness*, 238.

7. I. V. Popov, *St John Chrysostom and His Enemies*, 13–14; Chrysostom, 4:507–8.

8. Ibid.

9. Such as, for instance, Schopenhouer, Fichte, Helmholtz, and others. See G. I. Chelpanov, *The Brain and the Soul* (4th ed.), 200.

10. *Epigones* are followers of Kant, so-called neo-Kantians: Rickert, Cohen, and others.

11. Vladimir Ern, *Struggle for the Logos*.

12. Vyacheslav Ivanov, "On the Meaning of Vladimir Solovyov," in *Collections of Vladimir Solovyov*, 41.

13. We say that this knowledge of the laws of nature is only approximate because even the most adept scientists admit that fundamental scientific principles are *approximate truths*, barely true within fixed bounds. Outside these bounds they lose their exactness. See Lebon, *The Evolution of Matter*, 222.

14. Lodyzhenskii, *Super-Consciousness*, 21–24.

15. A. Besant, *Ancient Wisdom*, 21.

16. *Philokalia*, 3:279.

17. 1 Cor 8:1.

18. "Saying of the Ascetic Abba Evagrius," in *Philokalia*, 1:573.

19. *The Philosophy of Mysticism*, 306.

20. *Philokalia*, 2:670.

21. Ibid., 2:657.

22. L. N. Tolstoy, *Works*, (1886 ed.), 12:288. Italics ours.

23. Henri Bergson, *Creative Evolution* (trans. M. Bulgakov; Moscow, 1909), 228. Italics ours.

24. L. N. Tolstoy, *A Confession* (*The Mediator* [Posrednik]), ch. 12, 57. We quote this section from Tolstoy's confession: "During this whole year, when almost every minute I was asking myself whether to kill myself with a noose or a bullet, during all this time, alongside these thoughts and observations of which I spoke, my heart was anguished with a tormenting feeling. This feeling I cannot describe otherwise than as a searching for God. I say that this searching for God was not reasoning, but rather feeling, because this searching had *its source* not in the course of my thoughts—for it was even in indirect opposition to them—*rather it had its source in the heart*."

25. Lodyzhenskii, *Super-Consciousness*, 306–7.

26. In Christian history, we have an extraordinarily vivid example of such a rebirth in the conversion of the rabbi Saul into the Apostle Paul. "To the former rabbinic wisdom," says V. V. Rozanov, "he does not attach a new link—faith in Christ—no, he cast from himself rabbinism. The relation within himself is precisely that of Saul and Paul, mutually devouring one another's 'I.' And so it has been with everyone converting to Christ: devouring *of* the old by the new" (V. V. Rozanov, *Dark Visage*, 253).

27. I. V. Popov, *The Mystical Justification of Asceticism*, 29.

28. St Isaac of Syria, "Homily 43," in *Works*, 183.

29. *Philokalia*, chs. 13–16.

30. Lodyzhenskii, *Super-Consciousness*, chs. 13–6.

31. See further regarding these analogies in Chapter 2, 38–40.

32. Lodyzhenskii, *Super-Consciousness*, ch. 17. According to the teaching of St Macarius the Great, these faculties are called *charismas*; in them are revealed the mystical unity of the *soul* with God (Popov, *Mystical Justification*, 26).

33. *Philokalia*, 2:607.

34. Bishop Theophan, *The Path to Salvation* (9th ed.), 130–1.

35. K. P. Pobedonostsev, *Moscow Collection*, 115.

36. Popov, *St John Chrysostom and His Enemies*, 36.

37. Bishop Theophan, *The Path to Salvation*, 99.

38. Lodyzhenskii, *Super-Consciousness*, 327.

39. I. V. Popov, *The Concept of Deification in the Ancient Eastern Church*, 30–31.

40. Rozanov, *Dark Visage*, 265.

41. Ibid., 89.

42. William James, *The Varieties of Religious Experience*, 66.

43. Bishop Alexei, *Byzantine Church Mystics of the 14th Century* (Kazan, 1906), 27.

44. K. P. Pobedonostsev, *Moscow Collection* (Moscow, 1827), 106.

45. St Basil the Great, *Works of Farrar* (Deshyovaya Biblioteka Suvorina).

46. Although in the words of these ascetics we did not come across the expressions *higher reason* and *lower reason*, of which we spoke before, but judging by much data, it would appear that the concept contained in these words were undoubtedly well known to them. Only regarding these concepts, the ascetics had a completely different and also extremely varied terminology. Some of the ascetics called the higher reason the *higher mind*, others the *incorporeal mind*, still others *spiritual knowledge*, and so on. Regarding the ascetics' terminology, we have cited detailed information in Appendix 1 of this book. The ascetics' terminology concerning the lower reason is also cited there.

47. It would be appropriate here to make reference to the fact that the expression *mysticism* is understood differently by different writers and philosophers. For example, Professor Alexander Ivanovich Vedensky, in his book *Philosophical Essays* (1st ed.; St Petersburg, 1901, 44) says that mystical perception should be defined as direct (i.e., not acquired by means of any reasonings or deductions) knowledge of that which does not constitute part of the outside world, but which at the same time is not of ourselves and our emotional states, and also inner knowledge, that is, arising without the help of outer feelings. According to this understanding of mystical perception, Professor Vedensky excludes from the realm of mysticism clairvoyance,

telepathic, and mediumistic phenomena, because they are, in his opinion, external phenomena. Contrary to Vedensky's understanding of mystical perceptions, according to Vladimir Solovyov's definition of *mysticism*, cited in the text of the present book, mediumistic and telepathic phenomena (actions at a distance) and also animal magnetism and visions are all a part of mysticism.

William James, speaking of mysticism in *The Varieties of Religious Experience*, characterizes mystical states by two main indicators, their *inexpressibility* and *intuitiveness*, and these states relate to the *sphere of emotions*. Moreover, he generalizes these states quite broadly, reckoning among them all states of intoxication, even alcoholic intoxication.

Besides these, there are other definitions of mysticism by other authors, but we have confined ourselves to the aforementioned definitions as the most typical.

48. V. Solovyov, "Mystery and Mysticism," in *Dictionary of Brockhaus and Ephron*, 37:454.

49. Regarding super-consciousness, see *Super-Consciousness*, chs. 13–14.

50. Ibid., chs. 10–12.

51. Ibid., 298.

52. This word refers to the rites during the mysteries; the Greek ecclesiastical writers used this word when speaking of the sacraments: the Eucharist, baptism, and so forth.

Chapter 1

1. St Cassian the Roman, *Philokalia*, 2:125.

2. St Symeon the New Theologian, *Homilies* (1st ed.), 175.

3. Matt 11:28.

4. S. N. Syromiatnikov (Sigma) "Impenetrable Partitions" (*Russia*, April 8, 1912). This article castigates the modern-day haughty psychology of the rich bourgeoisie.

5. *Philokalia*, 5:344.

6. "The Sayings of St Anthony the Great," in *Philokalia*, 1:33.

7. William James, *The Varieties of Religious Experience*, 358.

8. "The Sayings of St Isaac of Syria," in *Philokalia*, 1:705.

9. "Life of Varlaam Khutynsky," in *Menologion*, 3:123.

10. "Address of Abba Isaiah," in *Philokalia*, 1:323.

11. Here it is interesting to note how vividly Tolstoy was able to express the contrast between our real life and the demands of that side of a man which we call morals, the basis of which lies in religion. For example,

Tolstoy, in describing his early years in *A Confession*, tells, in passing, a merciless truth that typifies the actual relationship to life in the environment in which he moved. Tolstoy writes, "Every time I attempted to say that I wanted to be morally good, I met with derision and mocking, but no sooner would I give myself up to vile passions, I was praised and encouraged. Ambition, love of power, mercenariness, sensuality, pride, anger, revenge— all this was respected."

12. Nicholas Berdayev, *Philosophy of Freedom*, 174–5.

13. By far the most striking example of this soulless heathen Caesarism we now see in the relations of England with her colonies in India, where the emperor of India (who is also the king of England) is the oppressor of the Indian people, exploited by the English in subtle forms, which are in essence even more cruel than the exploitation that was practiced by the Romans during the ancient Roman empire.

14. *New Times* (February 11, 1912).

15. A saint of the eleventh century, Symeon the New Theologian, spoke with special fervor against the selfish power of gold, the power of accumulating riches, although in his era this power was not nearly as strong as at the present time. But everything that Symeon said then, he could in all rights repeat now. He said, "The devil counseled us to acquire for ourselves, consider our own property, and to store up for ourselves that which God created for the general use of all men, through this love of gain to implant in us two sins and make us deserving of eternal torment. The first sin is heartlessness and mercilessness and the second sin is putting one's hope in one's possessions, and *not* in Christ" (*Homilies*, 192).

16. We took this expression *stony insensibility* from the famous prayer of St John Chrysostom, in which among twenty-four petitions raised to God, there is expressed the supplication for man's deliverance from *stony insensibility*, that is, from the extinguishing in man of the feeling of love for his neighbor. The expression *stony insensibility* vividly defines the bourgeois hardening of man that we see at every turn.

17. It does all it can in this direction, spending billions of our nation's savings on general armaments.

18. This is what the sixth-century ascetic St Isaac of Syria says about Christian patience: "Patience is the mother of consolation, a kind of strength usually begotten of expansiveness of heart. It is difficult for man to find this strength in his sorrows without its being granted by God, obtained through persistent *prayer*" (St Isaac of Syria, "Homily 79," in *Works*, 391).

19. Here is the place in St Isaac of Syria's work from which the analogy is taken. "Listen now," says St Isaac, "how a man becomes refined, comprehends spiritual things, how he becomes like the bodiless spirits.... When his soul, having abandoned everything earthly, begins with its consciousness to penetrate that world which is hidden from the physical eyes, when it is lifted up into a higher spiritual world, when it strives to feel through experiences the future spiritual life, longs for the coming of this life, strives to know its mysteries, then the experiential feelings of these mysteries descends upon this man and fills and devours his consciousness; then man becomes an entirely bodiless spirit.

"Then his consciousness can be carried away into the *bodiless (superphysical) realms, can touch the depths of the intangible sea*, know the wonderful wisdom of Divine activity, the wisdom of His governing in the natures of mental and sensual beings, comprehend spiritual mysteries with a simple and subtle mind. Then a man's inner feelings are awakened for those sensations which belong to the future life of immortality and incorruption. Then, even during a man's life in this world, impressions from the spiritual world are perceived by him as if he had finally passed over into it" (*Super-Consciousness*, 326).

20. Max Wilhelm Meyer, *The Making of the World* (trans. under editorship of Sergey Pavlovich Glazenap, St Petersburg, 1902), 84.

21. Ibid., 422.

22. The astronomical term *light-year* represents the distance that a ray of light travels in one year. In one second, light travels the equivalent of five circumferences of the earth, in other words, about 300,000 kilometers. In the course of a year, a ray of light travels the dizzying speed of about 10,000,000,000,000 kilometers. So as not to write this long number, it is accepted in astronomy to express the enormous distances between heavenly bodies using a particular unit—the light-year. Thus, the closest star to us in the constellation Centaurus is four light-years from the earth. Sirius is eight light-years from us, and so on. Now the majority of stars visible to the naked eye, to which number we could add the new star of which Azbelev speaks, are so far from the Earth (as he expressed it, from this tiny particle of matter in the universe) that the distance to these stars is determined in 200–300 light-years.

23. N. P. Azbelev, *Unity in the Structure of the Universe* (St Petersburg, 1902), 303.

24. Carl du Prel, *The Philosophies of Mysticism*, 67.

25. James, *The Varieties of Religious Experience*, 507.

26. St Isaac of Syria, "Homily 55," in *Works*, 251.

27. Regarding which of these two types of spiritual striving to give preference to in the ascetic's work of attaining perfection, the opinions of the ascetics themselves concerning this were different depending on their personal inclination to one or the other type of spiritual striving. In our book *Super-Consciousness* (257), we cited the opinions of Nilus of Sinai and Callistus of Talikud, expressing their preferences for asceticism and anchoritism. On the contrary, the active type of spiritual athletes such as, for example, Athanasius the Great, considered the active striving to be the higher path. Thus, in one of his letters to a monk–ascetic who refused the post of bishop, St Athanasius wrote that the ascetic life is less elevated and helpful than a life spent in fulfilling one's official duty (F. W. Farrar, *Lives of the Fathers*, 1:372.) We find a viewpoint that reconciles these two diverse opinions in St Gregory the Theologian, who in one of his writings expresses himself thus: "Do you wish to give preference to activity or contemplation? Vision is the work of the perfect, but action (activity) is for the majority. They are both lawful and excellent, but strive toward that which your nature requires" (ibid., 489). Finally, according to Macarius the Great, the main benefit of asceticism consists in this: (1) In solitude a person can examine himself attentively (clearly see his sin), (2) a person in seclusion concentrates his strength on the fight, and (3) a person who leaves the world delivers himself from the atmosphere of evil (I. N. Popov, *The Mystical Justification of Asceticism*, 85ff.)

28. We speak of a measure close to perfection, but not perfect, for according to the teaching of spiritual strivers, there can be no perfect people on earth. St Isaac of Syria says, "[T]here is no limit to perfecting oneself because perfection even of the perfect is in truth imperfect" (St Isaac of Syria, *Works*, 71:366.)

29. The development of these abilities is directly connected with various other abilities of a person and, mainly, with the strength of his emotional energy. This development depends on the degree of practice in spiritual endeavor and chiefly on man's cultivating within himself feelings of humility, during which divine grace overshadows a person and strengthens his natural energy to an extraordinary degree. St Isaac of Syria, speaking of the higher contemplative state of spiritual prayer, explains that the mental movements of this prayer, because of strict chastity and purity, are capable of receiving the action of the Holy Spirit (St Isaac of Syria, "Homily 21," in *Works*, 104).

30. Alexander Vedensky, *Philosophical Essays*, 45.

31. Vladimir Solvyov, "The Philosophical Bases of Integral Knowledge," in *Collected Works*, 1:289.

32. N. A. Berdyaev, *Philosophical Freedoms*, 242.

33. We cite the account of the event as it appears in the life of St Proclus, in *Menologion*, 3:563–6.

34. *Menologion*, 3:566.

35. *Menologion*, 3:449, 450.

36. I. V. Popov, *St John Chrysostom and His Enemies*, 14.

Chapter 2

1. Some of these spiritual instructions may be found in English in *Little Russian Philokalia*, Vol. 1, St Seraphim, 5th ed. (Platina, Calif.: St Herman of Alaska Brotherhood, 2008). —Ed.

2. P. D. Uspenskii, *Tertium Organum* (St Petersburg, 1911), 163–5.

3. About the higher reason, see Introduction, xx–xxx.

4. Seraphim explained that the acquisition of the Holy Spirit of God is the acquiring, the attaining of this, that "the Holy Spirit dwells in our souls." This is attained through the virtues and chiefly through prayer (Leonid Denisov, *The Life of St Seraphim, Wonderworker of Sarov*, 322–3). In our book *Super-Consciousness,* we said that the way of the ascetic begins with retraining the feelings of the heart and with the development of energy directed entirely toward the sensations of higher, altruistic emotions, and only then, when the heart is melted down and refined in its emotions, when it is kindled by the highest feeling of love, *then, according to the understanding of Christian ascetics, will come to dwell in man's heart the power of the Spirit*—a power, according to the religious experience of Christian ascetics, by far more powerful than man's cerebral energy, no matter how developed the latter may be (M. V. Lodyzhenskii, *Super-Consciousness*, 129).

5. Regarding the lower reason, see Introduction, xv–xx.

6. Letter 1463, in *Collected Letters of Bishop Theophan the Recluse* (8th ed.), 216.

7. Our research on the life of St Seraphim was facilitated by the richness of biographical material about him. Seraphim is the Orthodox saint closest to us in time, and information on him has not been obscured by legends. Seraphim's first biographers, Archimandrite Sergius, Archimandrite George, and Hieromonk Joseph, knew him personally; they even had the opportunity of living for a long time with Seraphim in the Sarov hermitage when they were monks. They gave much reliable information on his life of spiritual endeavor. Subsequently, in historical

and other journals over the past fifty years, there have appeared valuable reminiscences about Seraphim by people who met him personally. Therefore, we have in the *Menologion* (1904 ed.) a detailed description of Seraphim's life. Finally, in 1904 in Moscow a life of Seraphim was published that was compiled from primary sources by Leonid Denisov—a highly detailed and conscientious work (700 pages). For our account we have for the most part used material from the *Menologion* and from *The Life of St Seraphim* by Leonid Denisov.

8. Regarding contemplative faith, see *Super-Consciousness* (2nd ed.), 271.

9. Regarding the life of form and the life of the spirit, see *Super-Consciousness*, 45–48.

10. Prochorus's father died when Prochorus was only three years old.

11. Here is an excerpt from Seraphim's own account of this: "She put her right hand on my head, and in her left hand she held a crozier and with this crozier she touched wretched Seraphim." See Denisov, *The Life of St Seraphim*, 64.

12. Ibid., 78.

13. Seraphim's own account of this occurrence, as he himself told it, is presented in detail by one of Seraphim's first biographers, his contemporary, Igumen George, who knew Seraphim well, having lived at that time in the Sarov monastery under the name of *G'iri*. See Denisov, *The Life of St Seraphim*, 70–72. See also the account of Igumen George, 14–16.

14. St Isaac of Syria, *Works* 45.

15. Ibid., art. 17, 69

16. Concerning the heart, as the organ of spirituality, see *Super-Consciousness*, 129–31. The process of this vision is analogous to a sleepwalker's seeing through his solar plexus.

17. William James, *The Varieties of Religious Experience*, 412–3.

18. *Menologion,* 5:70.

19. Ibid., 71–72.

20. See *Super-Consciousness*, ch. 14.

21. To supplement that which we cited in *Super-Consciousness* concerning humility and repentance (261–2), we cite regarding this subject the words of one of the Eastern ascetics, Symeon the New Theologian. He says that man communicates of God's mysteries only if he ascends to the height of spiritual knowledge *by way of humility* without vainglory and self-love (St Symeon the New Theologian, *Homilies* [2nd ed.], 88) and that "*repentance* dispels our ignorance and brings us to a knowledge of human things, and later brings us to a knowledge of that which is higher than

us—Godly things, the mysteries of our faith, invisible and unknowable for the unrepentant" and those who repent of their sins "by the force of their repentance and to the extent they have acquired purification, they receive enlightenment" (ibid., 86). Concerning Seraphim, he has this to say about humility: "Let us love humility and we will see the Glory of God; for where humility flows forth there pours out the Glory of God" (Denisov, *The Life of St Seraphim*, 435.)

22. Regarding the Jesus prayer, see *Super-Consciousness*, 305–20.

23. *Menologion*, 5:87.

24. Regarding the lower reason and the higher reason, see Introduction, xv–xxx.

25. We have elaborated in detail on the psychology of this burning of the spirit and heart in *Super-Consciousness* in the rubric about spiritual prayer, 313–4.

26. Denisov, *The Life of St Seraphim*, 420.

27. As, for example, the testimony of the witnesses Monk Peter, Hierodeacon Alexander, and the superiors of the Lyskovsky community, Plescheyeva. See *Stories about Seraphim by His Contemporary, Monk-Priest Joasaph* (St Petersburg, 1885), 161–3, 167–8.

28. Denisov, *The Life of St Seraphim*, 82.

29. *Candid Accounts of a Wanderer to His Spiritual Father*, 31.

30. Denisov, *The Life of St Seraphim*, 426.

31. The monastery chronicle tells of the attacks on Seraphim by the evil spirit. These attacks were almost the same as those endured in the wilderness by St Anthony the Great.

32. *Menologion*, 5:76.

33. Merezkovsky, *Not Peace But a Sword*, 144–5.

34. See Introduction, regarding internal and external truth and conscience, xxv–xxvi.

35. "Sayings of Diadochos, Bishop of Photiki," in *Philokalia*, 3:65 .

36. James, *The Varieties of Religious Experience*, 348.

37. The essence of this latter spiritual struggle, as Leonid Denisov says, consisted not in outward withdrawal from sociability but in silence of the mind, in the renunciation of all worldly thoughts for the fullest devotion of oneself to God (Denisov, *The Life of St Seraphim*, 98).

38. *Menologion*, 5:83.

39. St Symeon the New Theologian, *Homilies*, 541–2.

40. *Menologion*, 92–93.

41. Ibid., 110.

42. Ibid., 88–89. This place later began to be called Fr Seraphim's near hermitage, and the spring called Fr Seraphim's well.

43. In this sack, Seraphim had a book of the Gospels and weight from rocks and sand for mortifying the flesh.

44. *Menologion*, 105.

45. Visokogorsky *pustyn'* (hermitage) is located in Vladimirsky province.

46. *Menologion*, 94.

47. Uspenskii, *Tertium Organum*, 225.

48. It is interesting here to compare Seraphim's clairvoyance with something similar attained through Raja yoga about which we spoke in detail in our book *Super-Consciousness* (218). There we cited instructions that Raja yoga exercises develop the so-called *astral vision*, that is, the ability of a person to see outwardly the astral and mental worlds and in these worlds or planes to see the *aura* of each person, which by changing its form and color reveals the secret movements of man's soul; but such *astral vision*, as A. Besant explains, is nothing like *spiritual vision;* this latter vision, by definition, is spiritual penetration by which a person instantly perceives the truth. St Isaac of Syria calls this penetration, or as he says, *knowledge,* supernatural, given by divine power (ibid., 298). Now it was precisely this knowledge, in this case clairvoyance, that Seraphim possessed.

49. *Menologion*, 93.

50. For example, there are interesting accounts about Seraphim in the records of Nevrov, printed in *Russian Antiquity* (June 1880), 234–8, and in the notes of Gen. Otraschenkov, printed in the *Russian Herald* (1879), 267–70.

51. It is mentioned in biographies that General L. later informed others that he had traveled throughout all of Europe and had seen a multitude of people of all different kinds, but this was the first time in his life that he had seen a man of such clairvoyance; the elder revealed to him his whole life.

52. Simplicity is a quality of the higher reason.

53. Denisov, *The Life of St Seraphim*, 275.

54. *Moscow Record* (July 18–20, 1903), nos. 195, 196, 197; also in Denisov, *The Life of St Seraphim*, 319–35. Published in English as *A Wonderful Revelation to the World* (Seattle, Wash.: St Nectarios Press, 1993).

55. It is obvious that Seraphim is talking here about the higher reason.

56. We speak in detail of similar states overshadowing ascetics in Chapter 6 ("Mystical Joys").

57. *Menologion*, 100–1.

58. I. V. Popov, *The Concept of Deification in the Ancient Eastern Church*, 41.

59. Ibid.

60. Ibid.

61. Denisov, *The Life of St Seraphim*, 317–8.

62. About mental prayer, see *Super-Consciousness*, 300–13.

63. *Menologion*, 107.

64. Ibid., 93.

65. James, *The Varieties of Religious Experience*, 347.

66. A week before his death, Seraphim beseeched Igumen Niphontius to bury him in the place he appointed in the monastery, in the coffin he had prepared for himself.

67. *Menologion*, 112.

68. Denisov, *The Life of St Seraphim*, 417.

Chapter 3

1. Vladimir Soloviev, "Philosophical Principles of Integral Knowledge," in *Collected Essays*, 1:289.

2. William James, *The Varieties of Religious Experience*, 66.

3. As, for example, the prerogatives of the Catholic clergy in the mystery of the Eucharist.

4. The principles of the books of the *Philokalia* have been summarized in M. V. Lodyzhenskii, *Super-Consciousness* (2nd ed.).

5. Regarding the life of the spirit and the life of form, see *Super-Consciousness*, 45–7.

6. This dogma, accepted at the second Ecumenical Council in 381, affirmed that "the Holy Spirit proceeds from the Father." But after several centuries, at a local council of a local Spanish Church, to be precise, an addition was made to this symbol in the article about the Holy Spirit. After the words *who proceeds from the Father* are inserted the words *and the Son* (the *Filioque*). The Western Church, with the pope at its head, accepted this addition, but the Eastern Church rejected it. The rupture between the churches began in the ninth century and was finally completed in the eleventh century.

7. We discuss in detail the character of Francis's humility in the next (fourth) chapter.

8. Our main source for information on Francis was the published research on Francis's life written by the Danish writer Johannes Jørgensen.

This research is based on earlier available information on the Catholic saint that has been critically verified anew. The aforesaid research is very complete; it contains everything that could be collected of a more or less reliable nature about Francis. Jørgensen's book came out in France in 1909; it was a great success, and in 1910 the eleventh printing of this work appeared (Johannes Jørgensen, *Saint François d'Assise*, Paris, 1910). Besides this research, we used for our work the books on Francis by the French theologian P. Sabatier and the Russian researcher V. Ger'e. Finally, we used some information from the work on Francis by Emile Jebar, *St Francis of Assisi*.

9. P. Sabatier, *Life of Francis of Assisi* (The Mediator [Posrednik], 1895), 32. We should mention here that at that time the thirst for gain and the striving for earthly goods became an everyday occurrence within the Catholic clergy. It reached the point that the Catholic Church, standing in the West between man and God, in essence, hid the Divinity from the face of men. In this church, everything was sold, beginning with the remission of sins and ending with the cardinal's cap.

10. Jørgensen, *Saint François d'Assise*, 16–17.

11. Ibid., 15. As can be seen from information in Sabatier's book, Francis in this respect did not lag behind his companions. According to his closest biographers, Thomas of Celano and three comrades (Leo, Angelo, and Rufinus), he even felt obliged to surpass his friends in unrestrained living (Sabatier, *Life of Francis of Assisi*, 8).

12. Jørgensen, *Saint François d'Assise*, 27.

13. Ibid., 20.

14. We speak of this trait of Francis further in Chapter 4.

15. Regarding Sergei of Radonezh and Alexei, Metropolitan of Moscow, refer to *Super-Consciousness*, 332–4, 338–9.

16. Jørgensen, *Saint François d'Assise*, 31.

17. Ibid., 32.

18. Ibid., 32.

19. Jørgensen refers here to one such incident of illness that happened earlier to Francis.

20. Ibid., 33–34.

21. Ibid., 35–36.

22. Sabatier, *The Life of Francis of Assisi*, 25.

23. V. Ger'e, *Francis, the Apostle of Poverty and Love* (Moscow, 1908), 18.

24. Sabatier, *The Life of Francis of Assisi*, 55.

25. Jørgensen, in his research on Francis, says that later the priest found this money and, when Francis's father arrived at the church of St Damian, he took this opportunity to return the money to Francis' father (Jørgensen, *Saint François d'Assise*, 59).

26. Ibid., 59.

27. Ger'e, *Francis, the Apostle*, 24.

28. Matt 10:9,10.

29. Jørgensen, *Saint François d'Assise*, 84. In Jørgensen's account, he says that all this is based on the testimony of Francis's closest biographers, his contemporary Thomas of Celano and three friends.

30. Ger'e, *Francis, the Apostle*, 26.

31. This day is considered to be the founding day of the Franciscan order.

32. Ger'e, *Francis, the Apostle*, 38.

33. Ibid., 38.

34. Ibid., 102.

35. Jørgensen, *Saint François d'Assise*, 435.

36. Ibid., 441.

37. Ibid., 443. Jørgensen took this quote from Francis's words, and also this account, from a book, the Italian name of which is *Fioretti*, that is, *flowers*. Jørgensen says that after studying the closest sources on Francis, he was convinced that this account and also the following account of Francis's main vision (accompanying the appearance of stigmata) were based on the testimony of brother Leo and other Franciscans, who lived then together with Francis on Mt Alverna (ibid., 448).

38. *Fioretti*, third consideration; Jørgensen acknowledges this to be a reliable source.

39. Regarding the meaning of the word *contempler* (to contemplate), see Chapter 5, 84–85.

40. Jørgensen, *Saint François d'Assise*, 446. Italics are Jørgensen's.

41. Ibid., 445–8.

42. Ger'e, *Francis, the Apostle*, 107.

43. A well-known position among Franciscans.

44. Ger'e, *Francis, the Apostle*, 112–3.

45. John 13:1.

46. Ger'e, *Francis, the Apostle*, 114–5.

47. Sabatier, 114–5

48. Jebar, *St Francis of Assisi*, 160–1.

Chapter 4

1. V. Ger'e, *Francis, the Apostle of Poverty and Love* (Moscow, 1908), 312–3.

2. Seventeen-year-old Louisa Lato, usually in good health, on "Fridays fell into a state of ecstasy; blood flowed forth from her left side, on her hands and feet, corresponding exactly to the position of the cross wounds on the body of the crucified Savior, in the form of the wounds represented on crucifixes."

3. Ger'e, *Francis, the Apostle*, 314–5.

4. Ibid., 308.

5. G. Dumas, "La stigmatisation chez les mistiques Chrétiens," *Revue des Deux Mondes*, May 1, 1907, taken from Ger'e, *Francis, the Apostle*, 315–7.

6. In support of Dumas' thesis, we cite here one fact analogous with stigmatization of which we were witnesses. This was in France (Algiers) at a private séance of a famous hypnotist, Pikman. At that time, we personally saw how he, by an act of his will, caused on the tips of his fingers (first on one finger, then on another, then on a third) bloody spots, giving forth even drops of blood. He achieved this owing to exercises in mental suggestion.

7. Ger'e, *Francis, the Apostle*, 315.

8. See note 37 for Chapter 3.

9. M. V. Lodyzhenskii, *Super-Consciousness*, 292–3.

10. See Chapter 2, 24.

11. Homilies of the Christian ascetic Elias Ekdikos, in *Philokalia* 5:378.

12. St Isaac of Syria, "Homily 8," in *Works* (4th ed.), 37.

13. *Philokalia*, 2:660. We should comment here that the cited analysis of St Isaac of Syria about the unexpectedness of spiritual visions need not be understood as an immutable law for all cases of such visions. In deviation from this generalization, there have been cases, however, of altogether exceptional phenomena in which some holy Christian ascetics had highly unusual visions that *they sensed in advance*. But they were sensed in advance as unconscious prophecy—as a prophecy of what must inevitably happen. Such an exceptional case of prophecy of a miracle that was to take place was experienced by St Sergius of Radonezh at the end of his life. We described in detail this case of a vision sensed in advance in our book *Super-Consciousness* (377). A similar vision at the end of Seraphim's life also descended upon this great ascetic (see Leonid Denisov, *The Life of St Seraphim, Wonderworker of Sarov*, 381).

14. Concerning the higher reason, see Introduction, xx–xxx.

15. Ger'e, *Francis, the Apostle*, 27.

16. Mark 6:7,12.

17. Ger'e, *Francis, the Apostle*, 115.

18. Ibid., 129.

19. Ibid., 129.

20. Denisov, *The Life of St Seraphim*, 435.

21. Ger'e, *Francis, the Apostle*, 103–4.

22. Ibid., 156.

23. Ibid., 67.

24. *Menologion*, 5:89. By the way, it is interesting to mention here the saying of a certain Russian Christian ascetic of the sixteenth century, St Nilus of Sora, a saying concerning an exhausting of his body, similar to which Seraphim subjected himself. St Nilus of Sora, in the directions he left after him, says that he who is healthy and has a strong body must exhaust it in every possible way so as to be delivered from passions and so that by the grace of Christ it may be submissive to the spirit.

25. See Chapter 2, 30–31.

26. Ger'e, *Francis, the Apostle*, 41–2.

27. Ibid., 170.

28. Ibid., 171.

29. See Chapter 2, 27.

30. Ger'e, *Francis, the Apostle*, 143.

31. Emile Jebar, *St Francis of Assisi*, 145.

32. See *Super-Consciousness*, ch. 14.

33. Regarding humility as emotion, see *Super-Consciousness*, 361–2.

34. Ger'e, *Francis, the Apostle*, 124.

35. St Isaac of Syria, "Homily 36," in *Works* (3rd ed.), 155.

36. The Christian ascetic of the Orthodox Church closest to us timewise, Bishop Theophan the Recluse, expresses himself in this very regard. He says, "The Lord accepts only those who come to Him with a feeling of sinfulness. He turns away from those who come to Him with a feeling of righteousness" (Bishop Theophan, Letter 261, *Collected Letters*, pt 2:103).

37. L. N. Tolstoy, *Posthumous Artistic Works*, 2:30. Italics ours.

38. *Philokalia*, 1:33.

39. Concerning mental passions, see *Super-Consciousness*, 65–74.

40. St Isaac of Syria, *Works*, 37.

41. P. Sabatier, *Life of Francis of Assisi* (The Mediator [Posrednik], 1895), 352.

42. The absolution of sins outside the mystery of confession and the Eucharist was in the Catholic world a prerogative of the papal authority. It

was this prerogative, as expressed in the granting of indulgences, that the Lutherans later rose up against.

43. *Menologion,* 11:119–20.

Chapter 5

1. In the mystical treatise "On the Reduction of Arts to Theology," St Bonaventure says that man has three eyes: the corporeal, the mental, and the contemplative; he develops this theme in detail.

2. Thanks to the assistance of the publicist S. N. Syromyatnikov (Sigma), we were able to obtain in St Petersburg two books on the subject of interest to us: The first book is a translation from Latin into French of Ignatius Loyola's original composition of *Spiritual Exercises* (translation published in 1817). The other, *Manrese,* is widespread in the Catholic world as a guide to understanding the aforesaid composition of Loyola. In the foreword to the ninth edition of this guide (which was printed in 1851), it says that the author of this guide is not named, yet it is a well known theologian belonging to the Jesuit order, who collected and united into the book *Manrese* what was established by the practice of Catholic asceticism, the most important commentaries on St Ignatius's work *Spiritual Exercises.*

3. M. V. Lodyzhenskii, *Super-Consciousness,* 176.

4. Ibid., 197.

5. *Manrese,* Introduction, 8.

6. Ibid.

7. *Manrese,* Introduction, 9.

8. Ibid.

9. *Manrese,* Introduction, 8.

10. *Manrese,* Introduction, 15.

11. "First Week, Fifth Exercise" in *Spiritual Exercises,* 70–71.

12. "Second Week, First Meditation," in *Spiritual Exercises,* 95–97.

13. "Colloque," in *Spiritual Exercises,* 56–57.

14. "Meditation on Hell," in *Spiritual Exercises,* 79.

15. Swami Vivekananda, *The Philosophy of Yoga,* 123.

16. Thomas à Kempis, *The Imitation of Christ* (trans. Count Speransky; Russian Pilgrim, 1893), 252–3.

17. William James, *The Varieties of Religious Experience,* 337. Italics ours.

18. Ibid., 401.

19. "Homily on Prayer," *Philokalia* 2, sec. 67, 215.

20. Ibid., sec. 66.

21. Ibid., sec. 115, 221.

22. Ibid., sec. 128, 222.

23. Ibid., 697.

24. Ibid., 5:463–4.

25. Ibid., 233.

26. Ibid., 224.

27. Bishop Alexei, *Byzantine Church Mystics of the 14th Century* (1906), 85.

28. Ibid., 45.

29. In Russian spiritual literature, the main and first preacher of Eastern mysticism was St Nilus of Sora (1433–1508). He lived on Mt Athos, studied there the lives of Athos monks, and in his *The Tradition of Skete Life* set forth the essence of the teaching of the Christian ascetics of the *Philokalia*, among them the views of Nilus of Sinai, Isaac of Syria, Symeon the New Theologian, and Gregory of Sinai.

30. Bishop Theophan, *Letters on Christian Living* (1st and 2nd printing, 2nd ed.; Moscow, 1900), 25.

31. Bishop Theophan, Letter 1063, in *Collected Letters* (7th printing), 24–5.

32. Here it is interesting to note that even Protestant mysticism, in the person of the famous seventeenth-century mystic Boehme, was against the manifestation of the working of the imagination and senses in states of ecstasy. Boehme speaks thus to a pupil striving to sense God: "When with abstract thought you *lock up the imagination and external senses,* then Eternal hearing, vision, and speech will open up within you and *God will* hear and see through you, because now you will be the organ of His Spirit" (P. D. Uspenskii, *Tertium Organum*, 225).

33. Regarding miracles of yoga, see *Super-Consciousness,* 212–32.

34. See Chapter 2, 38–40.

35. Emile Zola, *Lourdes* (St Petersburg: Komarov, 1894), 4.

36. Ibid., 282.

37. Ibid., 283.

38. Ibid., 284.

39. Ibid., 286.

40. Ibid., 288.

41. Ibid., 289.

42. Ibid., 289.

43. Ibid.

44. Ibid., 301.

45. Ibid., 301–2.

46. Ibid., 303.

47. In Zola, this girl is named Maria. Undoubtedly, he took this scene of Maria's healing from real life; the account of the internal psychological process of her healing in essence *repeats* the testimonies of healings of other sick people like Maria. It is not uncommon for such healings to be performed in Lourdes.

48. Zola, *Lourdes*, 303.

49. Ibid., 302.

50. Also striking for its simplicity is the miracle performed by Metropolitan Aleksei on the khan's wife, Taydula. See *Super-Consciousness*, 339.

51. Regarding the higher reason and lower reason, see Introduction, xv–xxx.

52. Excerpted from the book *Spiritual Exercises of St Ignatius*.

53. See *Super-Consciousness*, 301–2.

54. We speak about this government at the end of Chapter 9 of this book.

Chapter 6

1. It is impossible not to say here a few words regarding a certain book, *People of the Moonlight*, by the famous publicist V. Rozanov. In this book, Rozanov discusses with great originality the reasons leading Christian ascetics to the monastic spiritual struggle and the reasons influencing their preserving a life of virginity. In Rozanov's view, the idea of asceticism, the idea of a life of virginity, arose, so he thinks, from sexual perversion, from hermaphroditism, bisexuality, and homosexuality. In the aforesaid book, Rozanov says the following: "The turning to God of people in one way or another anomalous in sex, in a greater or lesser degree anomalous, unable to lead a normal family life, unable to function in married life—formed *all* of asceticism, ancient and modern, pagan and Christian. Except at that time, when in other religions it occupied a *corner,* was formed by *man*—Christianity in fact consists totally of *this alone,* with the addition of terms, condescending, semi-lawful and in essence *according to its strict inner meaning*—unlawful" (172–3).

In support of his position, Rozanov refers to the life of a certain Moses the Hungarian and to how his life is recounted in the Kiev Patericon. This life tells in detail how Moses the Hungarian, having become a slave to a young *lyakhin* (Polish) widow, not yielding to her desire to marry him, unseduced by her temptations, unafraid of her threats and torments, and despite all her coercion to satisfy her desire, he all the same preserved his virginity. From information in this life, Rozanov concludes that Moses the Hungarian was a man anomalous in sex. Rozanov says that in this life, "[H]e says the invincible—'I cannot'—which the compilers of the 'life' took for 'I do not want.' In this way," says Rozanov, "a fact of nature, unknown to the compilers of the life, was taken for an especially deep, for an especially pure confession of religious virginity." And in a footnote to the life of Moses the Hungarian, Rozanov underlines the fact that all this was presented "as instruction, as enlightenment" to the Russian people—to a child who chews that food that is put into his mouth. Meanwhile, the food is poisoned with the venom of those who practice castration and with revolt against the Lord's commandment "Bear fruit and multiply" (*People of the Moonlight*, 174, 175).

On the basis of this example, Rozanov even builds his conclusion that all Christian asceticism comes from people anomalous in sex. Obviously, Rozanov cannot conceive of another asceticism, cannot conceive of an ascetic who, being physically normal, would make the decision to reject married life for the sake of the interests of a special life that he chose for himself, for the sake of strengthening in himself the life of the spirit.

But in expressing such thoughts, Rozanov loses sight of the fact that the *Menologion* is full of examples of people who, being physically normal, manifested an inclination toward ascetic life solely as the result of a striving for God imprinted in their souls, as the result of a striving to sense spiritual super-consciousness. These strivings overpowered in them interest in the life of form, interest in acquiring property and worldly fame, and interest in the attractions of sex and family life. From *The Life of St Seraphim of Sarov*, we know that physically he was completely normal, but that for the sake of developing in himself spiritual life, he fought against his passions, and he strove to renounce feminine charms. In his directions to monks fighting against their passions, Seraphim expressed this view on the danger of feminine charms for monks: "One must especially keep oneself from associating with the female sex, for as a wax candle, though unlit, yet placed among burning ones, it melts, so the heart of a monk from conversing with the female sex imperceptibly weakens" (Leonid Denisov, *The Life of St Seraphim, Wonderworker of Sarov*, 426).

Yet this very same Seraphim of Sarov, as we know from his biography, regarded Christian marriage with great respect. "Virginity is glorious and marriage is blessed," he said to laypeople, "and God blesses them, saying: be fruitful and multiply." Yes, finally, our Eastern church, as we see from her history, has always placed Christian marriage on high. When at the Council of Nicea some of the members of the council, guided by a falsely understood zeal, tried to pass a resolution for celibate clergy, then against this rose up no other than the anchorite monk Bishop Paphnutius, who in a loud voice cried, "Do not impose this heavy burden on the clergy. Marriage is honorable for all and the bed undefiled. By exaggerated strictness you cause the Church more harm than good. Not everyone can endure such an ascetic rule" (F. W. Farrar, *Lives of the Fathers*, 338–9). Paphnutius's statement had total success at the council, and in the Eastern church it was made a fixed rule. In this church, marriage before ordination is not only approved of, but also made obligatory.

From all this information, it is obvious that Rozanov's conclusion—that Christian asceticism arises from people anomalous in sex—is in error.

2. Matt 19:24.

3. *Cuckle*: the headwear of a monk.

4. *Menologion*, 3:547–9.

5. This composition is recognized as the most remarkable of the works of Justin the Philosopher; it is called *Dialogue with Trypho*. In this composition, Justin recounts his conversation with an elder unknown to him, who influenced his conversion to Christianity.

6. See Chapter 2, 20.

7. *Menologion*, 10:8–11.

8. *Menologion*, 2:185–6.

9. Ibid., 185.

10. Ibid., 185–6.

11. Ibid., 186–7.

12. *Menologion*, 1:306.

13. I. V. Popov, *St John Chrysostom and His Enemies*, 41.

14. Palladius, Bishop of Helenopolis, *Lausiac History* (Russian trans., 1850), 216–63.

15. *Menologion*, 7:372.

16. Farrar, *Lives of the Fathers*, 2:469.

17. *Menologion*, 5:897–8.

18. "Life of Vitaly," in *Menologion*, 3:352,

19. John (II) the Merciful was patriarch from 609 to 620.

20. We suppose that the word *bean* means a large coconut or some other large arboreal fruit growing in Egypt.

21. *Menologion*, 8:352–3.

22. Ibid., 355.

23. *Menologion*, 2:55.

24. *Menologion*, 8:395–6.

25. *New Time* (November 28, 1910), no. 12470.

26. Italics ours.

27. L. N. Tolstoy, *Childhood* (1886), 1:42–44.

28. *Menologion*, 11:476.

29. Ibid., 478.

30. Ibid., 479.

31. Ibid.

32. Ibid., 494–5.

33. Ibid., 490.

34. Ibid., 490–1.

35. Ibid., 498.

36. *Menologion*, First Suppl., 548–50.

37. Bishop Philaret Gumilevsky, *Lives of the Saints* (December), 364–5.

Chapter 7

1. V. F. Chizh, "The Psychology of Our Righteous Ones," *Questions of Philosophy and Psychology* November–December (1906): 381–3.

2. I. V. Popov, *The Mystical Justification of Asceticism*, 47.

3. St Isaac of Syria, "Homily 56," in *Works*, 289–90.

4. *Philokalia*, 3:353.

5. Rom 8:26.

6. See M. V. Lodyzhenskii, *Super-Consciousness*, ch. 16.

7. We have taken this short biography from the life of Symeon the New Theologian composed by his disciple, Nikita Stifat. Refer to the life of Symeon located in *St Symeon's Homilies* (Moscow: Athonite Monastery, 1892).

8. St Symeon the New Theologian, "Homily 90," in *Homilies*, 483.

9. Ibid., 484.

10. Ibid.

11. Ibid., 487–9.

12. That is to say, invisible to the bodily eyes, but sensed by spiritual vision.

13. St Symeon the New Theologian, "Homily 90," in *Homilies*, 487–9.

14. By the word *darkness*, Symeon means here the darkness of his own eyes, which darkens his vision.

15. It is interesting to compare this with what St Isaac of Syria says in Homily 55: "No matter how much one tells a blind man about the glory of the sun and moon, about the multitude of stars, about the brilliance

of precious stones—and he accepts and judges and imagines to himself the beauty they have only in their names; his knowledge and reasoning is far from the delight given by the vision of them; so, in similar fashion, represent to yourself spiritual contemplation" (St Isaac of Syria, "Homily 55," in *Works*, 260).

16. St Symeon the New Theologian, "Homily 91," in *Homilies*, 496–500.

17. In Homily 58 of his *Works*, St Isaac of Syria says, "When your soul comes close to leaving the darkness, then here let this be a sign for you: your heart burns and like *fire* is enkindled. Suddenly you are given a stream of tears, like a flood, flowing without being forced" (St Isaac of Syria, "Homily 55," in *Works*, 316).

18. St Isaac of Syria, "Homily 89," in *Works*, 470.

19. Ibid., 471.

20. Ibid., 472.

21. Ibid., 473.

22. Ibid., 479–80.

23. See Introduction, xxiv.

24. St Symeon the New Theologian, "Homily 51," in *Homilies*, 473.

25. Ibid., 474.

26. Ibid., 476.

27. *Philokalia*, 5:393.

28. Popov, *Mystical Justification,* 31.

29. See Chapter 7, 130–1.

30. St Symeon the New Theologian, "Homily 45," in *Homilies*, 414.

31. Ibid., 415.

32. Evidently, by *eye of the heart* is understood here that same mystical sense about which we have spoken—a sense belonging to man's higher reason, that is, spiritual vision.

33. St Symeon the New Theologian, "Homily 45," in *Homilies*, 417.

34. St Isaac of Syria, "Homily 55," in *Works*, 263.

35. St Symeon the New Theologian (2nd ed.), 177–8.

36. St Symeon the New Theologian (1st ed.), 174.

37. Ibid., 173.

38. St Symeon the New Theologian (2nd ed.), 48.

39. Ibid., 318.

40. Popov, *Mystical Justification*, 35–36.

41. See Chapter 2, 36–37.

42. Bishop Alexei, *Byzantine Church Mystics of the 14th Century* (1906), 22.

43. Popov, *Mystical Justification*, 57.

44. *Menologion*, 4:232. (Taken from the life of Ambrose written by Paulinus.)

45. See Chapter 7, 129.

46. See Chapter 7, 129.

47. The aforesaid opinion is characteristic of the teaching about the Godhead as it developed among the Neoplatonists. This teaching is completely opposite to Christian teaching. Christianity never allowed and does not allow the thought that the divinity is always *inherent in man by his nature* or, similarly, that the human soul contains within itself an element *consubstantial with the Godhead*. According to Christian teaching, God remains God and man, man; only the one God/Man, Jesus Christ, is consubstantial with God the Father, Light from His light, God uncreated, but that very same God Himself. According to Christian teaching, man can merely be like God, can receive the grace of the Holy Spirit, given him by God, unite with this divine grace, but he himself is not transformed into God. The Apostle Paul says outright, "Or do you not know that your body is the temple of the Holy Spirit who is in you, *whom you have from God*" (1 Cor. 6:19); still further he says, "Now *we have received . . . the spirit who is from God, that we might know the things that have been freely given to us by God*" (1 Cor 2:12). Finally, he even says of himself that "*according to the grace of God which was given to me*, as a wise master builder, I have laid the foundation" (1 Cor 3:10). In this way, according to the teaching of the Apostle, the Spirit of God takes up its abode in man by the inscrutable consent of God. This is a gift of the Godhead, received by man during his endeavors of humility and repentance, during his striving toward the Godhead. This is a gift from God, and not an earned right to be divine by virtue of God's apparent presence in man's soul generally; that divinity is an inherent element belonging inalienably to man, but that only it does not always see its divinity (teaching of Plotinus).

48. The quotations from the works of Plotinus have been taken from the investigation of Popov, *Mystical Justification*, 13–17.

49. See Chapter 2, 32–33.

50. Bishop Nicanor, *St Athanasius the Great and Selected Works*, 298.

51. *Menologion*, 1:536.

52. Bishop Nikanor, *St Athanasius the Great and Selected Works*, 260–1.

53. *Menologion*, 1:537–8.

54. Ibid., 550.

Chapter 8

1. F. W. Farrar, *Lives of the Fathers*, 2:61.
2. *Rule*: a series of prayers established for certain occasions.
3. *Menologion*, First Suppl., 67.
4. *Menologion*, 3:474.
5. On acquisition of the Holy Spirit of God, see Chapter 2, 20–21.
6. St Isaac of Syria, "Homily 38," in *Works*, 159.
7. Ibid., "Homily 56," in *Works*, 279.
8. Ibid., "Homily 83," in *Works*, 398.
9. I. V. Popov, *The Mystical Justification of Asceticism*, 26.
10. See M. V. Lodyzhenskii, *Super-Consciousness* (2nd ed.), 10–11.
11. L. N. Tolstoy, mentioning here his ignorance, was speaking essentially of the state of his soul before the writing of *A Confession,* when he did not understand the meaning of life and when he considered life to be evil.
12. L. N. Tolstoy, *A Confession* (The Mediator [Posrednik]), 53.
13. From part 1 of Tolstoy's works (5th ed., 1886), 126–7.
14. See the collection *The Religion of Tolstoy* (published by The Way [*Put'*]), 237.
15. Tolstoy, *A Confession*, 5.
16. See Introduction, xxi.
17. Tolstoy, *A Confession*, 60.
19. L. N. Tolstoy, *Christian Teaching* (The Mediator [Posrednik]), secs. 35–6:16.
20. Here the theses of Tolstoy's teaching, relevant in this case, are taken from his book *Christian Teaching*. Tolstoy, saying that man is a spiritual being born of an animal (sec. 20 of the book), further explains that this spiritual being is born in man with the awakening and development of his rational consciousness. This rational consciousness, says Tolstoy, reveals to man that his spiritual being is this desire.
21. For example, Marcus Aurelius said, "The greatest good that man can obtain for himself is to act in conformance with the law of his reason, and this law commands that one, untiringly, do good to others, as the highest good for oneself" (see *Meditations of the Roman Emperor Marcus Aurelius* [The Mediator (Posrednik)], 20).
22. Bishop Theophan the Recluse, *Examples of Recording Good Thoughts* (Moscow, 1846), 40.
23. Tolstoy called the doctrine of the Holy Trinity a deception of faith (sec. 187 of his *Christian Teaching*). Tolstoy considered the suggestion to

people that the truth becomes known through revelation given by God to be a method of deception of faith (sec. 193 of *Christian Teaching*).

24. Here are excerpts from Tolstoy's theses on this subject in his *Christian Teaching*: "The essence revealed to man by his rational consciousness is the desire for good to all that exists" (sec. 25); "And the desire for good to all that exists is that which gives life to all existence, what we call God" (sec. 28); "Therefore, the essence revealed to man by his consciousness, giving birth to the essence, that is, what gives life to all existence, is God" (sec. 29); and "According to Christian [i.e., Tolstoy's] teaching, man knows God with his own consciousness within himself" (sec. 30).

25. John 14:6.

26. John 15:4.

27. In our book *Super-Consciousness*, when speaking of Tolstoy and Dostoyevsky (35–6), we also called Tolstoy a Christian at that time. We called him this because Tolstoy himself considered himself to be a follower of Christ and even wrote a book, *Christian Teaching*. He titled his book thus, thinking that he was explaining in it the true teaching of Christ. In reality, however, after a close study of Tolstoy's religion as expounded in this book, it turns out to be essentially anti-Christian teaching.

28. L. N. Tolstoy, *What I Believe* (The Mediator [Posrednik]), 109.

29. Tolstoy, *Christian Teaching*, sec. 401.

30. Ibid., sec. 404.

31. In the book *What I Believe*, Tolstoy says, "That my personal life perishes, and the life of the whole world by the will of the Father does not perish and that only merging with it gives me the possibility of salvation, of this I can have no doubt" (116).

32. See Chapter 7, 131.

33. Leonid Denisov, *The Life of St Seraphim, Wonderworker of Sarov*, 417.

34. This was agreed upon by letter by Countess Sophia Andrievna and my wife.

35. At that time I was preparing for print my book *Super-Consciousness*.

36. This treatise by Vivekananda gave me much material for my book *Super-Consciousness*.

37. The name of the estate where we were living that summer, 10 versts (6.6 miles) from Yasnaya Polyana.

38. Notwithstanding that Tolstoy had kindly invited me to his place, I was not fated to see him again. A few days after Tolstoy's visit, I fell seriously ill and was taken in this condition to Moscow.

39. Count Sergei Nikolayevich Tolstoy died August 27, 1904.

40. Concerning this event, here are the original words of Tolstoy's sister, the nun Maria, as told to Tolstoy's son, Ilia Lvovich. "You know how he [L. N. Tolstoy] amazed me at the death of brother Sergei. We were all afraid that he would talk him out of taking communion. But Maria Mikhaylovna [wife of the deceased Sergei Nikolayevich] and I wanted this so much! And can you believe it? When he [Sergei Nikolayevich] said to Lev that he wanted to take communion, Lev said to him: 'Splendid, I will tell this right now to Maria Mikhaylovna,' and Sergei confessed very well."

41. On October 29, Tolstoy arrived at his sister's, the nun Maria Nikolayevna, in Shamordino. Here is what the nun Maria Tolstoy recounted about this arrival later on to Tolstoy's son, Ilia Lvovich: "I was so glad that he had decided to settle here [in Shamordino]. He even rented a house for three weeks.... He even said to me: 'How pleasant, now we will see each other often."

42. This whole scene that we have recounted is based on two sources: (1) Makovitsky's account to the nuns of the Shamordino Convent; and (2) the words of Tolstoy's sister, Maria Nikolayovna, who asked Tolstoy himself why he did not visit the elders.

43. Here are the words of Maria Nikolayevna, Tolstoy's sister, written down by Poselyanin. Alexandra Lvovna said to her father, "Mama will most certainly come here and with this I frightened him."

44. That Tolstoy fell ill in Shamordino in the evening of October 30 is apparent from the doctors' record, written in Yasnaya Polyana on November 9, 1910.

45. On that day, that is, November 4, in the morning Tolstoy told Chertkov, who had come to Astapovo already on November 2, "It seems that I am dying."

46. Here the following words of Tolstoy call attention to themselves, to which Tolstoy's daughter, Tatiana Lvovna, ascribes great significance (see Chertkov's article printed in January 1911). Tolstoy said to the people taking care of him, "Only one thing I ask you to remember—in the world there is a multitude of people besides Lev Tolstoy, but you remember only Lev." In this phrase are expressed Tolstoy's lofty altruistic feelings. And when people were pestering him with their own cares, he became irritable, and when asked what he wanted, he answered, "I want people not to bother me."

47. Tolstoy, *A Confession*, 22.

48. In *Christian Teaching*, Tolstoy says this: "In order to be free from the deception of faith, man must acknowledge as true only that which is natural, that is, in agreement with his reason and acknowledge as false all

that is unnatural, that is, contradicts reason, knowing that all that presents itself as such is human deception ... same with the deception of miracles which are told about in the Gospels."

49. May you be responsible for this good news; I do not take upon myself the responsibility.

50. N. A. Berdyayev, *A. S. Khomyakov* (The Way [Put'], 1912), 70.

51. John 10:28.

Chapter 9

1. S. N. Bulgakov, "Early Christianity and Modern Socialism," *Questions of Philosophy and Psychology* May–June (1909), 239–40.

2. F. W. Farrar, *Lives of the Fathers*, 1:20–21.

3. Ibid., 22.

4. Ibid., 23.

5. *Menologion*, 1:ix–x.

6. *Menologion*, 1:346–7.

7. *Menologion*, 1:351. This answer is very characteristic. It vividly conveys to us the saint's whole psychology. This answer lets us feel whence came this inhuman strength of the martyr to overcome the torments. It proceeded from his sensing the help of the living God, that is, personal and true (really alive and giving strength to the martyr) .

8. Festival in honor of Castor and Pollux.

9. *Menologion*, 1:353.

10. St Cyprian, *Works* (Russian translation, [Kiev, 1891]), vol. 1, Epistle 8, 120–2.

11. *Menologion*, 4:505–9.

12. Ibid., 1:512–3.

13. Ibid., 514.

14. Paul Allard, *Christianity and the Roman Empire* (PTGD, 1898), 128.

15. Ibid.

16. For those who are interested in the details of the lives and activities of the Church fathers listed, we recommend that they acquaint themselves with the excellent work on this subject, *Lives of the Fathers* by Farrar.

17. According to the views of Theosophists, "That hidden God which is in the soul of every person, gradually, life after life, breaks its chains.... The path of searching and sorrows is crowned by heavenly joy, the joy of a man who has finally found himself, his hidden God," and so forth (excerpt from the speech by the chairman of the Russian Theosophical Society, A. Kamenskaya, given at the opening of this society on October 21, 1908).

18. According to Christian doctrine, the only one consubstantial with God the Father is the God–man Jesus Christ, uncreated—but that very same God. According to Christian doctrine, man can only be likened unto God and can become like God according to the grace given by God. And God's Grace grace takes up its abode in man in proportion to his development within himself of the feeling of humility. "Truly righteous men always think within themselves," says St Isaac of Syria, "that they are not worthy of God" (St Isaac of Syria, "Homily 36," in *Works*, 155). "If there is no humility in a person," says Anthony the Great, "then he will not inherit the kingdom of God" (*Philokalia* 1:33).

19. Farrar, *Lives of the Fathers,* 309.

20. Ibid., 310.

21. Ibid., 314.

22. Ibid., 315.

23. Ibid., 320.

24. Ibid., 336.

25. Here is the part of the Nicene Creed that relates to the dispute with the Arians: "And in one Lord Jesus Christ, the only-begotten Son of God, begotten of the Father, that is of the essence of the Father, God of God, Light of Light, true God of true God, begotten not made, of one essence with the Father" (Evgraf Smirnow, *History of the Christian Church* [2nd ed.], 232) .

26. Farrar, *Lives of the Fathers*, 347.

27. Thus, having returned to his cathedra in the beginning of Julian's reign, Athanasius first of all concerned himself with restoring in his bishopric the confession of the true faith. He confirmed it again at the Council of Alexandria in 362. This council, among other things, decided that Arians returning to Orthodoxy be accepted into church communion in their former hierarchical positions. This measure soothed the hostility of the Arians toward the defenders of the Nicene Creed.

28. Six years before Athanasius's death, the Emperor Valens was obliged against his own wishes to return Athanasius to his cathedra, because without Athanasius there was a great tumult in Alexandria.

29. Farrar, *Lives of the Fathers*, 403.

30. Ibid., 2:41.

31. Ibid., 43–44.

32. See Chapter 8, 147–8.

33. Bishop Theophan the Recluse, *The Path to Salvation* (Moscow, 1908), 91.

Afterword

1. Concerning the life of form and the life of the spirit, see *Super-Consciousness*, 45–48.

2. Matt 22:39.

3. Luke 6:27.

4. Concerning egotism and evil passions, see *Super-Consciousness*, chs. 3–4.

5. See Introduction, xviii–xix.

6. People of various eras and diverse views agree on the truth of this last position. Here are examples: One of the most recent philosopher-historians has said, "On the whole, humanity represents a multitude of egotists, standing higher than animals only in one respect, that their egotism is more thought out than with animals" (Ernst Renan, *The Life of Christ*, 356). Stoic philosophers have said, "Human nature is made in such a way that man loves nothing so much as his own flesh—neither father, nor brother, nor relative, nor homeland, nor God" (see Makovelsky, *The Morality of Epictetus* [Academic memoranda of the University of Kazan, August 1912], 14). Concerning the power of egotism, Christian ascetics speak thus: "He who himself wages war with himself, just the same wages it himself, and such a way, while he is acting against the self (egotism), in a certain way he is feeding it" (see Bishop Theophan the Recluse, *The Path to Salvation*, 393).

7. Bishop Theophan the Recluse, Letter 257, *Collected Letters*, 97.

Appendix 1

1. See Introduction, xxiii–xxiv.

2. *Philokalia*, 3:349.

3. It would be apropos here to point out an interesting connection between the thoughts of St Theodorus of Edessa in the aforesaid sayings and what P. D. Uspenskii expressed concerning the intellect in his book *Tertium Organum*. We happened to find there this idea: "The brain is that essential prism, passing through which, consciousness appears to us as intellect. Or to say it a little differently, the brain is a mirror that reflects consciousness in our three-dimensional world. The latter means that in our three-dimensional world not all consciousness is active, but only its reflection from the brain" (*Tertium Organum*, 138).

4. *Philokalia*, 2:660. And in several parts of his works, St Isaac of Syria also calls the *higher reason* the *spiritual mind*; see Introduction, xxiii–xxiv.

5. St Symeon the New Theologian, *Homilies* (1st ed.; trans. Bishop Theophan), 227.

6. Leonid Denisov, *The Life of St Seraphim, Wonderworker of Sarov*, 425. In addition, Seraphim of Sarov calls the higher reason *Godly reason*; see Chapter 2, 36–37, the conversation of Seraphim with the landowner Motovilov.

7. *Super-Consciousness* (2nd ed.), 292.

BIBLIOGRAPHY

Russian Secular Literature

Anthologies of the Publishing House Put [the Way]. (1) *Vladimir Soloviev.* Moscow, 1911. (2) *The Religion of Tolstoy.* Moscow, 1912.

Berdyayev, Nicholas A. *Philosophy of Freedom.* Moscow, 1911.

——. *A. S. Khomyakov*, Moscow, 1912.

Bulgakov, S. N. "Early Christianity and Modern Socialism," *Questions of Philosophy and Psychology* May/June (1909): 239–40.

Chelpanov, G. *The Brain and the Soul.* 4th ed. Kiev 1907.

Chizh, V. F. "The Psychology of Our Righteous Ones." *Questions of Philosophy and Psychology* November/December (1906).

Ern, Vladimir. *The Struggle for the Logos.* Moscow, 1911.

Ger'e, V. I. *Francis, the Apostle of Poverty and Love.* Moscow, 1908.

Logos, International Year-Book on the Philosophy of Culture, Book 1. 1911.

Makovelsky. "The Morality of Epictetus." Academic memoranda of the University of Kazan. August 1912.

Merezhkovsky, D. S. *Not Peace But a Sword.* St Petersburg, 1908.

Pobedonosetsev, K. P. *Moscow Anthology.* 4th ed. Moscow, 1897.

Popov, I. V. *The Mystical Justification of Asceticism* Trinity Lavra, 1905.

——. *The Concept of Deification in the Early Eastern Church.* Moscow, 1909.

Rozanov, V. V. *Dark Visage.* St Petersburg, 1911.

——. *People of the Moonlight.* St Petersburg, 1911.

Sabler, V. K. *The Peaceful Struggle with Socialism.* St Petersburg, 1908.

Soloviev, V. "Mysticism." Vol. 37 of *Dictionary of Brockhaus and Ephron.*

——. Vol. 1 of *Collected Works.*

Tolstoy, Leo N. Pt. 12 of *Works.* 1886 ed.

——. *A Confession.* The Mediator (Posrednik).

——. *Childhood* 1886.

——. *What I Believe*. The Mediator (Posrednik).

Uspenskii, P. D. *Tertium Organum*. St Petersburg, 1911.

Vedensky, Alexander. *Philosophical Essays*. 1st ed. St Petersburg, 1901.

Velichko, V. L. *Vladimir Soloviev: His Life and Works*. St Petersburg, 1904.

Writings on Natural Science

Azbelev, N. P. *Unity in the Structure of the Universe*. St Petersburg, 1902.

Lebon, Gustav. *The Evolution of Material*. St Petersburg, 1909.

Meyer, Max Wilhelm. *The Making of the World*. Translated under editorship of Sergey Pavlovich Glazenap. St Petersburg, 1902.

Orthodox Christian Spiritual Literature

Alexei, Bishop. *Byzantine Church Mystics of the 14th Century*. Kazan, 1906.

Denisov, Leonid. *The Life of St Seraphim, Wonderworker of Sarov*. Moscow, 1904.

Gumilevsky, Bishop Philaret. *Lives of the Saints Revered by the Orthodox Church*. 12 vols. St Petersburg, 1900.

St Isaac of Syria. "Homilies of Spiritual Endeavor," in *Works*. 3rd ed. Sergiev Posad, 1911.

Menologion in Russian. 12 vols. Moscow, 1900–1911.

Menologion. First Suppl. Moscow, 1908.

Nikanor, Bishop. *St Athanasius the Great and Selected Works*. St Petersburg, 1893.

Philokalia. 5 vols. Moscow, 1895–1905.

Popov, I. V. *St John Chrysostom and His Enemies*. Sergiev Posad, 1908.

Smirnov, Evgraf. *History of the Christian Church*. 8th ed. Vilna, 1907.

Symeon the New Theologian. *Homilies*. 2 parts. Translated by Bishop Theophan. Moscow, 1892.

Theophan the Recluse, Bishop. *Collected Letters*. 8 parts. Moscow, 1898–1902.

——. *Examples of Recording Good Thoughts*. Moscow, 1896.

——. *Letters on Christian Living*. 1st and 2nd issue. 2nd ed. Moscow, 1900.

——. *The Path to Salvation*. Moscow, 1908.

The Way of a Pilgrim. 3rd ed. Kazan, 1884.

Foreign Authors

Allard, Paul. *Christianity and the Roman Empire from Nero to Theodosius*. St Petersburg, 1898.

Aurelius, Marcus. *Meditations*. Moscow: The Mediator (Posrednik), 1911.

Bergson, Henri. *Creative Evolution*. Moscow: Sotrudnichestvo [Collaboration], 1909.

Besant, Annie. *Ancient Wisdom*. St Petersburg, 1910.

Copin-Albancelli. *Le pouvoir occulte contre la France*. 17th ed. Paris, 1908.

du Prel, Carl. *Philosophy of Mysticism*. Translated by M. S. Aksenov. St Petersburg, 1895.

Farrar, Frederick William. *Lives of the Fathers*. Translated by A. P. Lopukhin. 2 vols. 2nd ed. St Petersburg, 1902.

St Ignace. *Exercices spirituels: Traduits en français par M. l'abbé Clément*. Marseille, 1817.

——. *Manrese ou les Exercices spirituels de Saint Ignace mis à la portée de tous les fidèles dans une exposition neuve et facile*. 9th ed. Paris: Lion, 1851.

James, William. *The Varieties of Religious Experience*. Translated under the editorship of S. V. Lourie. Moscow, 1910.

Jebar, Emile. *St Francis of Assisi*. Book 6. Translated from the French. Suvorin's Popular Library.

Jørgensen, Johannes. *Saint François d'Assise: Sa vie et son oeuvre*. 11th ed. Paris, 1910.

Renan, Ernst. *The Apostles*. Translated by Svyatlovsky. St Petersburg, 1907.

Sabatier, P. *Life of Francis of Assisi*. Moscow: The Mediator (Posrednik), 1895.

Thomas à Kempis. *Imitation of Christ, and Other Essays*. Translated by Count M. M. Speransky. St Petersburg: Russian Pilgrim, 1893.

Vivekananda, Swami. *The Philosophy of Yoga*. Sosnitsa, 1906.

Zola, Emile. *Lourdes*. St Petersburg: Komarov Typography, 1894.

INDEX

absolution of sins, 80–81, 215n42
active type of ascetic
    description of, 6, 11, 19, 206n27
    St Seraphim of Sarov as, 21
Acts of the Martyrs, The, 176, 179
Aglaida, 179–80, 182
Alexander, Metropolitan, 185, 187
Alexander III, Pope, 57
Alexandrian Church, 186
Alexei, Metropolitan of Moscow,
    50
Ambrose of Mediolan, 139
analogies, 7, 10–11, 132, 134, 137
anchoritism, 25, 128, 206n27
animals, 75
Anin the Wonderworker, 113
Antioch, 109–11
Antony, 32–33
approximate truths, 201n13
aptitudes, 12, 33, 134, 195
Apulia, 50–51
Arcadius, Emperor, 14
Arianism, 183–9
Arius, 183–4, 186–8
Arsenius, 128
ascetic(s)
    active type of. *See* active type of
        ascetic

contemplative type of. *See*
    contemplative type of
    ascetic
description of, xii–xiii, xviii,
    xxiii, xxix–xxx, 3, 7
Eastern Christian. *See* Eastern
    Christian ascetics
foolishness for Christ in, 116
goal of, 21
joys of, 124–44
Nilus of Sinai, 90
nonresistance to evil by, 30
public service by, 31–32
terminology differences, 195–7
Tolstoy's conversations about,
    158–9
types of, 6, 11, 19
ascetic path, 6, 11
asceticism, 218n1
Asterius, 114
astral vision, 210n48
astronomy, 8–9
atheism, xvii
Aurelius, Marcus, 179, 183, 224n21
Azbelev, N. P., 9

Berdyaev, Nicholas, xiv–xv, 3, 13
Bergson, Henri, xx

234